WARM WISHES!

[signature]

Restless Skies

Restless Skies

THE ULTIMATE WEATHER BOOK

PAUL DOUGLAS

For Walt, Brett, and Laurie

Restless Skies

FIRST EDITION

2004 Barnes & Noble Books

Barnes & Noble Publishing
122 Fifth Avenue
New York, NY 10011

ISBN 0-7607-6133-2

First Printing

Printed and bound in China

Design: Richard J. Berenson
        BERENSON DESIGN & BOOKS, Ltd.,
        New York, NY

INTRODUCTION

"Hey, how's the weather?"

This question will be asked countless times today, from Boston to Baton Rouge to Bakersfield. Will it be rain, shine, or something else—something black, churning and windblown, something dark and dangerous that will ultimately chase us into the basement? Good question.

America's daily weather menu is not for the faint of heart. The global superpower is also home to some of the most severe weather on the planet. We supersize our storms, with terrifying, mile-wide tornadoes, Texas-size hurricanes, hundreds of millions of crackling lightning strikes, along with a dizzying parade of floods, droughts, blizzards, and heat waves. The same climate that has helped to make America's lush farmland the envy of the world can also turn fickle and capricious, capable of wiping out entire communities in the time it takes to read this sentence, flattening one house while leaving another across the street virtually untouched.

But for every severe storm there are countless days of backyard pleasure and pure weather bliss. A brisk northwest wind rustles autumn leaves as they ripen into rich Crayola colors; a flaming fire-engine-red sunset leaves us shaking our heads in wonder; popcorn-like cumulus clouds drifting over our heads look perfect enough to inspire a postcard. As much as we complain about the weather, we spend a fair amount of time admiring the sheer beauty it creates. Every day is new, a wonder to behold.

This display of changing weather has turned us into a nation of armchair meteorologists. Everyone has a stake in the weather. It's not idle interest. In many cases it comes down to pure survival: Will I get home before the ice storm hits? Will my elderly parents have to endure sizzling heat and humidity again today? Will the kids be OK at the ballgame? We want to know. We need to know.

Let's face it: Weather affects who we are, what we talk about, and even what we accomplish on a daily basis. From our work commutes to how we dress, what we eat, after-school sports, evening errands, and weekend playtime, the state of the weather tugs and pulls at our day planners and molds and shapes our lives. The weather unites us, bonding us all together as few other things can do.

What's the weather? Glorious. Inspiring. Changeable. Dreadful. Dangerous. You say you don't like the weather this morning. Don't worry. Just stick around for a few minutes and it will change. It's inevitable. The only predictable thing about the fickle sky overhead is that it will remain fairly unpredictable, a sobering thought for a man who makes his living predicting the weather.

It was a 1972 hurricane named Agnes that jolted me into the weather business. This dying tropical storm, a relatively mild hurricane when it first came ashore, did a loop over my home state of Pennsylvania, hitting us once, then hitting us again,

pouring down torrential amounts of rain and causing floods of almost biblical proportions. Agnes inundated the town of Wilkes-Barre, and flooded out the Governor's Mansion in Harrisburg. It turned our basement into a muddy swimming pool and sent cold murky water snaking up the steps into our living room. I was fourteen years old at the time and I vividly remember that a day after the storm, a drowning victim was pulled out of the Conestoga River, now in our backyard.

At least 117 people died in Agnes. It was the costliest disaster of its time, with damage estimated at $3 billion. It left me wide-eyed with wonder, amazed that a storm could have such an impact on our community. Suddenly I was obsessed with weather. I wanted to know as much as I could about it, and why no one had predicted the fury of this very unladylike storm. To this day I'm still wondering about the weather, still wide-eyed and incredulous at its power.

The weather story is even more interesting these days, with subtle shifts in climate and new technological breakthroughs. Now that we have better forecasting skills and tools, fewer people are caught unprepared in wild storms, but there are limits to what weather satellites, supercomputers, and Doppler radar can achieve. The severe storm forecasts get better and better, but the seven-day outlook is still as much an art as a science.

With the right information you can protect yourself and your family from severe weather and lower the probability of getting into trouble the next time the sky growls with thunder and the water begins to rise over your loafers. If you live long enough, chances are you'll be confronted with a dangerous weather situation, one which may become a matter of life or death. Across much of the United States an average of 30 to 50 days every year are potentially life-threatening, with some sort of weather watch, warning, or advisory in effect. On those days the weather could be more than just an inconvenience. But if you know what to look for, and what to do when skies turn severe, chances are you'll literally weather almost any storm.

In *Restless Skies* I'll attempt to capture the complicated beauty and magic of America's ever-changing and wide-ranging weather, from winter's wild storms to the soft lazy days of summer. Our atmosphere is a work in progress, constantly moving, morphing from one weather system to another, reacting to conditions hundreds, perhaps thousands, of miles away from where we stand. It is fascinating—and fun—to know about. You will also find in this book some facts and figures that may prove useful when the sky overhead does turn threatening. Keep the book handy, and if a friend or family member launches into Doppler-speak, trying to impress you with a mouthful of meteorological mush, you'll be ready!

The skies are restless. Look up. Mother Nature is at work.

CHAPTER ONE
Stormy Weather

"Don't knock the weather; nine-tenths of the people couldn't start
a conversation if it didn't change once in a while."—Kin Hubbard

N O, YOU'RE NOT IMAGINING IT. America's weather is changing, all
right. It's becoming more unpredictable and more severe—and in
our lifetime. More tornadoes are skipping across farmland into our
suburbs and cities. Hurricanes are growing stronger and more frequent. Floods of almost biblical proportion are chasing more people from
their homes, while wilting summer droughts and paralyzing winter blizzards
are in the news with alarming frequency.

It's as if Mother Nature has picked up the remote control and put our
nation's severe weather on fast-forward. Statistics kept by the National
Climatic Data Center in Asheville, North Carolina, show that since 1980 the
United States has endured a total of 58 weather-related disasters costing
$1 billion or more. The result: nearly a quarter of a trillion dollars' worth of
damage in less than 25 years.

The 10 most costly natural disasters ever reported in the United States
have all happened in the last 10 years. Scientists are growing increasingly
concerned that America has entered a stormier weather cycle, and the threat
of disaster is increasing as cities expand and more people move to coastal
areas to live and retire. Consider this: By the year 2019 an estimated 74 percent of Americans will live along or near coastal areas where hurricanes
threaten. As a nation we are more susceptible, more vulnerable to the elements
than ever before. The forecast: changeable, and increasingly dangerous.

America's weather has always been wild, with frequent storms and
bizarre swings in temperature and moisture. The term "normal weather" is
wishful thinking, a statistical aberration. Usually we just go from one
extreme to another. We are, after all, captives of our unique geography. Dry

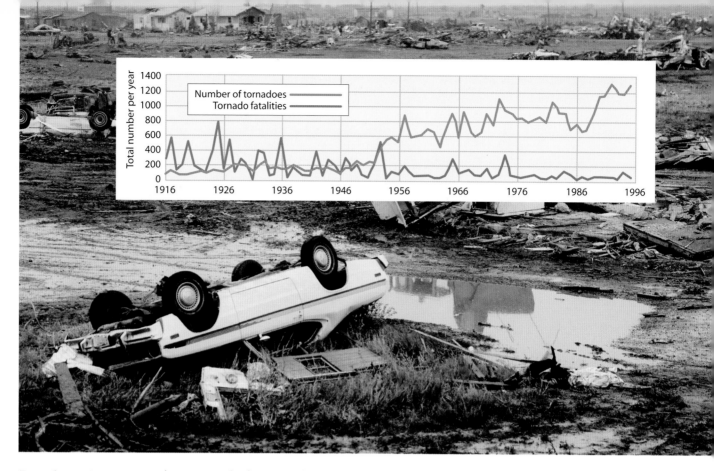

Data shows that even as the number of observed tornadoes has increased, the death toll has dropped dramatically since the early 1900s, the result of technological advances, drills, and the use of the mass media to get warnings to threatened areas.

air streams in from the Desert Southwest, mixing with thick, moisture-rich air flowing out of the Gulf of Mexico. Throw in a dash of Canadian chill, mix it up with jet-stream air flowing along at a brisk 150 mph, and you have all the atmospheric ingredients for big trouble, possibly a monster storm, that will lead the news and could chase you into the basement!

Here's something to ponder: As the nation's population grows and shifts, new housing developments are being built on farmland, in the path of tornadoes. More people are living along the floodplain, and development along the coast has put tens of millions of Americans in the potential path of hurricanes. Have we set ourselves up for weather disaster? Is more extreme weather part of a natural cycle or a symptom of larger climate change? While experts debate the issue, it's up to every one of us to make wise weather-related decisions and lower our potential for danger. The forecast for the future is uncertain, and maybe dangerous, but if you know what to do you can lower your own risk of getting into trouble.

The good news is that technology is playing a remarkable role in bringing down the death toll from severe storms. It wasn't all that long ago that swarms of tornadoes routinely killed many hundreds of American people every year. A single hurricane could claim thousands of lives. Today, Doppler radar, sophisticated weather satellites, automated ground sensors, and supercomputers have revolutionized the tracking and prediction of dangerous storms. In spite of an upward spike in severe weather, today's death toll is a fraction of what it was at the turn of the twentieth century.

America's National Weather Service, a division of the National Oceanic and Atmospheric Administration (NOAA), issues more than 734,000 forecasts every year. A longer warning period gives people more time to prepare. A few extra minutes can mean the difference between life and death. Hurricanes that were once a deadly surprise are now methodically forecast and tracked. Snowstorms and blizzards are forecast days or weeks in advance, and tornadoes are detected an average of 12 minutes before they hit the ground. NOAA's warning and forecast system isn't perfect, but it's generally regarded as the best in the world. Considering the state of the agitated weather floating above our heads, we require nothing less.

Top 15 U.S. Weather and Climate Disasters

How severe can our weather get? Here is a list of America's worst weather disasters compiled after reviewing NOAA's data—deaths, injuries, disruptions of daily life, and the toll on the economy. The list is subjective and in no particular order, but certainly these are some of the most unforgettable storms that have occurred in just over a century.

1888	Blizzard of '88	1992	Hurricane Andrew
1900	Galveston, Texas, hurricane	1988	Heat Wave and Drought
1930s	Dust Bowl	1938	New England Hurricane
1974	Super Tornado Outbreak	1925	Tri-State Tornado
1969	Hurricane Camille	1996	Great Eastern Blizzard
1993	Midwestern Flood	1999	Hurricane Hugo
1983	El Niño Events	1889	Johnstown Flood
1993	"Storm of the Century"		

March 12, 1888, 7 A. M.

Philadelphia

**Blizzard
of 1888**

Recipe for snow.
A weather map from
March 12, 1888,
showing an intense area
of low pressure off the
coast of New Jersey.

March 11–14, 1888
The Great Blizzard of 1888

It was dubbed the "Great White Hurricane," and this epic blizzard has become the stuff of weather legend. It was a severe blizzard, as defined by the National Weather Service—sustained winds of 45 mph, visibility under a quarter of a mile, and temperatures colder than 10 degrees.

The days leading up to the blizzard had been unusually mild, with temperatures in the 40s and 50s along the East Coast. People thought that spring was just around the corner. They couldn't have been more wrong. On March 12 torrential rains began to turn to snow as a harsh north wind kicked in. A blinding snow continued for the next 36 hours. As much as 50 inches of snow fell in Massachusetts and Connecticut, with more than 40 inches in New York and New Jersey. Winds blew as fast as 48 mph, carving out impenetrable snowdrifts 40 to 50 feet high! The resulting transportation gridlock underscored the need for a subway in New York City, and one was hastily approved in 1900. Railroad service was halted, businesses shut down, and people were imprisoned in their homes, unable to go anywhere.

New Yorkers who were unaware of the intensity of the blizzard became stranded by the thousands. Many risked their lives by walking over the ice-clogged East River to Brooklyn, trying desperately to reach their homes. Little did they know that they were living through what is generally regarded as New York City's greatest weather disaster.

Two hundred ships were grounded offshore, and at least a hundred seamen died. Fire stations were snowed in, and blazes burned unchecked. Overall more than 400 deaths were reported, and it would take over a week for the East Coast to dig itself out from two-story drifts.

September 8–9, 1900
The Galveston, Texas, Hurricane

As the twentieth century dawned, a renewed sense of expectation and optimism was abroad in the United States, especially in the great state of Texas. As a senior employee at the weather bureau in the popular coastal city of Galveston, Isaac M. Cline (forever immortalized in the book *Isaac's Storm*) was confident that he could warn of any impending hurricane in time to evacuate nearby beaches. It turned out that Isaac Cline was tragically wrong.

The low pressure and high winds, estimated as high as 135 mph, carved out a 20-foot dome of water, which slammed into Galveston Island.

In late August weather forecasters in Cuba were nervously tracking a new tropical storm entering the Gulf of Mexico. As it passed over water with the temperature of bathwater, the storm intensified explosively, reaching category-4 strength, on a scale ranging from 1 to 5. On the evening of September 8, the nameless storm howled into southern Texas. The low pressure and high winds, estimated as high as 135 mph, carved out a 20-foot dome of water, a looming storm surge, which slammed into Galveston Island in a grinding

Men use ropes to pull away the debris of houses to look for bodies, after the Galveston Hurricane of 1900.

blur of wind-whipped water, foam, and debris. About 3,600 homes on the island and in nearby Galveston City were swept off their foundations. Survivors told harrowing stories of floating for hours on doors and improvised rafts made of furniture, with people holding on for their lives. Over 6,000 died on Galveston Island in only a few hours that night, with another 2,000 deaths on nearby islands and the mainland, making this America's worst weather disaster in terms of life lost.

1930s
America's Dust Bowl

The 1930s will be remembered as years of blistering heat and baking drought. At the height of the Heat Wave of '36, an estimated 50 million acres of land lay parched and unproductive. Afternoon temperatures reached 120 to 125 degrees over the Great Plains, but suffocating heat spread as far north as Minnesota and as far east as New Jersey. Some 15,000 Americans died from heat-related ailments. John Steinbeck captured the horror and fascination of dust storms in his epic novel, *The Grapes of Wrath,* as millions of tons of precious topsoil were stripped from the land and blown hundreds of miles downwind, adding to the growing misery. These boiling, churning curtains of soil reached as high as 16,000 feet above the ground. Called "black blizzards," they came on with little warning, triggering massive crop losses, respiratory ailments for millions, and a nagging sense of dread. Many Americans were convinced that the world was coming to an end.

Arthur Rothstein's photograph of a farmer and his sons walking in the face of a dust storm in Cimarron County, Oklahoma, became an iconic image of the Dust Bowl era.

In her *Dust Bowl Diary,* Ann Marie Low, a woman who lived on the plains of North Dakota in the 1930s, captured the dark feelings of those times:

"April 25, 1934, Wednesday. Last weekend was the worst dust storm we ever had. We've been having quite a bit of blowing dirt every year since the drought started, not only here, but all over the Great Plains. Many days this spring the air is just full of dirt coming, literally for hundreds of miles. It sifts into everything. After we wash the dishes and put them away, so much dirt sifts into the cupboards we must wash them again before the next meal. Clothes in the closets are covered with dust. Last weekend no one was taking an automobile out for fear of ruining the motor. I rode Roany to Frank's place to return a gear. To find my way I had to ride right beside the fence, scarcely able to see from one fence post to the next. Newspapers say the deaths of many babies and old people are attributed to breathing in so much dirt."

A wall of dust
approaches Stratford, Texas, on April 18, 1935. Inset, newspaper head-lines from the period.

Killer tornado.
Top, a mile-wide tornado approaches Xenia, Ohio. Inset, aerial view of the Arrowhead subdivision of Xenia, leveled by tornadic winds, which may have exceeded 300 mph.

April 3–4, 1974
The Super Tornado Outbreak

Spring is tornado season, but nothing had prepared America for the onslaught of killer funnels that ripped across the nation one April day in 1974. Meteorological conditions were ripe: moisture flowing northward out of the Gulf of Mexico, dry air aloft, a powerful storm approaching from the Great Plains, and an inversion "capping" the atmosphere. Rising air currents broke through that cap, resulting in rotating, long-lasting "supercells" that spawned families of tornadoes during the afternoon and evening hours. A record number of tornadoes touched down, 148 in two days! At the height of the outbreak a new tornado was reported on average every three minutes. The swarm of lethal twisters skipped across 13 states and 2 Canadian provinces, killing 330 people and injuring another 5,400, with damages estimated at $600 million. One of the most destructive tornadoes was on the ground for two hours, raging across northwest Alabama into south-central Tennessee, killing 63 people. Had it not been for improved civil-defense communications, dedicated teams of the National Weather Service's Skywarn weather spotters, National Weather Service radar, and the media's quick response, the toll would have been much higher.

One of the hardest-hit towns was Xenia, Ohio, which was all but leveled by a monstrous, mile-wide tornado. It shredded this town of 130,000 people, destroying half the buildings and leaving more than 10,000 people homeless. The black, swirling curtain of debris ripped up nine schools, nine churches, and 180 businesses, killing 33 people. Recovery efforts were hampered when a freight train moving through the center of town was blown over by the tornado, blocking routes for fire and rescue.

August 17–18, 1969

Hurricane Camille

Hurricane forecasters in Miami knew that a potentially catastrophic weather scenario was brewing. On the morning of August 17, 1969, an Air Force reconnaissance aircraft reported a central pressure in the storm's eye of 26.84 inches of mercury—dangerously low pressure—and sustained winds of 200 mph. That report prompted feverish last-minute evacuations away from the coast, which may have saved tens of thousands of lives. Hurricane Camille was the strongest hurricane to hit the U.S. mainland in the twentieth century—a rare category-5 storm, on a scale ranging from 1 to 5. Camille slammed into coastal Mississippi with sustained winds approaching 200 mph, shoving a 24-foot-high wall of water ashore. The water inundated popular coastal resorts and wiped hundreds of homes and businesses right off the map. Camille killed 256 people, primarily in Mississippi from the storm surge and then days later from intense flash flooding as the storm weakened over Virginia.

From air photos and ground surveys after the storm, the storm surge of Hurricane Camille seemed without parallel. No other storm had ever submerged so much land so quickly and to such a great depth. In one harrowing tale a survivor told of sitting at home during Camille, watching the ocean water flood through his yard and eventually seep up into the first floor of his home. Panicking, he retreated to the attic, where the water quickly became neck-deep, forcing him to kick out a small attic window and swim to a large transmission tower located at the rear of his property. As he struggled to climb up the tower, he watched in horror as the roof of his home slipped under water. He lived two miles from the Gulf of Mexico.

This historic home along the Mississippi coast was scheduled to open as an Episcopal school in September 1969. That was before Camille reshaped the coastline with 200-mph winds and a storm surge estimated as high as 24 feet.

A 24-foot storm surge produced some very strange sights indeed.

17

1993
The Great Midwest Flood

Aerial view of the Missouri River flooding on July 30, 1993, north of Jefferson City, Missouri. The river now resembled a lake, 4 to 6 times wider than normal, producing some of the highest crests ever witnessed in the twentieth century.

"The Mississippi River cannot be tamed, curbed or confined," Mark Twain once wrote. "You cannot bar its path with an obstruction which it will not tear down, dance over and laugh at. The Mississippi River will always have its own way; no engineering skill can persuade it to do otherwise."

In 1993 the Mississippi and Missouri rivers proved Twain right. The Great Flood of '93 swamped 20 million acres in nine states, claiming 50 lives and costing the nation an estimated $50 billion. Some 54,000 people were chased from their homes by the muddy floodwaters; at least 50,000 homes were destroyed or damaged. As many as 75 towns were completely deluged. Some riverside communities gave up after the flood, either abandoning their towns altogether or relocat-

ing to higher ground. In many areas the harvest of 1993 and '94 was a total loss because of persistent water. Amazingly, some locations on the Mississippi River were flooded for almost 200 days.

Heavy March rains combined with rapidly melting snow to set the stage for the watery disaster. Instead of fluctuating, jet-stream winds kept guiding storms over the same central states. In some areas a normal year's worth of rain fell in less than four months. The Mississippi River crested as high as 22 feet above flood stage. The flood was so widespread and immense that new bodies of water showed up on weather satellites. In some cases the river was 3 to 5 times wider than usual, a flood of historic proportion.

High-resolution NASA imagery showing the Mississippi River flowing out of its banks, resulting in severe flooding around St. Louis, Missouri. Over 1,000 levees were damaged or topped, eroding an esimated 600 billion tons of valuable topsoil and inundating many farms under a layer of silt and sand, wiping out the 1993, and in some cases the 1994, harvest.

1982—83
A Devastating El Niño

El Niño is a complex domino effect of unusually warm water and light winds that slowly evolves over the Pacific Ocean once every 4 or 5 years, throwing a meteorological monkey wrench into the world's weather downwind. Named after the Christ child, El Niño often becomes apparent around Christmas. Peruvian fishermen in the late 1800s first noticed the phenomenon of warm water displacing the normally chilly waters of the Pacific. The result is fewer fish, along with torrential rains where skies are usually sunny.

A witches' brew of ingredients goes into a strong El Niño, starting with trade winds mysteriously dropping off near Australia. That in turn allows a stain of unusually warm ocean water to spread east, with water temperatures as much as 4 to 8 degrees higher than normal. This abnormally warm water tends to pull the jet stream, the highway for storms, farther south, wracking California with wild storms and soaking much of the southern United States, while northern latitudes remain relatively mild and dry.

The most severe and devastating El Niño on record, responsible for more than a thousand deaths and as much as $10 billion in damage to property and livestock worldwide, occurred in 1982–83. (Another strong El Niño developed in 1997–98, resulting in the worst spring tornado season in 14 years and the warmest first half of the year, globally, since weather records were first kept.)

There is no known direct link between El Niño and global climate change or global warming. If anything, El Niño increases jet-stream winds near the equator, reducing the risk of hurricanes. There is a high correlation between El Niño and drought in Australia as well as floods, mud slides, and even tornadoes in California. Recently National Weather Service forecasters have been able to issue 6- to 9-month advance warnings that El Niño is brewing in the Pacific, giving Americans more time to prepare for the bad weather to come.

NASA satellite data showing sea surface temperatures in the Pacific Ocean. The red and white regions are areas of unusual warmth, with ocean water 4 to 8 degrees warmer than normal, producing a domino effect on the world's weather downwind.

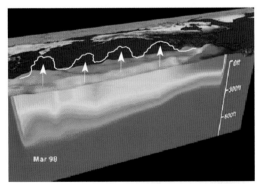

A warm, growing stain of water. This March 1998 simulation shows abnormally warm El Niño ocean water collecting as deep as 300 feet beneath the surface of the ocean off the coast of Central America.

20

Satellite image from March 13, 1993. This infrared image measures the temperatures of the clouds. The tallest, coldest clouds, producing the heaviest precipitation, show up as purple and blue. New York City, top left, was buried under 1 to 2 feet of snow.

March 12–14, 1993
"The Storm of the Century"

An amazingly powerful and destructive storm, dubbed the "Storm of the Century," battered the entire Eastern United States in mid-March 1993 with tornadoes, violent winds, record low pressure, and heavy snows. For the first time on record a single storm closed every airport on the East Coast at one time or another. Snow fell at the rate of 2 to 3 inches an hour, crushing hundreds of roofs. In warmer climates straight-line winds blew in with a hurricanelike ferocity, gusting well over 100 mph and pushing a 10-foot-high storm surge ashore in Western Florida. A total of 15 tornadoes killed 15 people in Florida, while to the north a half foot of snow fell in the Florida Panhandle! As many as 50 tornadoes may have been spawned by the storm. These tornadic thunderstorms moved into Dade County, near the Miami area. One of the tornadoes touched down on a recovery site, built to house victims of Hurricane Andrew, which had struck just six months earlier. The site was destroyed. Many people had to start rebuilding their lives for a second time. High winds blew over thousands of trees, cutting off power to at least 3 million people along the storm's path. More than a foot of snow fell from Alabama to Maine, and intense cold followed the storm, with at least 145 record lows over two days. According to the National Disaster Survey Report, at least 26 states were impacted, disrupting the lives of about 100 million Americans, approximately half the nation's population. The 1993 storm is thought to be the worst blizzard to hit the Northeast in a century. The National Weather Service is now developing a scale of 1 to 5 to grade winter storms, as it does hurricanes. On that scale, this one gets a 5! In all, at least 270 people were killed, and damage ultimately topped $3 billion.

"STORM OF THE CENTURY" HIGHLIGHTS	
Recorded Wind Gusts	*Mph*
Mount Washington, NH	144
Franklin County, FL	110
Dry Tortugas, FL	109
Flattop Mountain, NC	101
Recorded Sea-Level Pressures	*Inches*
White Plains, NY	28.28
Philadelphia, PA	28.43
New York, (Kennedy Airport)	28.43
Dover, DE	28.45
Recorded Snowfall Totals	*Inches*
Mt. Mitchell, NC	50
Grantsville, MD	47
Snowshoe, WV	44
Syracuse, NY	43

Atmospheric time bomb. A satellite timeline showing the track of Hurricane Andrew, the first category 5 storm to hit the USA since Camille, in 1969. Andrew blew into southern Florida and then moved out into the Gulf of Mexico before delivering a second blow to Louisiana.

Landfall. Below right, high resolution infrared satellite image taken at the time of maximum winds in the Miami area. The doughnut-shaped hole at the center of Andrew is the eye of the storm. Immediately surrounding the eye, the bright white clouds are rapidly rotating thunderstorms, the "eyewall," containing sustained winds of 150 to 165 mph. Unofficially, winds in the eyewall may have approached 200 mph.

August 1992
Hurricane Andrew

Hurricane Andrew was one of the most intense and destructive hurricanes to ever hit the U.S. mainland. It battered the Bahamas with a storm surge 23 feet high and then smashed into southern Florida on August 24, 1992. Coastal marine weather buoys recorded maximum sustained winds of 141 mph and a peak of 169 mph. The National Hurricane Center in Coral Gables had sustained winds of 115 mph with gusts of up to 164 mph. The shrieking winds leveled many of the subdivisions just south of Miami. The town of Homestead was virtually wiped out. More than 120,000 homes were severely damaged or destroyed, leaving a quarter of a million Floridians homeless.

Andrew continued into the Gulf of Mexico and swept into Louisiana, claiming more lives and triggering more severe flooding. At least 23 people lost their lives in Florida and Louisiana. The total cost of cleanup from Andrew approached $30

HURRICANE ANDREW
24 AUGUST 1992
5 AM EDT   926 MB

billion, making it America's costliest storm. Hurricane experts estimate that had the storm tracked only another 10 to 20 miles farther north and hit downtown Miami, the damage toll could have hit $100 billion.

In 2002 hurricane scientists announced that Hurricane Andrew, when it hit southern Florida, was even stronger than originally believed. It was initially thought to be a category-4

Remains of a trailer park
near Homestead, Florida, ravaged
by Hurricane Andrew.

Anatomy of a weather monster.
Unusually warm ocean water fueled
Andrew, and light winds aloft meant that
the storm could continue to strengthen
unchecked. This is a three-dimensional
model view of the hurricane approaching
the Florida coast in August 1992. In this
illustration winds in excess of gale force
are indicated by the white and red arrows
at the surface and top of the storm,
respectively. The color shading at the
earth's surface represents the precipitation
rate. Note the intense precipitation (red)
surrounding the storm center and the rain
bands (green) in the outer regions of the
storm. The tan, three-dimensional
cloudlike feature is the 85 percent
relative-humidity surface, cut away on its
southern side to reveal the hurricane's
interior structure. The tubelike feature
extending upward near the center of the
storm encompasses an eyelike region of
drier air and weak sinking motion.

storm, but new research upgraded it to a rare category-5 hurricane, only the third cat-5 hurricane to hit the United States in recorded history. In its re-analysis of Hurricane Andrew's maximum sustained surface-wind speeds, NOAA's National Hurricane Center Best Track Committee, a team of hurricane experts, concluded that winds were 165 mph—20 mph faster than earlier estimated—as the storm made landfall. When Hurricane Andrew hit southeast Dade County on August 24, 1992, flying debris from the storm's winds knocked out most ground-based wind-measuring instruments, and widespread power outages caused electric-based measuring equipment to fail. The winds were so strong that many wind-measuring tools were incapable of registering their speed. Surviving wind observations and measurements from aircraft reconnaissance, surface pressure, satellite analysis, and radar, along with the distribution of debris and structural failures, were used to estimate the surface winds.

July 13–14, 1995
Chicago's Sweltering Heat Storm

There are heat waves that creep up gradually and linger for days or weeks. And then there are rare heat storms, sudden outbreaks of life-threatening heat and humidity that can, overnight, overwhelm a city and its population. On July 13, 1995, Chicago's mercury peaked at 106 degrees. Dew-point temperatures in the 70s made the heat feel more like 120 to 125 degrees on the streets of Chicago—suffocating levels. Nighttime lows did not drop below 80 for several nights in a row that week, turning many Chicago apartments into deadly ovens. People were simply unable to find any kind of relief when they opened their windows. Extreme heat made the roads buckle and the train tracks warp, and the city set new records for electricity use.

On July 13, 1995, Chicago's mercury peaked at 106 degrees.

According to Eric Klinenberg, in his book *Heat Wave: A Social Autopsy of Disaster in Chicago,* people swarmed to the beaches to cool down. More than 3,000 fire hydrants were illegally opened, causing some neighborhoods to lose water pressure on top of losing electricity. City workers hosed down the bridges, hoping to prevent them from buckling when the plates expanded from the intense heat. Kids riding home in school buses became so hot, dehydrated, and nauseated that they had to be hosed down by local firefighters.

The death toll from the heat, directly and indirectly, may have reached 739 from July 14 to July 21. Most of the victims were older, living alone, sick, or bedridden, lacking access to transportation or air conditioning, with many afraid to open doors or windows for fear of crime. In contrast, during the heat waves of the 1930s many Chicagoans found relief by sleeping outside in parks or along the Lake Michigan shoreline.

Some experts warn that what happened in Chicago may not be an aberration, that in a world warmed by greenhouse gases the frequency and intensity of these sudden heat storms will be on the rise, posing the greatest threat to inner-city residents who lack the means or ability to cool their dwellings.

September 21, 1938
The Great New England Hurricane

Before sophisticated weather satellites beamed down pictures of the weather from space every 15 minutes, hurricane forecasters had to rely on reports from islands and ships caught in the middle of these fearsome storms.

As the decade of the '30s came to a close, New Englanders could be forgiven for being a bit complacent when it came to hurricanes. It had been many years since a major storm swept off the Atlantic, and 150 years since a hurricane cut a swath of destruction through the interior.

In her book *Sudden Sea: The Great Hurricane of 1938,* R. A. Scotti tells readers that *hurricane* was a foreign word in New England at the time. People didn't even know how to pronounce it. They didn't know what it meant, and whatever it meant, they were sure it couldn't happen to them. They had no idea what was brewing to their south and the path this raging storm would take.

Late on September 20, 1938, a tropical storm was reported in the eastern Bahamas. Forecasters assumed that this storm, like most others, would recurve to the northeast, moving harmlessly out to sea. But a large area of high pressure was located over the Atlantic Ocean just east of the coast, which kept the storm close to the coast and moving northeastward.

An aerial view of a once palatial estate in Westhampton, Long Island, New York, as it appeared on September 22, 1938 after howling winds and pounding waves had done their work of destruction. The home and swimming pool in the foreground are total wrecks. Note also the complete washout of the bridge in the background.

25

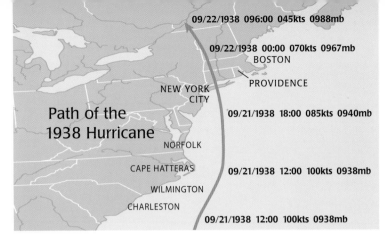

Path of the
1938 Hurricane

09/22/1938 096:00 045kts 0988mb

09/22/1938 00:00 070kts 0967mb
BOSTON

PROVIDENCE

NEW YORK
CITY

09/21/1938 18:00 085kts 0940mb

NORFOLK

CAPE HATTERAS

09/21/1938 12:00 100kts 0938mb

WILMINGTON

CHARLESTON

09/21/1938 12:00 100kts 0938mb

A trainman surveys the damage done to a Long Island Railroad train after it had been derailed as a result of the hurricane that struck here with its full force. The rails were torn from the ties and twisted into grotesque curlicues.

The map, above right, shows the track of the Great Hurricane of 1938. With no weather satellites, no Doppler radar, no offshore weather buoys transmitting real-time information, and few ships offshore, forecasters had no idea that a severe hurricane was racing up the Eastern Seaboard.

Charlie Pierce, a young research forecaster for the U.S. Weather Bureau, concluded that the storm would not curve out to sea but would instead track due north. He was overruled by more senior meteorologists, and so the official forecast was for cloudy skies and gusty conditions—but no hurricane. Because the official forecast was not cause for alarm, even as the winds picked up speed and the waves rolled in, nobody realized that a catastrophe was only a few hours away. But a trough of low pressure literally sucked the growing storm due north, where it accelerated to speeds as high as 70 mph, more than a mile a minute, the fastest hurricane ever observed up to that time!

This nameless storm, later dubbed the "Long Island Express," sliced across Long Island around mid-afternoon, just a few hours before an astronomical high tide. The calm eye of the hurricane was estimated to be 50 miles wide and the entire storm nearly 500 miles in diameter, monstrous in scope and intensity. Waves between 30 and 50 feet pounded the coastline with millions of tons of sea-water, sweeping entire homes and families into the ocean. The impact of the storm surge was so powerful that it was recorded on the earthquake seismograph at Fordham University in New York City.

Most people did not realize that a hurricane was upon them, even as the waters began flooding their coastal homes. The hurricane had traveled up the coast and smashed into Connecticut before any kind of formal warning could be issued. Winds gusting as high as 186 mph stripped the paint off cars. People fled the rising water by hiding in their attics, only to have their entire homes swept away by the storm surge. Winds gusting as high as 150 mph pushed a 20-foot wall of water and debris into Rhode Island, and wind-whipped waves rose as high as 30 feet, inundating coastal communities. Downtown Providence was deluged with 20 feet of churning, muddy water. At least 380 people died in Rhode Island alone, a total of more than 600 people perished, and nearly 2,000 were injured.

The hurricane produced the greatest storm tides ever witnessed in southern New England, destroying nearly 9,000 homes. With an estimated price tag of a third of a billion dollars, the Great Hurricane of '38 was the costliest storm the United States had ever experienced, a grim reminder of the sheer unpredictability of nature's most fickle storm.

Ruins of the Baptist Church at Murphysboro, Illinois. A funeral was in progress when the tornado hit around 2:30 p.m. The church was a casualty of the Tri-State Tornado, the longest-lived and with the longest path of any recorded tornado. It traveled over 219 miles from southeast Missouri to Indiana and killed 695 people.

March 18, 1925
Tri-State Tornado

The tornado that tore across three states on March 18, 1925, remains America's deadliest single tornado. Touching down around 1:00 p.m. in the Ozarks of Missouri, the mile-wide funnel clung to the ground for 219 havoc-ridden miles. It had an average forward speed of 63 mph but accelerated to 73 mph at times, giving surprised residents little time to reach a safe shelter. By the time this monster tornado dissipated near Petersburg, Indiana, at 4:30 p.m., it had killed 695 people, at least 600 of them in Illinois. It wiped the towns of Murphysboro, Illinois, Gorham, Missouri, and DeSoto, Indiana, off the map, injuring over 2,000 people and destroying 15,000 homes.

In his book *The Tri-State Tornado: The Story of America's Greatest Tornado Tragedy,* Peter S. Felknor describes the horrific scene that survivors confronted in the southwestern Indiana town of Griffin: "When the cloud, bloated with debris and tons of river mud, had passed over a slight rise of land to the east of the village, it

Touching down around 1:00 p.m. in the afternoon in the Ozarks of Missouri, the mile-wide funnel clung to the ground for 219 havoc-ridden miles.

Members of an engineering committee examining a 1- by 5-inch board, which was driven through a 2- by 6-inch plank.

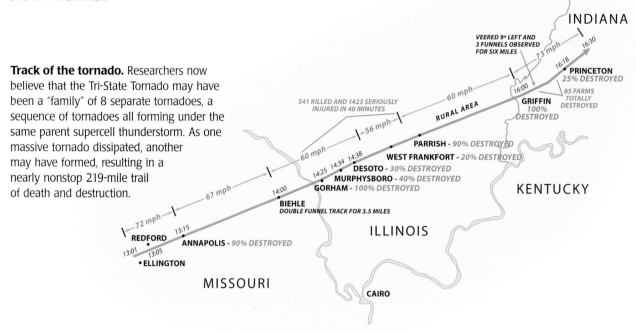

Track of the tornado. Researchers now believe that the Tri-State Tornado may have been a "family" of 8 separate tornadoes, a sequence of tornadoes all forming under the same parent supercell thunderstorm. As one massive tornado dissipated, another may have formed, resulting in a nearly nonstop 219-mile trail of death and destruction.

INDIANA

VEERED 9° LEFT AND
3 FUNNELS OBSERVED
FOR SIX MILES

73 mph

16:30

16:18

• PRINCETON
25% DESTROYED

60 mph

16:00

85 FARMS
TOTALLY
DESTROYED

GRIFFIN
100%
DESTROYED

RURAL AREA

541 KILLED AND 1423 SERIOUSLY
INJURED IN 40 MINUTES

56 mph

PARRISH - 90% DESTROYED

WEST FRANKFORT - 20% DESTROYED

KENTUCKY

60 mph

14:25 14:34 14:38

DESOTO - 30% DESTROYED

MURPHYSBORO - 40% DESTROYED

GORHAM - 100% DESTROYED

67 mph

14:00

BIEHLE
DOUBLE FUNNEL TRACK FOR 3.5 MILES

ILLINOIS

72 mph

13:15

REDFORD

ANNAPOLIS - 90% DESTROYED

13:05

13:01

• ELLINGTON

MISSOURI

CAIRO

It was a bubbling, churning wall of debris, a swirling landfill of sharp objects rotating at close to 300 mph.

left behind a landscape that passed beyond the bounds of despair into unreality. The handful of unscathed citizens from Griffin and surrounding districts were confronted with destruction so complete that some could only guess where they had once lived. The search for family and friends had a special hellishness, as fires flickered over the ruins and the injured wandered about in a daze, mud so thoroughly embedded in their skin that identification was all but impossible."

Felknor's book has a quote from a survivor that was printed in the *St. Louis Post-Dispatch* of March 20, 1925: "All morning, before the tornado, it had rained. The day was dark and gloomy. The air was heavy. There was no wind. Then the drizzle increased. The heavens seemed to open, pouring down a flood. The day grew black. . . . Then the air was filled with 10,000 things. Boards, poles, cans, garments, stoves, whole sides of the little frame houses, in some cases the houses themselves, were picked up and smashed to earth. And living beings, too. A baby was blown from its mother's arms. A cow, picked up by the wind, was hurled into the village restaurant."

A "wedge tornado," the storm didn't even resemble the classic funnel that people knew as a "cyclone," the term used for tornadoes during that era. It was a bubbling, churning wall of debris, a swirling landfill of sharp objects rotating at close to 300 mph. Despite the fact that an F-5 tornado touches down every year or two somewhere in the United States, there has never been a tornado to rival the viciousness of the Tri-State Tornado of 1925.

There was very little left of Desoto, Illinois, after the F-5 Tri-State Tornado swept into town.

In his book *Significant Tornadoes,* Thomas P. Grazulis writes that the Tri-State Tornado was America's deadliest. It also had the longest track, 219 miles.

Getting to work in New York City. Three-to four-foot snow piles, which buried cars and curtailed public transportation, were common in Manhattan.

An enhanced infrared satellite image. The coldest clouds producing the heaviest snow show up as green, yellow, and orange. From space powerful storms often appear to look like "comma clouds."

January 6–8, 1996
The Blizzard of '96

A parade of wild winter storms plagued much of the eastern United States with record snow and ice during the winter of 1995–96. A paralyzing blizzard, a classic nor'easter, swept up the East Coast from January 6 to January 8, dumping 1 to 3 feet of snow in its wake. Many cities east of the Mississippi River picked up 3 to 4 times their normal winter allotment of snow. Accidents and heart attacks from shoveling are thought to have been responsible for as many as 100 deaths, with damage estimates of $2 billion.

Philadelphia and parts of New Jersey were hammered by the greatest one-storm snowfall totals ever. In Philadelphia, the storm left 30.7 inches of snow, breaking the old one-storm snowfall record by 9.4 inches. This blizzard also exceeded the 12 inches of snow left during 1993's so-called "Storm of the Century." The all-time record snowfall for New Jersey, 34 inches in coastal Cape May in February 1899, was beaten by 1 inch at Whitehouse Station in northeastern Hunterdon County, New Jersey, which received 35 inches of snow through January 9. Central Park in New York City was buried under 20.2 inches of snow, making it the third-greatest snowfall in the city's history.

Snowfall amounts were even more impressive just inland, with 24.6 inches at Dulles International Airport, west of Washington, D.C. But the "Golden Snow Shovel" award goes to Pocahontas County, West Virginia, where an astounding 48 inches of snow was reported; that's without the drifts!

29

September 21, 1989
Hurricane Hugo

Hurricane Hugo, a very powerful category-4 hurricane, struck Charleston, South Carolina, on September 21, 1989. Hugo's storm surge was the highest ever recorded on the East Coast of the United States, estimated at 20 feet above normal sea level just north of Charleston. The hurricane had a 150-mile-wide swath of severe destruction, and the damage path extended hundreds of miles inland. An estimated 1 billion board feet of timber were destroyed by the hurricane's relentless winds. Hugo killed 504 people, 82 of those deaths in the U.S., and the damage estimates have approached $7 billion. Hurricane Hugo ranked as the 11th most intense hurricane to strike the U.S. mainland during the twentieth century and the most intense hurricane to strike Georgia and the Carolinas in the last 100 years.

Hurricane Hugo was twice the size of Hurricane Andrew, which slammed into southern Florida in August 1992.

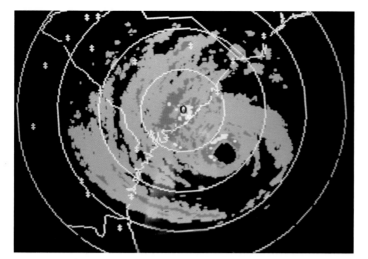

Weather beast. National Weather Service radar showing Hugo's eye approaching the South Carolina coast. The strongest winds were just north of the eye in the doughnut-shaped "eyewall." Sustained winds of 135 mph were reported as the eye came ashore, but winds may have gusted as high as 150 mph. Charleston reported a wind gust of 108 mph. Luckily the strongest winds hit a relatively rural area well north of Charleston; otherwise the death toll would have been much higher.

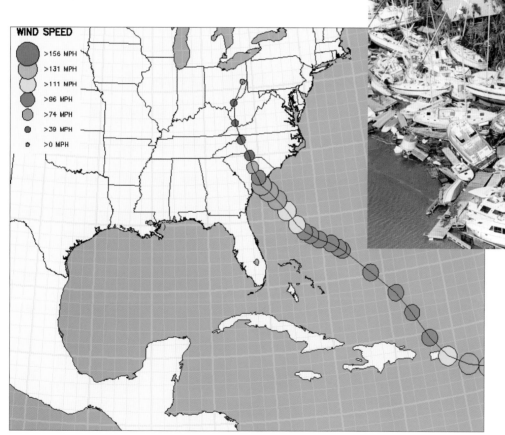

WIND SPEED
- >156 MPH
- >131 MPH
- >111 MPH
- >96 MPH
- >74 MPH
- >39 MPH
- >0 MPH

Boats piled up at Isle of Pines, South Carolina. Total damage from the storm was $7 billion.

Hugo's track. The National Hurricane Center uses satellite imagery and manned flights into hurricanes to estimate the intensity and direction of tropical systems. On September 15, 1989, a NOAA reconnaissance aircraft flew into Hugo, expecting to find winds in the 100–115 mph range. But satellite photographs had greatly underestimated Hugo's fury. What the crew found when it entered the "eyewall" was sustained winds of 190 mph and a central barometric pressure of 27.1 inches, a category-5 storm. The NOAA aircraft was damaged by extreme turbulence. It was forced to dump 50,000 pounds of fuel while inside the eye of Hugo. The crew and aircraft of this mission were nearly lost.

May 31, 1889
Johnstown Flood

Two thousand two hundred and nine residents of Johnstown died on that fateful Friday,

Let's end where we began, in the nineteenth century.

The rains were relentless, the ground hopelessly waterlogged, when a telegraph warning went out to the residents of Johnstown, Pennsylvania. The old South Fork Dam might not be able to hold up under the strain of the weather, it warned. Scores of men rushed into the fray and worked around the clock to try to fortify the dam, but the sheer volume of muddy water was overwhelming. On that fateful Friday 2,209 residents of Johnstown died, making this one of America's worst weather-related tragedies.

Johnstown in 1889 was a steel company town with a German and Welsh population. With 30,000 inhabitants, it was a growing and industrious community known for the quality of its steel.

There was one small drawback to living there. Johnstown had been built on a floodplain at the fork of the Little Conemaugh and Stony Creek rivers. Because the growing city had narrowed the riverbanks to gain building space, the heavy annual rains had caused increased flooding in recent years. There was another thing. Fourteen miles up the Little Conemaugh was the three-mile long Lake Conemaugh, an abandoned reservoir, held on the side of a mountain—450 feet higher than Johnstown—by the old South Fork Dam. The dam had been poorly maintained, and every spring there was talk that it might not hold. But it always had, and the supposed threat became something of a standing joke around town.

At 4:07 p.m. on the chilly, wet afternoon of May 31, 1889, the inhabitants heard a low rumble that grew to a "roar like thunder." Some knew immediately what had happened: After a night of heavy rains, the South Fork Dam had finally broken, sending 20 million tons of water crashing down the narrow valley. Churning with huge chunks of debris, the wall of floodwater grew at times to 60 feet high, tearing downhill at 40 mph, leveling everything in its path.

Thousands of people desperately tried to escape the wave. Those caught by the wave found themselves swept up in a torrent of oily, muddy water, surrounded by tons of grinding debris, which crushed some but provided rafts for others. Many became helplessly entangled in miles of barbed wire from the destroyed wireworks. It was over in 10 minutes, but for some the worst was still to come. Darkness fell, thousands were huddled in attics, and others were floating

House ripped from its foundation by the flood, with a tree trunk sticking out of a window.

on the debris, while many more had been swept downstream to the old Stone Bridge at the junction of the rivers. Piled up against the arches, much of the debris caught fire, entrapping 80 people who had survived the initial flood wave.

Many bodies were never identified; hundreds of the missing never found. Emergency morgues and hospitals were set up, and commissaries distributed food and clothing. The nation responded to the disaster with a spontaneous outpouring of time, money, food, clothing, and medical assistance.

The cleanup operation took years, with bodies being found months, and in a few cases years, after the flood. The city regained its population and rebuilt its manufacturing centers, but it was five years before Johnstown was fully recovered from the devastation.

In the aftermath, most survivors laid the blame for the dam's failure squarely at the feet of the members of the South Fork Fishing and Hunting Club. They had bought the abandoned reservoir and then repaired the old dam, raised the lake level, and built cottages and a clubhouse in their secretive retreat in the mountains. The members were wealthy Pittsburgh steel and coal industrialists, including Andrew Carnegie and Andrew Mellon, who had hired one B. Ruff to oversee the repairs to the dam. There is no question about the shoddy condition of the dam, but no successful lawsuits were ever brought against club members for its failure and the resulting deaths downstream. Many locals still believe that although this may have been a "natural" disaster, surely man was an accomplice.

A wall of water and debris estimated to be 40 to 60 feet high swept through the center of town with a thunderous roar at 4:07 p.m., moving at 40 mph. The grinding roar of water and debris somersaulting and churning downstream drowned out the screams of residents. In less than 10 minutes it was over, and survivors who had been fortunate enough to take shelter on higher ground emerged to the flattened, muddy remains of Johnstown below.

CHAPTER TWO

Seasons of Change

"There is no season such delight can bring,
as summer, autumn, winter and spring."—William Browne

Winter

ADMIT IT, I ENJOY WINTER. Canada sneezes a numbing air mass south of the border, and those jagged blue triangles invading from the north have us piling on layers of clothing and darting from one heated space to another. And leave it to the meteorologists to make us feel even more uncomfortable. Before we

even stick a toe out the front door, we've been clubbed over the head with the windchill and the perils of frostbite. Yes, it's cold out there, a character-building day. But with a modicum of sense we can take it all in stride.

We all learned in the third grade why the seasons change, and probably forgot it by the fourth grade. Our earth moves around the sun in an elliptical orbit. One complete orbit equals one full year, a little over 365 days. While it orbits, the earth is also turning on an axis. One complete turn equals 24 hours, day and night, as we turn away from and then back to the sun.

The seasons are the result of the earth being

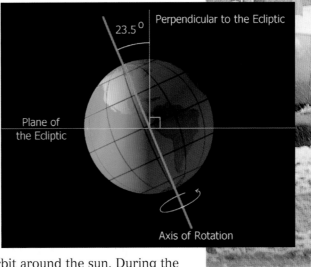

tilted on that axis 23 1/2 degrees as it makes its orbit around the sun. During the summer months the Northern Hemisphere tilts toward the sun, receiving direct and intense sunlight. During the winter the Northern Hemisphere tilts away from the sun, so the sun's energy is more diffuse and washed out.

Because of that elliptical orbit, the earth is a few million miles closer to the sun in winter than it is in summer. But the backward tilt of the axis keeps it cold—sometimes very cold—in our part of the world.

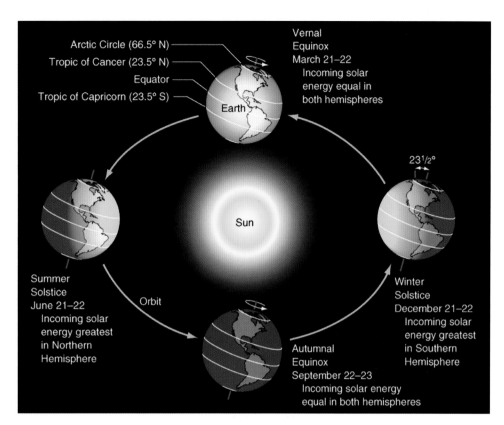

Every state in America has experienced snow, even Florida, where the Panhandle has picked up enough to shovel and plow. Although it's rare, even Los Angeles has been pelted with ankle-deep drifts. Snow can be too plentiful over the Rockies, resulting in deadly avalanches, while fat nor'easters grinding up the Atlantic Seaboard, dripping with moisture from the Gulf of Mexico and the Atlantic Ocean, are capable of piling up snow not only by the inch, but also by the foot! No one is immune from the wicked winds of winter.

But how often do you take a few extra minutes to enjoy the icy wonders unfolding outside your window? A fresh snow coats the world outside with white wonder and new possibilities, icicles drip, and the sky sparkles with crystalline radiance. After a fresh blast of arctic air, the snow squeaks underfoot and a deep breath will bring a jolting surge of ice crystals into your nose, both tip-offs that the mercury in your thermometer is close to zero.

America has thrived for many reasons. We are a creative, resilient, and tenacious people, and some of that has probably come about thanks to our winters. We not only survive, but thrive, as the flakes race past our windows. In spite of a weariness born of countless traffic reports, spin-outs and fender-benders, Americans are still optimistic about the state of the weather. And if you don't like the sky draped over your house right now, don't worry. Give it a few minutes, and it's bound to change.

DO VEHICLES "FEEL" THE WINDCHILL, LIKE PEOPLE AND PETS DO?

Unless your vehicle perspires, the short answer is no. Remember that evaporation of perspiration off your skin is the basis for the windchill formula. Since cars and trucks don't perspire, metal and plastic won't feel any colder than the actual air temperature. One caveat: A strong wind will cool your vehicle's engine down to the current air temperature faster than if there were little or no wind.

A New Windchill Formula

Meteorologists are fond of reciting the latest windchill, and there is a reason why. A steady wind will make you feel colder than you would otherwise. Evaporation has a cooling effect, and the stronger the wind the more perspiration evaporates off your skin, leaving you feeling chilled to the bone.

Until recently, the windchill formula we used was based on the work of two Antarctic explorers, Paul Siple and Charles Passel. In the 1940s, the two experimented with water-filled plastic cylinders, noting how long it took the water to freeze under various combinations of temperature and wind.

The problem? Siple and Passel based their findings on winds 33 feet off the ground. And the human face is quite different from a plastic cylinder. A new and refined windchill formula was needed. Volunteers were recruited, with temperature sensors attached to their faces to test different combinations of wind and temperature in a wind tunnel!

The new windchill formula takes into consideration temperature and wind, a lack of sunlight, and gives a more realistic prediction of what it really feels like out there.

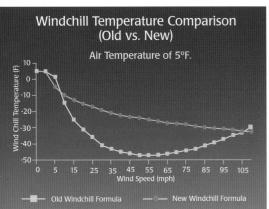

Windchill Temperature Comparison (Old vs. New)
Air Temperature of 5°F.

The new windchill formula. T is temperature in degrees Fahrenheit and V is wind velocity in mph. This new formula, developed with the National Weather Service and the Meteorological Services of Canada, went into effect in the fall of 2001.

The new windchill formula is warmer than the old formula. You can see this in the graph above, which assumes an air temperature of 5 degrees. So, a particular windchill index doesn't feel quite as cold as it used to.

At right, the new windchill chart in use today.

$$\text{Windchill}(^\circ F) = 35.74 + 0.6215T - 35.75(V^{0.16}) + 0.4275T(V^{0.16})$$

	Temperature (°F)																
Calm	40	35	30	25	20	15	10	5	0	-5	-10	-15	-20	-25	-30	-35	-40	-45
5	36	31	25	19	13	7	1	-5	-11	-16	-22	-28	-34	-40	-46	-52	-57	-63
10	34	27	21	15	9	3	-4	-10	-16	-22	-28	-35	-41	-47	-53	-59	-66	-72
15	32	25	19	13	6	0	-7	-13	-19	-26	-32	-39	-45	-51	-58	-64	-71	-77
20	30	24	17	11	4	-2	-9	-15	-22	-29	-35	-42	-48	-55	-61	-68	-74	-81
25	29	23	16	9	3	-4	-11	-17	-24	-31	-37	-44	-51	-58	-64	-71	-78	-84
30	28	22	15	8	1	-5	-12	-19	-26	-33	-39	-46	-53	-60	-67	-73	-80	-87
35	28	21	14	7	0	-7	-14	-21	-27	-34	-41	-48	-55	-62	-69	-76	-82	-89
40	27	20	13	6	-1	-8	-15	-22	-29	-36	-43	-50	-57	-64	-71	-78	-84	-91
45	26	19	12	5	-2	-9	-16	-23	-30	-37	-44	-51	-58	-65	-72	-79	-86	-93
50	26	19	12	4	-3	-10	-17	-24	-31	-38	-45	-52	-60	-67	-74	-81	-88	-95
55	25	18	11	4	-3	-11	-18	-25	-32	-39	-46	-54	-61	-68	-75	-82	-89	-97
60	25	17	10	3	-4	-11	-19	-26	-33	-40	-48	-55	-62	-69	-76	-84	-91	-98

Wind (mph)

Frostbite Times   30 minutes   10 minutes   5 minutes

Layering for Warmth

Your mother was right. Dressing in multiple layers of clothing will do a better job of keeping you warm than putting on one big overcoat. Layers of underwear and outerwear hold on to your body's warmth more effectively, trapping insulating air between the layers and cutting down on heat loss. The goal is to wear clothing that allows ventilation as well as insulation. This will enable the sweat to evaporate into the air instead of lingering and making you feel chilled.

Winter Dressing Tips

Don't overdress. Heavy clothing can increase perspiration and have a cooling effect. The advantage of layering is that clothing can be removed as the body warms up. It's also important to remove wet clothing immediately, as dampness will leave you more vulnerable to windchill and hypothermia. Use your head. Remember that most of the heat leaving your body goes through the top of your head. Consider wearing a hat and scarf. Avoid cotton because it absorbs perspiration, leaving you more vulnerable to catching a chill over time.

Don't forget to cover your extremities; don't count on the sun to keep you warm. The best choices for hats and gloves are fleece, wool, and polypropylene. Mittens tend to be warmer than gloves, because less area is exposed. Pick the right shoes, socks, and boots. Too much covering and warmth on your feet can be just as bad as not enough; too much covering can trap heat, increase perspiration, and cause a chill. Wear shoes with thick soles if you are physically active.

Frostbite

Frostbite is, literally, frozen body tissue, usually on the surface of the skin, but sometimes going much deeper. It most commonly affects extremities: toes, fingers, earlobes, the chin, cheeks, and the nose—body parts often left uncovered in

WEATHER-PROOFING YOUR PETS

• Don't leave dogs outdoors in cold weather. Most dogs, and all cats, are safer indoors, except when taken out for exercise. Regardless of the season, shorthaired, very young, or old dogs and all cats should never be left outside without supervision. Short-coated dogs may feel more comfortable wearing a sweater during walks.

• No matter what the temperature, windchill can threaten a dog's life . . . If your dog is an outdoor dog, he/she must be protected by a dry, draft-free doghouse large enough to allow the dog to lie down comfortably, but small enough to hold in his/her body heat. The floor should be raised a few inches off the ground and covered with cedar shavings or straw.

• Warm engines in parked cars attract cats and other small mammals, which may crawl up under the hood. To avoid injuring any hidden animals, bang on your car's hood to scare them away before starting your engine.

• The salt and other chemicals used to melt snow and ice can irritate the pads of your pet's feet. Wipe the feet with a damp towel before your pet licks them and irritates his/her mouth.

• Antifreeze is a deadly poison, but it has a sweet taste that may attract animals and children. Wipe up spills and store antifreeze (and all household chemicals) out of reach. Better yet, use antifreeze-coolant made with propylene glycol; if swallowed in small amounts, it will not hurt pets, wildlife, or children.

State-by-State Low Temperature Records

Washington
-48
Dec. 30, 1968
Mazama,
Winthrop

Montana
-70
Jan. 20, 1954
Rogers Pass

North Dakota
-60
Feb. 15, 1936
Parshall

Oregon
-54
Feb. 10, 1933
Seneca

Idaho
-60
Jan. 18, 1943
Island Park Dam

Wyoming
-66
Feb. 9, 1933
Riverside

South Dakota
-58
Feb. 17, 1936
McIntosh

Nebraska
-47
Feb. 12, 1899
Camp Clarke

Nevada
-50
Jan. 8, 1937
San Jacinto

Utah
-69
Feb. 1, 1985
Peter's Sink

Colorado
-61
Feb. 1, 1985
Maybell

Kansas
-40
Feb. 13, 1905
Lebanon

California
-45
Jan. 20, 1937
Boca

Oklahoma
-27
Jan. 18, 1930
Watts

Arizona
-40
Jan. 7, 1971
Hawley Lake

New Mexico
-50
Feb. 1, 1951
Gavilan

Alaska
-80
Jan. 23, 1971
Prospect Creek

Texas
-23
Feb. 8, 1933
Seminole

Hawaii
12
May 17, 1979
Mauna Kea

IT COULD BE WORSE, MUCH WORSE.

The Russian research facility at Vostok, Antarctica, holds the record for the world's coldest air temperature, −129° F. on July 21, 1983.

Minnesota
-60
Feb. 2, 1996
Tower

Wisconsin
-54
Jan. 24, 1922
Danbury

Michigan
-51
Feb. 9, 1934
Vanderbilt

Iowa
-47
Feb. 3, 1996
Elkader

Illinois
-36
Jan. 5, 1999
Congerville

Indiana
-36
Jan. 19, 1994
New Whiteland

Ohio
-39
Feb. 10, 1899
Milligan

Missouri
-40
Feb. 13, 1905
Warsaw

Kentucky
-34
Jan. 28, 1963
Cynthiana

West Virginia
-37
Dec. 30, 1917
Lewisburg

Virginia
-30
Jan. 22, 1985
Mountain Lake

Arkansas
-29
Feb. 13, 1905
Pond

Tennessee
-32
Dec. 30, 1917
Mountain City

North Carolina
-34
Jan. 21, 1985
Mt. Mitchell

Mississippi
-19
Jan. 30, 1966
Corinth

Alabama
−27
Jan. 30,1966
New Market

Georgia
-17
Jan. 27, 1940
N. Floyd County

South Carolina
-19
Jan. 21, 1985
Caesars Head

Louisiana
-16
Feb. 13, 1899
Minden

Florida
- 2
Feb. 13, 1899
Tallahassee

Vermont
-50
Dec. 30, 1933
Bloomfield

New Hampshire
-47
Jan. 29, 1934
Mt. Washington

Maine
-48
Jan. 19, 1925
Van Buren

New York
-52
Feb. 18, 1979
Old Forge

Massachusetts
-35
Jan. 12, 1981
Chester

Pennsylvania
-42
Jan. 5, 1904
Smethport

New Jersey
-34
Jan. 5, 1904
River Vale

Connecticut
-32
Feb. 16, 1943
Falls Village

Rhode Island
-25
Feb. 5, 1996
Greene

Delaware
-17
Jan. 17, 1893
Millsboro

Maryland
-40
Jan. 13, 1912
Oakland

the cold. Frostbite must be handled very carefully to prevent permanent tissue damage or loss. Children are at greater risk than adults, both because they lose heat from their skin more rapidly and because they may be reluctant to go inside and warm up.

> ## WHAT DOES FROSTBITE FEEL LIKE?
>
> "The temperature was −47°F and I was fool enough to take my hands out of my mitts to haul on the ropes to bring the sledges up. I started away with all ten fingers frostbitten. They did not really come back until we were in our tent for our night meal, and within a few hours there were two or three large blisters, up to an inch long on all of them. For many days those blisters hurt frightfully." —Apsley Cherry Garrard, in his book about Antarctic exploration, *The Worst Journey in the World*

Symptoms of frostbite can include:
- A tingling, "pins and needles" sensation.
- A numb or waxy feel to the skin.
- Skin that turns white or a grayish-yellow.

What do you do if you suspect frostbite?
- Bring the person indoors into a warm room.
- Make sure the person affected does not try to walk on frostbitten toes; this can increase damage.
- Remove wet clothing and gently warm the affected area in lukewarm (but not hot!) water. If fingers are showing signs of frostbite, you can also place them under your armpits to speed the warming process.
- Don't rub the affected area. Do not rub snow on the affected area! This remedy is an old wives' tale that will only increase pain and possible damage.
- Don't heat the affected area in front of a furnace or flame. Because of numbness the victim is much more vulnerable to burns.
- Wash the area gently and put a sterile bandage on the frostbitten area. Keep the area clean to avoid possible infection.
- Call a doctor immediately and get the affected person to the emergency room.

The cold facts: Cold weather kills an average of 700 Americans every year, according to the Centers for Disease Control and Prevention. About 50 percent of all winter fatalities from hypothermia are people over 60, with 75 percent of these being male. The elderly and children less than a year old are most susceptible to the cold. For people in these age groups, indoor temperatures should be kept above 69 degrees, and they should dress appropriately when going outside. Check in on older family members and neighbors when a frigid wind is blowing.

What Is Snow?

A snowflake is a unique collection of ice crystals that stick together as they fall to earth. Microscopic bits of dust, clay, leaf particles, and sea salt provide the nuclei on which ice crystals begin to form when the atmosphere is supersaturated, a relative humidity above 100 percent. Snowflakes are really soil particles that have been dressed up in an icy cloak. In a ripe environment, with a high ice content, a typical snowflake can grow from 1 to about 10 millimeters in less than 20 minutes. Snowflakes vary in size, lacy structure, and surface markings.

Example of a "dentritic crystal."

Every snowflake is made up of from 2 to 200 ice crystals. A snowflake's ultimate shape depends on several factors, including the air temperature, the type of nucleus, and the humidity of the air the flake is falling through. The result can be a "dendrite," "needle," "plate," or "prism."

Signs of an Impending Heavy Snowfall

It's cold out there! An estimated 80% of all snowstorms occur between 24 and 32 degrees; the heaviest wet snows occur close to 32 degrees.

- Winds are blowing from the northeast. If winds are blowing from the east or southeast, there's a good chance that warm air will change the snow over to ice or rain in the short term. A northwesterly wind often means that the storm has already passed and that colder, drier air is blowing back into town.
- The projected storm track is south and east of your location, keeping you on the "cold side" of the storm.
- The barometer is falling rapidly.
- The air is dry. Evaporative cooling, the reason we feel chilled when a strong wind is blowing, often changes rain over to snow if the air is dry.
- Temperatures throughout the lowest mile of the atmosphere are below 32 degrees. Even a thin layer of warmer air near the ground can change precipitation to sleet or rain.

SNOWY TRIVIA

- More snow falls each year in southern Canada and the northern U.S. than at the North Pole.
- Large snowflakes can measure up to 2 inches across and can contain hundreds of individual crystals.
- The largest snowflake ever found was 8 inches by 12 inches. It was reported to have fallen in Bratsk, Siberia, in 1971.
- The heaviest snowfall in 24 hours was 76 inches at Silver Lake, CO, on April 15, 1921.
- The heaviest snowstorm occurred Feb. 13–19, 1959, at Mt. Shasta Ski Bowl, CA: 189 inches of snow fell.

Nationwide the average amount of snow that falls is about 28 inches. The record snowfall for a single winter season is a whopping 1,140 inches, about 95 feet, which fell during the winter of 1998—99 at Mount Baker, in Washington State.

Not All Snows Are Created Equal

Meteorologists have specific definitions when discussing snowfalls. Snow flurries, obviously, are those light snowfalls with little or no accumulation. "Light snow" means the falling snow allows for visibility greater than 5/8 of a mile. "Moderate snow" means visibility is restricted to between 1/4 mile and 5/8 of a mile. "Heavy snow" means visibility is under a quarter mile. That's when you stay home if you can!

A blizzard is defined as falling or blowing snow with visibility under 1/4 mile and sustained winds of 35 mph or higher, with dangerous windchills for a period of at least three hours. A severe blizzard requires winds of 45 mph or higher, along with temperatures colder than 10 degrees.

The word *blizzard* was originally a boxing term used to describe a flurry of punches. But in 1870 a newspaper reporter at the Easterville, Iowa, *Vindicator* used the word to describe a storm that had delivered a "knockout punch" to the area. Within a few years the big East Coast newspapers had picked up the term, and *blizzard* had become the word for wild winter storms.

Winter Watches, Warnings, and Advisories: The Difference

Ever wonder what the meteorologists mean when they use terms like "warnings" and "advisories"? Here's what they're saying:

WINTER STORM WATCH   Announced when there is a likelihood a "warning" will eventually be issued. Watches are normally valid for events possibly occurring within 12 to 48 hours, but they may be pushed to 6 hours before if uncertainty still exists.

WINTER STORM WARNING   Heavy snow expected, 6 inches or more within 12 hours or 8 inches within 24 hours. Warnings may also be issued for smaller amounts if there is significant blowing snow, low windchills, sleet, freezing rain, and the like.

BLIZZARD WARNING and **GROUND BLIZZARD WARNING**   Expected: sustained winds or frequent gusts of 35 mph or higher, and falling or blowing snow with visibility less than one-quarter mile for at least three hours. Ground blizzards deal only with blowing snow.

ICE STORM WARNING   Ice accumulations of at least 1/4 inch expected.

WINDCHILL WARNING   Widespread windchills of at least 35 degrees below zero, with winds greater than 10 mph. In some parts of the southern U.S., the threshold for issuing a warning can be warmer than minus 35 degrees.

WINTER WEATHER ADVISORY   Normally issued for weather that may cause inconvenience or require caution. Issued for up to six inches of snow, freezing rain/drizzle, sleet, blowing snow, or a combination of weather elements. Typically issued for the upcoming 12-hour period but sometimes extends into the second 12-hour period.

WINDCHILL WATCH   Typically issued when windchill values of minus 35 degrees with a 10 mph wind are possible 12 to 48 hours in the future.

WINDCHILL ADVISORY   Widespread windchills of at least 25 degrees below zero with winds at least 10 mph. In some parts of southern Minnesota, the threshold may be 20 below.

FREEZE WATCH   Typically issued when low temperatures of 32 degrees or lower will be possible in the next 12- to 48-hour period, during the growing season.

FREEZE WARNING   Low temperatures are expected to be 32 degrees or lower during the growing season.

> **WHEN IS ICE SAFE TO WALK ON?**
>
> Don't even think about walking on ice that is less than 2 inches thick. In fact, you would be well advised to wait until there is at least 4 inches of clear, solid ice. A 4-inch thickness will provide a valuable margin of safety. Snowmobiles and ATVs need at least 5 inches, and cars and light trucks need at least 8 to 12 inches of good clear ice.

Avalanche Weather

Avalanches pose a significant threat across the western United States and New England, claiming more lives every year than earthquakes. An avalanche is truly a force of nature, capable of snapping mature pine trees like matchsticks and crushing reinforced buildings. When an avalanche finally stops, the snow often has the consistency of concrete, making search-and-rescue efforts difficult or even making them impossible.

Avalanches are difficult to predict. The threat of a slide depends on the weather, the steepness of the slope, and the exposure to wind and sunshine. A weak layer of snow—snow crystals shaped in a way that makes it difficult for them to bond together—within a thick snow pack can set the stage for disaster. If a weak layer is buried deep within a slab of snow, and a trigger is present, such as a skier or snowmobiler above, the slab can break off and surge down the hillside. A majority of avalanche victims travel in backcountry, and many of these people trigger the slides that ultimately claim their lives. Nearly all avalanche accidents could be avoided if people would read the signs on the mountains and avoid steep slopes of 35 degrees or more when conditions are favorable for slides.

Avalanches are most likely after rapid and extreme changes in the weather. Heavy snow, rain falling on snow, high winds, a quick thaw—any of these conditions hitting a slope of 30 to 45 degrees can increase the risk of a devastating and deadly avalanche. Under the right conditions massive slabs of snow can break off and hurtle down the slopes at an astounding 60 mph.

Oddly enough, rescue techniques for avalanche victims remain nearly as crude and limited as they were centuries ago. In spite of new sophisticated tracking and GPS location technology that skiers and hikers can carry on to the slopes, the rescuer's best tool is still a long, thin pole used for probing the packed snow for its victims.

SNOWFALL IN AMERICA

The northern two-thirds of America receive, on average, at least 10 inches or more of snow every winter. The heaviest amounts of snow are over the Rocky Mountain Range and downwind of the Great Lakes, where "lake effect" can wring out snow at the rate of 3 inches an hour.

AMERICA'S SNOWIEST CITIES

1. Valdez, AK	326.0
2. Blue Canyon, CA	240.3
3. Marquette, MI	141.0
4. Sault Ste. Marie, MI	117.4
5. Syracuse, NY	115.6
6. Caribou, ME	111.6
7. Mount Shasta, CA	104.9
8. Lander, WY	100.4
9. Flagstaff, AZ	100.3
10. Sexton Summit, OR	97.8
11. Muskegon, MI	96.1
12. Buffalo, NY	93.6
13. Rochester, NY	92.3
14. Erie, PA	88.8
15. Alpena, MI	84.6
16. Binghamton, NY	84.2

Snow, Sleet, and Freezing Rain

For precipitation to fall as snow, temperatures throughout the lowest mile or so of the atmosphere need to be below freezing. Often snowflakes melt within a warm layer aloft

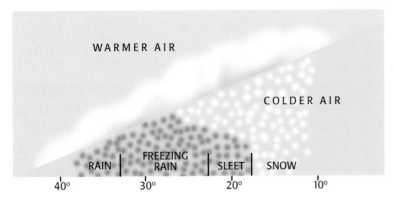

WARMER AIR

COLDER AIR

| RAIN | FREEZING RAIN | SLEET | SNOW |

40°   30°   20°   10°

Icy precipitation. When snowflakes melt while falling through a warm layer and refreeze, the result is sleet—ice pellets. If snow melts into rain and then freezes on contact with cold ground, freezing rain, or glaze ice, results, the most difficult form of winter precipitation to drive on.

Glaze. Freezing rain creates a coating of glaze ice that can make for treacherous travel.

and then refreeze into tiny ice pellets called sleet.

If rain freezes on contact with cold surfaces, roads, trees, and power lines, the result is freezing rain, which poses the greatest danger to commuters and pedestrians. Front-wheel and even four-wheel drive will not provide much additional traction on glaze ice triggered by freezing rain. The only solution: Slow down dramatically when driving, and help older friends and family members when they are walking on icy sidewalks and driveways.

The Perils of Predicting

Predicting how much snow will fall is fraught with peril. Every storm is different, and although computer models give us a rough idea of what may happen, a tiny swerve in the storm track can make the difference between heavy rain and six inches of heavy wet snow. Are temperatures in the lowest mile going to stay below freezing? If not, even a thin layer of milder air may change snow over to sleet or rain, keeping snowfall amounts lower.

As meteorologists, our biggest fear is predicting "partly sunny," only to wake up the next morning to 12 inches of "partly sunny." As a result weather forecasters tend to overestimate snowfall amounts. The truth is that there are limits to the science of snow prediction. Most days it's more of an art than a science. We can't usually pin down a snowfall to a specific inch amount, and even a range of inches can be far off the mark.

Is there a better way to predict snowstorms? Pennsylvania State's Professor John Cahir may be on to something. Here is the scale he devised, a way of rating potential snowstorms:

Nuisance Snow Light coating of snow or slush, no significant impact on transportation.

Plowable Snow Enough to shovel, scrape, and plow. Commutes are affected. Walking is difficult, but it is possible to get around.

Crippling Snow A paralyzing snowstorm capable of halting most ground and air travel. Just getting around town becomes difficult. Schools and businesses are closed.

45

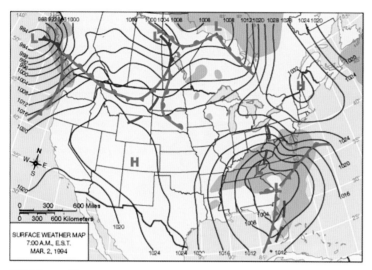

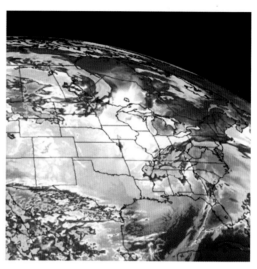

NOAA weather map and an infrared satellite image from a developing nor'easter on March 2, 1994.

The Nor'easter

A nor'easter is a powerful area of low pressure that usually forms or intensifies off the Carolina coast before tracking toward Long Island and New England. It gets its name from the howling winds that often blow in from the northeast as the storm is strengthening and tracking along the coastline.

Because nor'easters can tap moisture from the Gulf of Mexico, rainfall and snowfall amounts inland can be very significant. The greatest blizzards on record—1888, 1993, and 1996—were all extreme examples of nor'easters. A fresh surge of cold air approaching from the northwest, combining with warm, moist air offshore and warm Gulf Stream waters sets the stage for explosive intensification. Air pressure drops dramatically, forcing more moisture to spiral into the center of this area of low pressure. The air converges, rises, and cools rapidly. Since cool air can't hold as much water as warm air, the result is rain, snow, and ice.

Nor'easters are most likely between October and April, when moisture is abundant and large temperature contrasts are present—potential fuel for a deepening low-pressure system. In addition to producing heavy snow, ice, and rain, they can result in near-hurricane force winds capable of severe beach erosion and coastal flooding. In rare instances nor'easters have been even more damaging than hurricanes, affecting tens of millions of Americans.

> **NOTABLE NOR'EASTERS**
>
> March 1993
> ('Storm of the Century')
> Snow, tornadoes, and flooding from Alabama to Maine; damages in excess of $1 billion
>
> Halloween 1991
> More than 1,000 homes damaged from the Carolinas to Maine
>
> Presidents' Day 1979
> Shut down Washington, D.C.
>
> Ash Wednesday 1962
> Northeast coastline hit for five days

A Maine forest, left, mangled by heavy ice. Above: Two inches of ice and more accumulated on power lines across a huge portion of northern New England and eastern Canada in the Ice Storm of '98.

The Ice Storm of '98

In early January of 1998 heavy rain fell on New England and much of eastern Canada, freezing into glaze ice on contact. As much as three inches of ice accumulated on trees and power lines, crushing roofs and throwing hundreds of thousands of people into the dark for weeks. At least 11 deaths were blamed on the unusually severe ice storm, and thousands of New Englanders were forced to flee their homes until full power was restored.

In Quebec, Canada, at least two million people were left without power by the freak storm. Residents of Maine are accustomed to heavy snow (an average of 72 inches falls every year), but the Ice Storm of '98 was one of the worst to ever hit the region. One storm after another crashed in, with no chance for the ice to melt in between systems. As a result most of New England became encased in a thick shell of solid ice. Thirty-seven counties were declared disaster areas. The U.S. Department of Agriculture estimated that 18 million acres of forestland were damaged by the heavy coating of ice.

Lake-Effect Snows

Lake-effect snows, sometimes called squalls, are most likely to form downwind of the Great Lakes, the result of icy winds passing over open water that is, in some cases, 10 to 30 degrees warmer than the air temperature. One-hundred-inch snowfalls are common from the suburbs of Cleveland into western New York, and

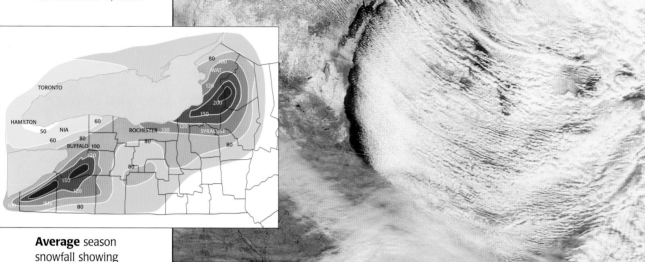

A spectacular satellite image of lake-effect snow bands setting up on December 5, 2000.

Average season snowfall showing enhanced totals due to lake-effect snows in New York State. During Christmas break, 2001, a total of seven feet of snow buried the Buffalo, New York, area. Travel bans went into effect and at least 70 percent of the highways in western New York State were impassable.

many towns routinely shovel out from 200 inches or more every winter.

How do these wild snows form? As cold air is moistened and heated from the lake below, the atmosphere in the lowest couple of miles becomes highly unstable and capable of heavy downpours of snow. This agitated, churning air reaches the shoreline, where it is forced to rise up and over hilly terrain. This added upward motion squeezes even more snow out of the atmosphere. On rare occasions snowfall rates as high as 5 to 10 inches an hour have been observed, along with lightning and thunder.

LAKE-EFFECT SNOWS

68"
Adams, New York
January 9, 1976

102"
Oswego, New York
January 27–31, 1966

467"
Hooker, New York
Winter of 1976–77

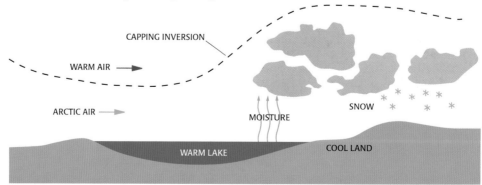

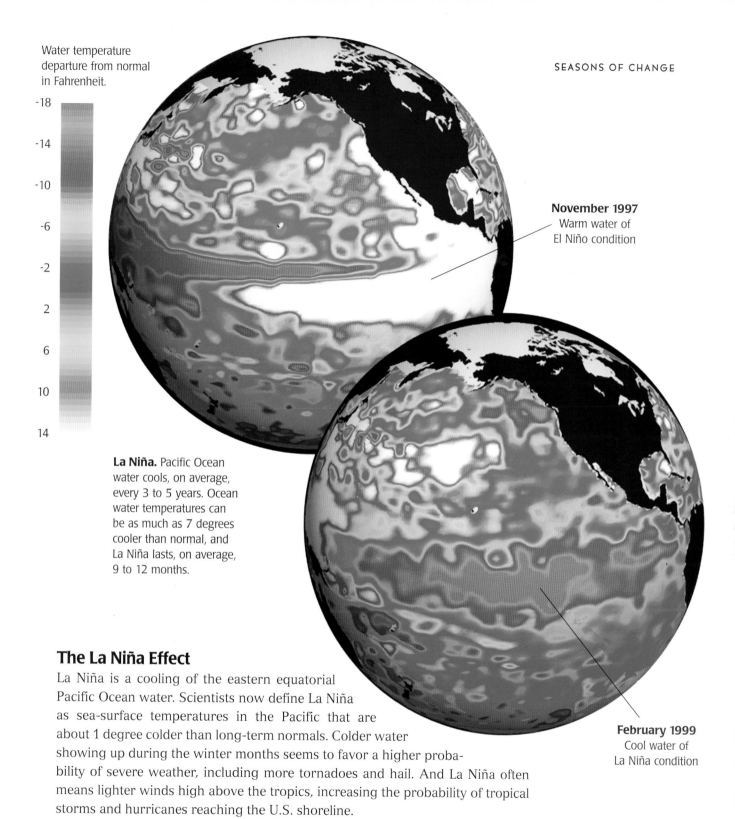

Water temperature departure from normal in Fahrenheit.

-18
-14
-10
-6
-2
2
6
10
14

November 1997
Warm water of
El Niño condition

La Niña. Pacific Ocean water cools, on average, every 3 to 5 years. Ocean water temperatures can be as much as 7 degrees cooler than normal, and La Niña lasts, on average, 9 to 12 months.

February 1999
Cool water of
La Niña condition

The La Niña Effect

La Niña is a cooling of the eastern equatorial Pacific Ocean water. Scientists now define La Niña as sea-surface temperatures in the Pacific that are about 1 degree colder than long-term normals. Colder water showing up during the winter months seems to favor a higher probability of severe weather, including more tornadoes and hail. And La Niña often means lighter winds high above the tropics, increasing the probability of tropical storms and hurricanes reaching the U.S. shoreline.

La Niña, which means "little girl" in Spanish, produces the opposite weather of El Niño, including wetter-than-normal weather for the Pacific Northwest and warmer, drier weather for most of the southern United States.

49

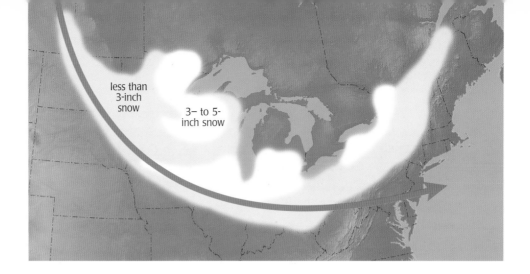

less than 3-inch snow

3– to 5-inch snow

An Alberta clipper diving southeastward out of Canada, spreading snow into the Great Lakes and New England.

The Alberta Clipper

Storms can approach from virtually any direction, but for much of the Midwest, the Great Lakes region, and New England, fast-moving storms sweeping out of Canada can bring sudden snows and high winds capable of severe blowing and drifting. Alberta clippers are named after the clipper ships of the nineteenth century, the fastest vessels of their times.

Clippers have limited moisture, but they can often whip up 30 to 60 mph winds, stirring up snow already on the ground. Cold, northwesterly exhaust on the back of these fast-moving storms can trigger sudden lake-effect snows. Although generally not as severe as nor'easters, clippers are capable of wreaking their own unique brand of meteorological trouble.

Some Sobering Winter Storm Facts and What to Do About Them

Statistics show that 70 percent of winter-storm deaths are automobile related. One-fourth of winter-storm fatalities are the result of individuals being stranded in a storm, and more than 50 percent of these deaths involve males.

"Black ice" is one of winter's worst hazards. When air temperatures fall close to zero, water in your vehicle's exhaust is unable to evaporate into the air. It freezes directly onto the highway surface, creating a thin layer of ice, even when skies overhead are crystal clear. Black ice is most likely to be found where cars and trucks idle, at intersections and metered ramps. Ice can come from rather unlikely sources!

Too many people wind up injured, or worse, when their cars are disabled in a snowstorm. If you are in an urban or a suburban area, walk to a house or business, but only if it's so close that you can see its lights.

If you are in the country and no lights are visible nearby, wait for help to reach you. Statistically, you are far safer if you stay with your vehicle and wait for help.

Here's what you can do to increase your odds of survival:

- Tie something colorful onto your vehicle's antenna, to signal that you are having trouble.
- Run your engine and heater sparingly, to conserve fuel.

- Crack your window to let fresh air into the vehicle. If your vehicle's exhaust pipe is buried in the snow and you run the engine, the risk of carbon monoxide poisoning is considerable.
- Do not attempt to go through fields to reach help. In a heavy snowstorm or blizzard it's easy to become disoriented, frostbitten, and hypothermic.

Before heading out on a long cross-country drive in the cold weather, put together a winter survival kit, just in case you get stuck. Here is what you should include:

- Shovel
- First-aid kit
- Nonperishable food, such as granola bars and peanuts
- Flashlight with extra batteries
- Candles and matches
- Extra clothing, and sleeping bags or blankets for everyone
- Tire chains
- Battery-operated radio with batteries
- Empty coffee can to be used to burn the candles or to melt snow for water
- Booster cables
- Cell phone with fully charged batteries

Simply Refueling Your Car Can Be a Winter Hazard

You may be surprised to hear that just getting back into your vehicle to warm up while the gas is pumping greatly increases the risk of igniting gas fumes, with potentially catastrophic results. The reason for the threat: The simple act of opening the door and getting back into your seat creates static electricity, which under certain circumstances may be enough to ignite gasoline fumes coming from the gas tank. The threat of static electricity is higher during the winter months, when the relative humidity is low.

Mobile cell phones can also ignite gasoline fuel or fumes. Mobile phones that light up when switched on, or when they ring, release enough energy to provide a spark for ignition. Cellular phones should not be used in filling stations, or when fueling lawn mowers, boats, or portable containers. Mobile phones should not be used, or should be turned off, around other materials that generate flammable or explosive fumes or dust, such as solvents, chemicals, gases, and grain dust.

The Four Rules for Safe Refueling

- Turn off your engine.
- Do not smoke.
- Do not use your cell phone—leave it inside the vehicle or turn it off.
- Do not re-enter your vehicle during fueling.

Spring

Across much of America spring comes tentatively, teasing us with moments of soft warmth, then dashing our hopes in rainy downpours.

The transition from winter to summer can leave the atmosphere irritable, unstable, and capable of unspeakable wrath. The earth begins to tilt back toward the sun, warming the ground and the air near it to balmy levels. But the upper atmosphere is still feeling a chill, a winter hangover of sorts, and this imbalance, cold air above warm air, sets the stage for violently rising thermals, intense updrafts capable of hail, and, on rare occasions, tornadoes. That's why severe weather peaks during the spring months, when the temperature profile over our heads is most lopsided, unstable and primed for thunderstorms.

The severe weather season starts early in the year along the coastline of the Gulf of Mexico, from Texas to Georgia and Florida, and then works its way north with the rising sun. Dry air swirling in from the west at mid levels of the atmosphere mix with a moist southerly wind coming up from the

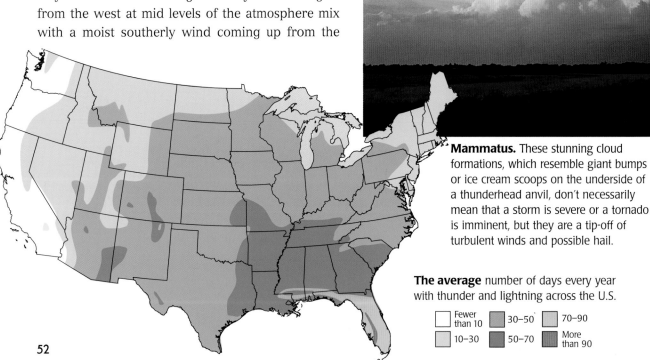

Mammatus. These stunning cloud formations, which resemble giant bumps or ice cream scoops on the underside of a thunderhead anvil, don't necessarily mean that a storm is severe or a tornado is imminent, but they are a tip-off of turbulent winds and possible hail.

The average number of days every year with thunder and lightning across the U.S.

Fewer than 10	30–50	70–90
10–30	50–70	More than 90

bayous of Louisiana. Throw in a dash of jet-stream winds speeding along at 125 mph and you have a ripe environment for thunderstorms. When these rapidly rising fingers of warm, moist air begin to twist and turn, rotating violently, the stage is set for atmospheric fireworks below.

Tracking the Unstable Atmosphere

How do meteorologists know when the atmosphere is unstable and capable of thunderstorms, hail, and tornadoes?

National Weather Service meteorologists release weather balloons into the atmosphere and track them as they drift downwind. A radiosonde is a balloon-borne weather-instrument platform with radio transmitting capabilities. Tiny radio transmitters onboard transmit temperatures, humidity, and pressure data back to National Weather Service offices, giving meteorologists a thumbprint of what the atmosphere overhead looks like. How quickly are temperatures dropping off as the balloons lose altitude? Is there dry air aloft? Is there a warm "cap," an inversion that can help the atmosphere build up energy? If a rising thermal of warm, moist air finally breaks through, the result can be a thunderstorm with explosive upward motion, capable of spinning up a tornado. A rawinsonde is a radiosonde with special radar reflectors that can be tracked from the ground, permitting forecasters to calculate wind speed and direction as it rises through the atmosphere.

The weather balloons, which are made of latex or synthetic rubber (neoprene), are filled with either hydrogen or helium. The balloons start out measuring about 6 feet wide in diameter before release and expand to about 20 feet as they rise. These instruments will endure brutal conditions: temperatures as cold as minus 139 degrees, relative humidities from zero to 100 percent, air pressures only a few thousandths of what is found on the earth's surface, ice, rain, thunderstorms, and wind speeds of almost 200 mph. A transmitter on the radiosonde sends the data back to tracking equipment on the ground every one to two seconds.

Launching a weather balloon from the South Pole. Twice a day, every day of the year, weather balloons are released simultaneously from almost 900 locations worldwide. This includes 92 released by the National Weather Service in the U.S. and its territories. A typical balloon flight lasts for around two hours. During that time the balloon can drift as far as 125 miles away and rise up to over 100,000 feet (about 20 miles) in the atmosphere.

A parachute attached to the end of the weather balloon allows it to fall slowly to the ground at speeds of less than 22 mph after the balloon bursts. Each and every weather balloon contains a mailing bag and instructions on what to do if one is found. About 20 percent of the 75,000 rawinsondes sent up each year in the United States are found and returned. These instruments are fixed and reused, saving the government money.

Weather balloons are the primary source of data above the ground. They provide information for computer forecast models and provide data for meteorologists to make forecasts. Without weather balloons accurate forecasts beyond a few hours would be almost impossible.

Floods: An Alarming Trend

In spite of vastly improved technology and mass media warnings, the number of Americans killed by flooding has been on the rise since the 1940s.

FLOOD-RELATED FATALITIES IN THE UNITED STATES	
Decade	Deaths
1940–49	619
1950–59	791
1960–69	1,297
1970–79	1,819
1980–89	1,097
1990–99	994

Scientists estimate that river flooding costs the United States an average of $6 billion every year. During an average year flooding claims more lives in this country than hurricanes, tornadoes, and lightning combined.

Why is the flooding toll so high? There is some evidence that much of America is experiencing snowier winters, which means more potential moisture to be released during a sudden thaw or rain. And that rain isn't falling nearly as gently as it did a century ago. Research shows that in the United States, heavy one-day rainfalls have become 20 percent more common in the last 90 to 100 years. Add to that the fact that much of what was once farmland is now suburban subdivisions and parking lots. Rainwater and melting snow can't soak into the paved-over ground, so they run off into streets, storm sewers, and rivers faster than ever, increasing the risk of disaster.

Both economic and human losses caused by floods have been increasing in the latter half of the twentieth century. But in spite of the increased flooding, more people than ever are moving into or near floodplains, precariously close to streams or rivers. For many it's a matter of aesthetics. Yes, the view out the window overlooking the water is beautiful, but it comes with a cost.

THE WORST CONDITIONS FOR RIVER FLOODING

Heavy snow cover, with 3 to 8 inches of water contained in a 1- to 4-foot snowpack.

A rapid thaw, with temperatures rising into the 40s and 50s.

Heavy rain, which can accelerate snowmelt and make a bad situation much worse.

The Red River Flood

During the spring of 1997 the Red River, which flows north into Canada, experienced a devastating flood. The flood was a catastrophic event for Grand Forks, North Dakota, and East Grand Forks, Minnesota. Thousands of homes and businesses were inundated by the floodwaters, and the damage toll is thought to have been close to $2 billion. Immediately following the flood, local, state, and federal officials began to point fingers at the flawed flood predictions as a factor that made the damage much worse.

The winter of 1996–97 had broken records for snowfall throughout the region. The *Grand Forks Herald* had popularized the practice of naming blizzards in a

fashion similar to hurricanes. In April 1997 blizzard Hannah brought winds of over 60 mph to the Red River Valley, along with more than 20 inches of snow, the most severe blizzard since March 1941. This record snowfall set the stage for the record floods that were to follow.

In early March, the National Weather Service was predicting a major flood with a crest of 49 feet at East Grand Forks, and officials planned accordingly. The additional moisture deposited from the early April blizzard boosted the eventual flood crest to 54 feet in mid April. The Flood of '97 showed what the limits of science were and highlighted the inherent difficulties of flood prediction.

A Flood Watch or Warning Has Been Issued. What Should I Do?

In preparation for a river flood, follow these guidelines from the National Weather Service:

- Know your elevation compared to flood stage.
- Keep your automobile fueled. Gas stations may not be able to operate gas pumps for several days after the flood.
- Store drinking water in clean bathtubs or in containers. Water service may be interrupted for days.
- Maintain a reserve of food that requires little, if any, cooking and no refrigeration.

Here is what the Flood of '97 looked like. Nearly all of the 50,000+ residents of Grand Forks, ND, and East Grand Forks, MN, had to be evacuated. More than 90 percent of the 10-square-mile city was underwater. Inset, a screen shot from a WCCO-TV helicopter in Minnesota's Twin Cities showing the Red River bursting through the levees surrounding Grand Forks, ND.

- Keep on hand a battery-powered radio and plenty of batteries.
- Install check valves in sewer traps to prevent floodwaters from backing into drains in your home.

During a river flood, follow these safety tips:
- If you come upon a flowing stream where the water is above your ankles, stop, turn around, and go the other way.
- Do not attempt to drive over flooded roadways.
- Never allow children to play near high water, storm drains, or viaducts.
- Follow all evacuation orders.

After the flood is over many dangers still remain. Remember these safety rules after river floods end:
- Throw out any fresh food that came in contact with floodwaters.
- Boil all water before drinking it.
- Test well water for purity before drinking.
- Do not visit disaster areas; you may hinder emergency operations.
- Dry and check electrical equipment before using it.
- Use flashlights—not lanterns, torches, or matches—to examine buildings. Flammable materials may be inside.
- Report downed utility lines to appropriate authorities.

Pothole Weather

During the early spring, when the temperature fluctuates to either side of 32 degrees, conditions are ripe for the creation of potholes. The freeze-thaw cycle is prime time for highway havoc. The reason? During the day snow melts and seeps into tiny cracks in the highway. At night, as the mercury dips below freezing, water freezes and expands. Over time this can literally pulverize the roadway surface and carve out crater-size potholes.

A pothole big enough to fish in!
Crater-size potholes are most likely over the northern-tier states of America, where the freeze-thaw cycle can last for several months in the spring, and again in the fall.

Rainbow Time

One benefit of April showers is the rainbow that may follow the storm. But the sun has to be low in the sky, usually within a couple hours of sunrise or sunset for this beautiful optical illusion to be visible. Rainbows are created by white sunlight being refracted, or bent, within a tiny, prism-like raindrop. If the light is bent once, a single rainbow is visible; twice, and you can see a rare double rainbow. Triple rainbows are extremely rare, but they do occur.

57

A towering thunderhead.
Usually, the higher a storm reaches into the atmosphere, the greater the potential for flooding rains, hail, high winds, and tornadoes.

Summer

America's summers are typically long and luxurious. A bright sun warms the lower 48 states, and moisture streams out of the Gulf of Mexico to create a hazy stew of tropical heat. By evening many of us are secretly praying for a cooling thundershower. Some of us will get our wish, and then some.

Although the atmosphere isn't as agitated as it was back in April and May, late-day cauliflower-clouds can shoot skyward, dropping rain and hail, and thus cooling the earth below by 20 degrees in a few seconds and providing precious water for farmers. Every once in a great while a thunderstorm will encounter a wind field that sets it spinning like a top. The storm mutates into a "supercell," a rotating, 6-mile-wide, 12-mile-tall tower of trouble that could evolve into a tornado. Sirens sound, and television meteorologists interrupt shows with warnings showing the track of the storm right down to street level. About 20 percent of the time a tornado does skip across the ground.

As the air becomes stuffy and inflamed and the mercury rises through the 90s, we take off to the beach or the pool or huddle indoors in air-conditioned comfort, wondering where the Canadian cool fronts are when you really need them! That heat poses a slow-motion, insidious form of danger, directly or indirectly claiming over a thousand lives every summer, far more than hurricanes, tornadoes, and lightning combined. We remove too much clothing, chug gallons of water, and avoid the midday sun, and yet there are still some days when relief is just nowhere to be found.

Heat Index and Dew Point: Do They Matter?

The heat index, the combined effect of temperature and relative humidity, gives a more accurate measure of how we're going to feel outside than temperature alone does. A heat index over 105 represents significant danger; one over 125 can lead to dangerous and even fatal heat-related ailments within minutes, especially if heavy exercise is involved. The elderly, infants, and people with medical conditions, such as heart and respiratory ailments, are most at risk for heat exhaustion and heatstroke.

Dew point is an absolute measure of how much water is in the air, and how uncomfortable it really feels outside. The higher the number, the greater the amount of water in the air and the more likely you are to overheat.

The dew point is different from relative humidity, which, as the name implies, is relative to the temperature. The relative humidity can be a bit misleading. For example, if the temperature is 94 but the relative humidity is 50 percent, the apparent temperature, or heat index, is 103, in the danger zone! A relative humidity of 50 percent doesn't sound that bad, but coupled with hot temperatures it can be life threatening.

Many people expect to see the relative humidity displayed during the nightly weather report, but increasingly the dew point temperature is being accepted as an effective way to communicate the comfort level—just how sticky it feels outside.

Relative Humidity (%)

HEAT INDEX (apparent temperature)

Air Temperature (°F)	40	45	50	55	60	65	70	75	80	85	90	95	100
110	136												
108	130	137											
106	124	130	137										
104	119	124	131	137									
102	114	119	124	130	137								
100	109	114	118	124	129	136							
98	105	109	113	117	123	128	134						
96	101	104	108	112	116	121	126	132					
94	97	100	103	106	110	114	119	124	129	135			
92	94	96	99	101	105	108	112	116	121	126	131		
90	91	93	95	97	100	103	106	109	113	117	122	127	132
88	88	89	91	93	95	98	100	103	106	110	113	117	121
86	85	87	88	89	91	93	95	97	100	102	105	108	112
84	83	84	85	86	88	89	90	92	94	96	98	100	103
82	81	82	83	84	84	85	86	88	89	90	91	93	96
80	80	80	81	81	82	82	83	84	84	85	85	86	87

EXTREME DANGER
Heatstroke or sunstroke highly likely

DANGER
Sunstroke, muscle cramps, and/or heat exhaustion likely

EXTREME CAUTION
Sunstroke, muscle cramps, and/or heat exhaustion possible

CAUTION
Fatigue possible

DEW POINT SCALE

40s	Dry, crisp and comfortable
50s	Comfortable for most people
60s	Sticky and uncomfortable
70s	Tropical and potentially dangerous (consider limiting outdoor activities)
80+	Rare and extreme, danger level is off the charts (stay inside an air-conditioned room!)

JUNE BRIDES, BEWARE!

For much of America east of the Mississippi River, June is the wettest month of the year. A total of 3 to 7 inches of rain falls on much of the eastern United States, and Pacific storms drop the heaviest precipitation on the Pacific Northwest.

Heat Risks

Every year, either directly or indirectly, extreme heat claims more than a thousand lives in the United States. A single heat wave in 1980 is thought to have claimed 1,250 lives across the nation. A single heat storm in Chicago over the span of three days in July 1995 took 739 lives. Researchers estimate that worldwide the death toll from heatstroke may exceed 20,000 people annually, deaths that in many cases could have been prevented if people had taken even minimal precautions.

Here's the problem. When it's not only hot but humid, all that extra water in the air makes it difficult for your body to cool itself. All of us have natural thermostats wired into our systems that cause us to perspire when the mercury rises to high temperatures. The evaporation of sweat from your skin has a cooling effect (that's the concept behind windchill). The more you sweat, the cooler you feel, up to a point.

But when the relative humidity is high, when dew point temperatures are already in the 70s and a thick pall of moisture hangs in the air, your body's natural defense system begins to break down. If the weather's already sticky and humid, simply perspiring won't have much of a cooling effect, and that can have serious consequences.

It's important to understand the difference between various heat-related disorders, so you know what to do if you come across someone who has symptoms. Making the right choices can have life-saving implications.

THE HOT FACTS

America's hottest official temperature: 134°F at Death Valley on July 10, 1913.

The hottest temperature recorded on earth: 136 at Al'Aziziyah, Libya, in September 1922.

The summer of 1995 was so hot that freshly cut bales of hay in Missouri began emitting methane, causing some of them to spontaneously combust!

Heat Disorders

Sunburn

Symptoms: Redness and pain. In severe cases, swelling of skin, blisters, fever, headaches.
First Aid: Ointment for mild cases if blisters appear. If blisters break, apply dry sterile dressing. Serious, extensive cases should be seen by a physician.

Heat Cramps

Symptoms: Painful spasms, usually in muscles of legs and abdomen. Heavy sweating.
First Aid: Firm pressure on cramping muscles, or gentle massage to relieve spasm. Give sips of water; if nausea occurs, discontinue.

Heat Exhaustion

Symptoms: Heavy sweating; weakness; skin cold, pale, and clammy. Pulse thready. Normal temperature possible. Fainting and vomiting.

First Aid: Get victim out of sun. Have person lie down, and loosen clothing. Apply cool wet cloths. Fan victim or move him or her to air-conditioned room. Give sips of water; if nausea occurs, discontinue. If vomiting continues, seek immediate medical attention.

Heatstroke or Sunstroke

Symptoms: High body temperature (106 degrees or higher). Hot dry skin. Rapid and strong pulse. In some cases unconsciousness.

First Aid: Heatstroke is a severe medical emergency. Summon medical assistance or get the victim to a hospital immediately. Delay can be fatal.

Move the victim to a cooler environment. Remove clothing, and reduce body temperature with cold bath or sponging. Use fans and air conditioners. If temperature rises again, repeat process. Do not give fluids.

DID YOU KNOW?

Tree crickets chirp faster when days are hotter, allowing you to compute the current temperature accurately to within a degree or two. Count the number of chirps in 15 seconds, and then add 37. You'll be amazed at how close this is to reality!

In Germany, frogs were once kept as pets because they croaked more loudly when air pressure fell, signaling bad weather. The frogs were primitive living barometers.

PETS FEEL THE HEAT TOO!

Overheating can kill your pet. Never leave an animal in a car since the temperature can rise rapidly even with windows open.

Do not leave a dog outside on hot tar surfaces. He's much lower to the ground than you are and heats up faster.

Be watchful of pesticides. Your pet doesn't wear shoes on his feet or pants to keep these things off his body. Weed killers and insecticides can make your pet sick or even kill him.

A well-brushed pet will be cooler, but never shave an Arctic breed dog short. This breed's skin has a blue and pink cast to it and burns easily.

Never let your dog ride unsecured in a pickup truck. A crate is the best and safest way for a dog to travel. In Massachusetts, it's illegal to keep your dog in a pickup unless secured in the back of the bed equally on both sides. This prevents the dog from jumping or falling out.

If your dog or cat is hot, place a cool rag on the belly, head, and paws. This will help bring the animal's temperature down. Also, everyone loves a nice cool drink. When you get ice for your drink, throw some ice cubes in your pet's dish as well.

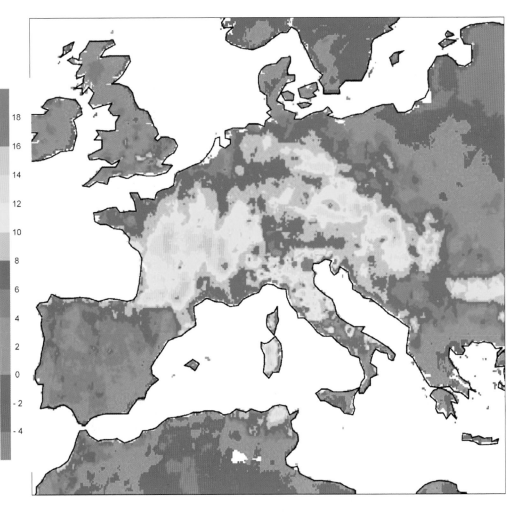

European heat storm.
This map shows the difference in temperature from 2002 to 2003. Over much of central Europe temperatures from August 10 to August 15, 2003, ran 10 to 20 degrees Centigrade, almost 20 to 40 degrees Fahrenheit, hotter than during the same period in 2002, reaching 105 to 115 degrees Fahrenheit in some areas of France, Spain, and Italy.

Temperature in Centigrade

18
16
14
12
10
8
6
4
2
0
- 2
- 4

Europe's Heat Wave

Heat can be deadly, not just in America, but around the world. During the summer of 2003, a scorching heat wave gripped Europe, with several weeks of 100-plus-degree heat. The death toll is now estimated at 35,000, according to the Earth Policy Institute in Washington, D.C., with the greatest loss of life reported in France, where more than 14,800 died.

August 2003 was the hottest August ever recorded in the Northern Hemisphere, and the heat wave of 2003 in Europe was the deadliest ever recorded anywhere on the planet. And this may be a harbinger of things to come. According to the World Meteorological Institute, the number of heat-related deaths worldwide could double in fewer than 20 years as global temperatures continue to slowly rise.

To Lower Risks in Hot Weather:
- Increase your intake of nonalcoholic, noncarbonated, caffeine-free drinks like water and juice.
- Wear lightweight, loose-fitting, light-colored clothing.

> **KOREY STRINGER'S LEGACY**
>
> Korey Stringer was a talented and caring player on the Minnesota Vikings football team. Korey was active in the community, a role model for people of all ages. He died during a workout at the Vikings training camp on August 1, 2001, from heatstroke. The previous day the temperature had reached 99, with a heat index of 111. Korey had displayed some of the symptoms of heat exhaustion and heatstroke, including vomiting and weakness, but he continued to practice. Walking off the field, he collapsed, and he was rushed to a hospital. Minutes after his arrival in the emergency room, his core body temperature was 108 degrees. A few hours later his organs began to fail, and he died.
>
> Some in the sports world have speculated that Stringer knew he was in trouble but tried to play through the nausea and disorientation. His death is a poignant reminder to coaches and players at all levels—from professional on down to peewee leagues—of certain basic rules of common sense in hot weather. Players need adequate water at all times. Doing without it doesn't "toughen" one up. That is a potentially lethal mistake. Trying to sweat or starve down to a specific weight is another dangerous exercise.
>
> Korey Stringer was a professional athlete, surrounded by professional and experienced coaches and an esteemed team doctor. And yet he's dead. He pushed too hard, under terrible weather conditions, and now a good man is gone.

- Stay in an air-conditioned environment, if possible. If your home isn't air-conditioned, go to some place that is, such as a movie theatre, a store, or a shopping mall.
- Curtail strenuous activity like running, biking, and even lawn care until a cooler front arrives.
- Cut down on your protein intake; eat less meat and more salads. This will decrease metabolic activity and heat production and leave you feeling a bit more comfortable.
- Check on older friends, family members, and neighbors. They are most susceptible to heat-related ailments.

Beware the Flash Floods of Summer

Unlike river flooding, which can take weeks to unfold, giving people time to prepare and evacuate, a flash flood can occur in a matter of minutes.

Flash floods are most likely during the summer months, when the strongest jet-stream winds aloft retreat northward. Weak steering currents high overhead can allow thunderstorms to stall or redevelop over the same counties, dumping one or two months' worth of rain in a few hours.

Unlike a gentle rainfall, torrential rains can't soak into the ground. Most of the water runs off into streets, storm sewers, and streams, and this can cause water

The Big Thompson flood of July 31, 1976, may have been a 1-in-10,000-year flash flood, according to the United States Geological Survey. The force of the water coming down the canyon was almost inconceivable, a raging tidal wave of water, rocks and debris. The flood killed 139 people; 6 others were never found. It destroyed 418 houses and damaged 138 more. Fifty-two businesses were wiped out. Damage was estimated at $35.5 million.

levels to rise to dangerous levels in a very short period.

Keep in mind that only six inches of rapidly moving water can knock you off your feet. Only two feet of rapidly moving water can turn your vehicle into a boat! Never try to cross a road that is flooded. It is impossible to estimate how deep the water is, especially at night. Flash floods claim half of all their victims in cars or trucks.

The National Weather Service issues river watches for specific rivers and tributaries, while flash flood watches can cover hundreds of thousands of square miles and highlight areas that are ripe for later flooding from heavy rainfall. If flooding is actually occurring, a flood warning or flash flood warning will be issued for specific areas along a river or for a specific county where deadly flooding is imminent.

On July 31, 1976, the Big Thompson River, near Denver, overflowed after an extremely heavy storm. A wall of water 19 feet high roared down the Big Thompson Canyon, where many people were camping. One hundred and thirty-nine people perished and millions of dollars in property were lost.

How Far Away Is That Lightning Strike?

Thunder travels at the speed of sound, covering roughly 1 mile in 5 seconds. So count the number of seconds between seeing the flash and hearing the boom, then divide by 5 to get how many miles away the strike is. For instance, if you count 15 seconds, the lightning bolt was 3 miles away. Only 3 seconds? That strike was just over a half mile away, uncomfortably close!

Another way of telling how close you are to a thunder-and-lightning storm is right in your own vehicle. Lightning creates pulses of charged electromagnetic particles, which you can pick up on your car's AM radio. To see if there are storms nearby, tune your AM radio to the far left end of the dial, around 600 to 700 kHz, but not to a particular station. Those annoying crackles of static are probably individual lightning strikes within 100 to 150 miles of your position. If you hear continuous static, then a line of strong thunderstorms may be nearby.

THE DOG DAYS

Some people think the term Dog Days refers to weather so hot it isn't fit for a dog, or that it means people wind up panting, or that they're about to endure the kind of weather where dogs go mad. Actually, it's none of the above.

The Dog Days are defined as the period of summer that goes from about July 3 to August 11. During this time the brightest star in the nighttime sky, Sirius, is rising in conjunction with the sun. It was once thought that the combination of the rising sun and Sirius created the most extreme heat of summer. Sirius is called the Dog Star (it resides in the constellation Canis Major, the Greater Dog). So for this reason these hot, hazy, lazy days were called the Dog Days of Summer. Our ancestors linked the Dog Star to more than just severe summer heat. They also thought the early morning appearance of Sirius could set off droughts, plagues, even madness!

WEATHER MYTH:
HOT WEATHER CAN TRIGGER HEAT LIGHTNING

Not true. In fact there is no such thing as heat lightning. On a clear night lightning from a distant thunderhead or line of storms can be visible hundreds of miles away. But you only hear the thunder from that lightning when the storm is less than 10 miles away. So the illusion is that the warm, sultry winds are triggering lightning, when in reality what you're seeing is distant lightning flashes from storms too far away for you to hear the accompanying thunder. Spread the word: heat lightning is a myth!

State-by-State High Temperature Records

Washington
118
Aug. 5, 1961
Ice Harbor Dam

Montana
117
July 5, 1937
Medicine Lake

North Dakota
121
July 6, 1936
Steele

Oregon
119
Aug. 10, 1898
Pendleton

Idaho
118
July 28, 1934
Orofino

Wyoming
114
July 12, 1900
Basin

South Dakota
120
July 5, 1936
Gannvalley

Nebraska
118
July 24, 1936
Minden

Nevada
125
June 29, 1994
Laughlin

Utah
117
July 5, 1985
Saint George

Colorado
118
July 11, 1888
Bennett

Kansas
121
July 24, 1936
Alton

California
134
July 10, 1913
Death Valley

Arizona
128
June 29, 1994
Lake Havasu

New Mexico
122
June 27, 1994
Lakewood

Oklahoma
120
June 27, 1994
Tipton

Alaska
100
June 27, 1915
Ft. Yukon

Texas
120
Aug. 12, 1936
Seymour

Hawaii
100
April 27, 1931
Pahala

Minnesota
114
July 6, 1936
Moorhead

Wisconsin
114
July 13, 1936
Wisconsin Dells

Michigan
112
July 13, 1936
Mio

Iowa
118
July 20, 1934
Keokuk

Illinois
117
July 14, 1954
E. St. Louis

Indiana
116
July 14, 1936
Collegeville

Ohio
113
July 21, 1934
Gallipolis

Missouri
118
July 14, 1954
Warsaw and Union

Kentucky
114
July 28, 1930
Greensburg

West Virginia
112
July 10, 1936
Martinsburg

Virginia
110
July 15, 1954
Balcony Falls

Pennsylvania
111
July 10, 1936
Phoenixville

New York
108
July 22, 1926
Troy

Vermont
105
July 4, 1911
Vernon

New Hampshire
106
July 4, 1911
Nashua

Maine
105
July 10, 1911
N. Bridgton

Massachusetts
107
Aug. 2, 1975
New Bedford and Chester

New Jersey
110
July 10, 1936
Runyon

Connecticut
106
July 15, 1995
Danbury

Rhode Island
104
Aug. 2, 1975
Providence

Delaware
110
July 21, 1930
Millsboro

Maryland
109
July 10, 1936
Cumberland and Frederick

Tennessee
113
Aug. 9, 1930
Perryville

North Carolina
110
Aug. 21, 1983
Fayetteville

Arkansas
120
Aug. 10, 1936
Ozark

Mississippi
115
July 29, 1930
Holly Springs

Alabama
112
Sept. 5, 1925
Centerville

Georgia
112
July 24, 1952
Louisville

South Carolina
111
June 28, 1954
Camden

Louisiana
114
Aug. 10, 1936
Plain Dealing

Florida
109
June 29, 1931
Monticello

67

Autumn

In the blink of an eye, it seems, summer is over. The school buses are rolling once more, and shadows are growing longer. Across much of America, September and October are glorious months with lower humidity and less chance of a sudden deluge.

There are, of course, huge exceptions to the rule. These exceptions have names, like Alice and Fran and Hugo. Ocean temperatures peak in September, potent fuel for one of nature's most fearsome of storms, the hurricane. Thanks to satellite technology and fearless aviators who fly into the raging hearts of these weather beasts, we can track them as never before, giving people ample time to move out of harm's way. The only thing we can't predict is whether people will heed the warnings or stay put and take their chances with Lady Luck.

Less daylight means that leaves are ripening into a colorful smorgasbord of lemon, rust, and pumpkin colors, and soon a shower of crunchy leaves will be stirred up by the first tentative gust of cold from Canada. Flurries will come sweeping into the northern-tier states by October, and by November lake-effect snow squalls will pummel the suburbs of Chicago, Cleveland, and Buffalo, with snow accumulating not by the inch, but by the foot!

Autumn may be my favorite season. The heat and booming thunder is history, and this intermission of blue, lukewarm sky is a tonic for the soul, giving us all a little break before the first icy blast arrives like a cold smack across the face. It's as if Mother Nature is giving us one last meteorological vacation, a reprieve of sorts, allowing us to catch our collective breath and accumulate warm clothes for the numbing winter winds to come.

Cirrus horsetail clouds, composed of ice crystals suspended 25,000 feet above the ground, can take on some interesting shapes.

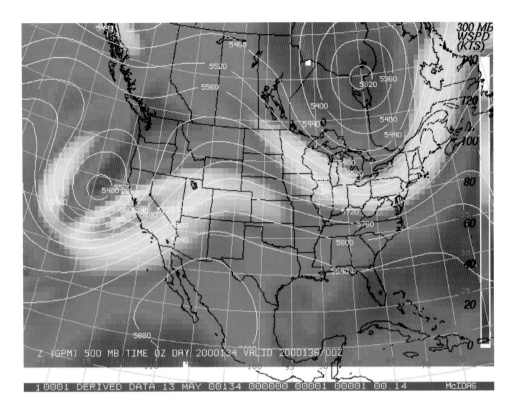

Jet stream. This is a computerized plot of high-altitude winds, roughly 30,000 feet above the ground. The yellow-shaded areas highlight the core of the strongest jet stream winds. The "wrinkle" of yellow over the Great Lakes and New England is a trough of low pressure, a potential breeding ground for low pressure systems. The trough off the west coast is "cut off", or temporarily stalled, suggesting an even stronger storm for California. The red and magenta colors show a jet streak, the most powerful surge of wind energy coming ashore. A strong storm at ground level is most likely to spin up just north of this jet streak, capable of high winds, heavy rains and mountain snows below. In between the slight bulge in the jet stream is a ridge, where drier weather is favored, possibly with a little sunshine.

The Jet Stream

What we know as "weather" takes place in the lowest 12 miles of the atmosphere, what meteorologists call the troposphere. A river of fast-moving air is constantly in motion high over our heads, blowing strongest in the winter months. The greater the contrast in temperature from north to south, the stronger the howling winds above. When the jet stream buckles in the fall and spring, the result can be rapidly intensifying storms.

The term "jet stream" originated at the end of World War II. The U.S. Air Force was flying a new plane, the B-29, at a higher altitude than any previous aircrafts. On November 4, 1944, 94 B-29 Superfortress bombers were approaching Japan on the first mass bombing assault of the war on Tokyo. These raids were conducted at high altitudes to avoid anti-aircraft fire and Japanese fighter aircraft. At altitudes between 27,000 and 33,000 feet, the planes turned east over Mount Fuji and began their bombing run. Suddenly, the startled pilots found themselves roaring

B-29 Flying Superfortress aircraft flew roughly 30,000 feet above the ground, making them the first aircraft to encounter the full fury of what became known as the "jet stream."

Meteorologists were intrigued. They had stumbled upon something truly inexplicable. What could explain a river of air at high altitudes ripping along at some 140 mph?

past landmarks at a speed of almost 450 mph, about 90 mph faster than the theoretical top speed of the aircraft. It was too late for most bombardiers to make adjustments, and most bombs fell miles beyond the intended target. Of the more than 1,000 bombs dropped, only 48 fell anywhere near the objective.

From the military viewpoint, the mission was a dismal failure, but meteorologists were intrigued. They had stumbled upon something truly inexplicable. What could explain a river of air at high altitudes ripping along at some 140 mph?

After the war, high-altitude aircraft and balloons confirmed the existence of relatively narrow ribbons of rapidly moving air, normally 180 to 300 miles wide and up to 2 miles thick. The average speed of these jet streams, as they came to be known, was between 60 and 115 mph. Some with speeds in excess of 290 mph were recorded. They were found to blow worldwide, and the shape of these ribbons could determine the characteristics of the weather below.

Meteorologists use computer models to predict the future shape and intensity of the jet-stream winds and thus extrapolate what the weather may be on the ground. A simple west to east flow implies relatively mild, storm-free weather. But when sharp troughs and ridges show up on the jet-stream maps, significant storms are likely to develop.

Why Do Leaves Change Color in Fall?

Leaves are food factories, absorbing water from the ground and carbon dioxide from the air to produce glucose, a kind of sugar, which provides the fuel that trees need to grow. This chemical conversion of carbon gas and water into sugar is called photosynthesis; it takes place with the help of something called chlorophyll, which gives leaves their green color.

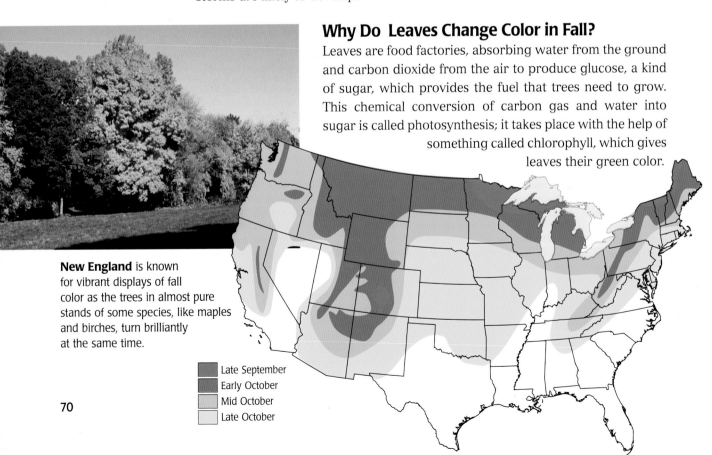

New England is known for vibrant displays of fall color as the trees in almost pure stands of some species, like maples and birches, turn brilliantly at the same time.

- Late September
- Early October
- Mid October
- Late October

70

Less daylight and cooler temperatures during the autumn months send a signal to the leaves to stop producing chlorophyll. As chlorophyll breaks down, yellow-producing xanthophyll and orange-producing carotenes, which are always present within the leaves, are no longer obscured, and so those wonderfully vivid colors begin to emerge.

Weather is a factor. Believe it or not, gray, rainy days tend to intensify the fall colors. And a combination of warm sunny days and chilly autumn nights can reveal anthocyanin, a pigment that gives leaves their reddish color, one that completes a rich crescendo of colors!

Fog

Fog is most likely in September and October, when the combination of longer nights and lingering summer moisture creates a perfect stew for lazy clouds. That's all fog is: a cloud that forms on the ground as the temperature falls to the dew point, the relative humidity reaches 100 percent, and the air becomes saturated. Fog is most likely within an hour or two of sunrise, especially when skies are clear and winds are light, allowing the mercury to drop off more rapidly.

Average number of days every year with dense fog (visibilities under 1/4 mile)

More than 40.4
35.5–40.4
30.5–35.4
25.5–30.4
20.5–25.4
10.5–20.4
5.5–10.4
less than 5.5

The foggiest weather is along the Pacific Northwest coastline, where cold ocean water chills relatively mild air above. But fog is quite common over interior New England and over the central Appalachians as well. The least fog can be found over the Rocky Mountains and the Desert Southwest.

Fog rolling into San Franciso Bay, a common sight. Fog is typical, but snow in the Bay Area is rare; National Weather Service records show that flakes have only been observed 10 times since the mid 1800s.

WEATHERFACT
One pail of water can theoretically produce enough fog to cover 105 square miles to a depth of 50 feet!

71

The Deadly Inversion

Normally temperatures in the atmosphere cool with altitude, at the rate of 3 to 5 degrees for every 1,000 feet you rise up through the air. But sometimes the temperature a few thousand feet up is warmer than at ground level. This is known as an inversion, and it can prolong cloudiness and keep the air below stale and increasingly polluted. Some of America's worst air pollution outbreaks have occurred during autumn, when winds are relatively light and inversions are quite common.

Donora, Pennsylvania at noon, October, 1948

"We all live downwind."
—1980s bumper sticker

In the 1940s the towering smokestack was a symbol of national pride, progress, and unlimited prosperity. So the town of Donora, Pennsylvania, a suburb of Pittsburgh, gave little thought to the smoke and ash billowing from the Donora Zinc Works. But in October of 1948 a strong inversion stalled over the Northeast, trapping pollutants near the ground and creating a thick, choking curtain of gray.

Streetlights came on at noon, but the town still held its Halloween parade. At the annual homecoming game, people in the stands couldn't see the players on the field. Firemen groped their way from house to house carrying oxygen bottles so residents could have a few sips of clean, untainted air. Still, the Zinc Works stayed open for several days after the stalled inversion. When rain finally broke the sulfur cloud on a Sunday night, 7,000 people, half the town's population, were ill, and 20 people had died.

The slow-motion suffocation of Donora shocked the nation and marked a turning point in our complacency about industrial pollution and its effect on health. States began to control air pollution, and in 1963 Congress passed the first federal Clean Air Act, which was amended and strengthened in 1970. States were now required to put pollution-reduction plans in place to meet federal clean-air standards. In spite of lingering issues, we've come a long way in cleaning up our air since the 1940s.

The Barometer and Grandma's Bones

In forecasting, meteorologists plot barometric readings—air pressure—to help determine if a storm is approaching. It isn't the precise value of barometric pressure that is important, but rather the trend. Is air pressure rising or falling, and if so, how quickly? A rapidly falling barometer is a tip-off that a soggy front or a storm may be approaching.

Many people are literally walking, talking barometers, able to feel subtle changes in atmospheric pressure ahead of a change in the weather. As the air pressure overhead falls, fluids in joints can swell, causing discomfort or even intense pain. Arthritis and bursitis sufferers, along with people who have recently suffered a broken bone, are more apt than others to be affected by these changes in pressure. The next time Grandma complains of a pain in the neck or her trick knee, heed the warning and batten down the hatches!

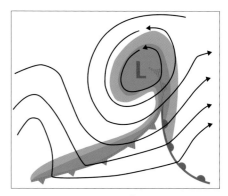

A classic low-pressure system, or cyclone. Storms become better organized during autumn as the north-south contrast in temperature becomes sharper and more extreme. Rain or snow will be heaviest and steadiest to the north and northeast of the center of low pressure, near and along the warm front. The cold front, marking the leading edge of colder air and a wind shift to the northwest, usually produces brief, heavy, showery precipitation.

The Gales of November

The transition from summer to winter can create temperature extremes, which in turn can whip up violent winds, especially when storms strengthen explosively, a rare phenomenon meteorologists call "bombogenesis." Sustained winds on the Great Lakes can easily top 60 mph. In a disastrous encounter with furious winds—captured by Gordon Lightfoot in a haunting melody—the SS *Edmund Fitzgerald* sank in Lake Superior on November 10, 1975, killing all 29 crew members onboard. A powerful low-pressure system had whipped up sustained winds of close to 50 mph, with gusts close to hurricane force. When the winds shifted around to the northwest, it meant they would blow over a longer fetch of Lake Superior, carving out towering 16-foot waves.

The 729-foot vessel, labeled the "Pride of the American Flag" when it was launched in 1958, left Superior, Wisconsin, loaded with 26,000 tons of iron ore, bound for Detroit, Michigan. Though it was the largest carrier on the Great Lakes, in the end it was no match for the gales of November.

Storm Track
November 8–10, 1975

All Times
Eastern Standard Time

7 p.m. Nov. 10 — 28.88
1 p.m. Nov. 10 — 23.95
7 a.m. Nov. 10 — 28.99
1 a.m. Nov. 10 — 29.24
7 p.m. Nov. 9 — 29.33
7 a.m. Nov. 8
7 a.m. Nov. 9 — 29.53

Deadly voyage. Track of the low-pressure system that produced sustained winds estimated at 50 mph and 16-foot waves that sank the SS *Edmund Fitzgerald*.

Southern California wildfires rage in the San Bernardino National Forest. The hot Santa Ana winds drove the ravaging fires to leap over fire breaks and roads.

Santa Ana Winds

"Those hot dry Santa Anas … come down through the mountain passes and curl your hair and make your nerves jump and your skin itch. On nights like that every booze party ends in a fight. Meek little wives feel the edge of the carving knife and study their husbands' necks. Anything can happen." That was Raymond Chandler's take on the Santa Ana winds in his short story "Red Wind."

Nothing strikes dread faster in the hearts of Californians than a prediction of Santa Ana conditions. Occurring from October into February, the Santa Ana is most likely to whip up during December, dropping relative-humidity levels to single digits, and in many cases fanning ferocious wildfires that threaten buildings and people.

When high pressure sets up near Salt Lake City, a clockwise wind flow causes the air to descend and warm as it reaches California. Winds howl from the east, reaching speeds as high as 100 mph. The air originates over the central mountains, near Salt Lake City, and it warms almost 30 degrees for every mile it drops, picking up more speed as it accelerates and spreads out through passes and canyons into the neighborhoods of Los Angeles and San Diego.

These wicked winds get their name from the Santa Ana Valley, where they blow especially hard. They dry out vegetation and ultimately spread wildfires rapidly in their wake. Many local residents associate the hot, dry winds with homicides and earthquakes, but these connections are probably just urban legends.

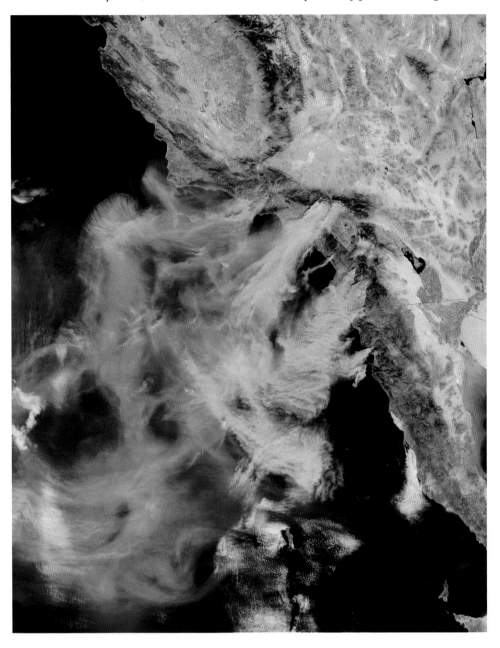

Whipped by Santa Ana winds, several massive wildfires raged across Southern California in October 2003. This satellite image captures the fire and clouds of smoke that spread over the region. Moving southeast along the coast, the first cluster of red dots is a combination of the Piru, Verdale, and Simi Incident fires; the next cluster to the east of Los Angeles is the Grand Prix (west) and Old (east) fires; to their south is the Roblar 2 Fire; next is the Paradise Fire; then the massive Cedar Fire, whose thick smoke is completely overshadowing the coastal city of San Diego; finally, at the California-Mexico border, is the Otay Fire. At least 13 people lost their lives because of these fires, which officials attribute to carelessness and arson.

CHAPTER THREE

Tornado
Nature's Evil Wind

"Nothing in the earth's atmosphere so uniquely combines spectacle, terror and random violence against unsuspecting and innocent people as the tornado. Few other phenomena can form so quickly, vanish so suddenly, leave behind such misery and yet still be seen as beautiful ."—Tom Grazulis, *Significant Tornadoes*

WHEN DISCUSSING THE WILDEST, most dangerous wind on the planet, it helps to keep some sense of perspective. Unless you live in what we call Tornado Alley, you will probably never see a tornado, even from a distance. Tornadoes do, however, make news more often than many other natural disasters. We have a morbid fascination with these fingers of extreme wind that seemingly spin up out of nowhere.

We're fascinated for good reason. Nothing is more terrifying than witnessing a writhing, churning landfill of airborne debris swirling around at four times the legal speed limit of an automobile. The tornado threat is not being sucked up into the heavens like Dorothy in *The Wizard of Oz*, but being hit on the head by a flying piece of glass whizzing along faster than a Formula 1 race car. It's not the tornado that kills; it's the junk swept up in the whirlwind. A pebble is transformed into a bullet; a nail into a spear. Blunt head trauma is the cause of most tornado-related injuries and fatalities.

There is no reason for too much complacency, either. You may not live in Tornado Alley, but these unpredictable storms can strike in unexpected places. In recent years tornadoes have hit the suburbs of Washington, D.C., and have smashed into downtown Nashville, Miami, Fort Worth, Texas, and even Salt Lake City, Utah. Tornadoes can cross rivers and mountains; they can swirl into suburbs; and a few urban high-rise buildings won't stop them.

If this is a typical year, about 1,200 tornadoes will form nationwide. Damage from these violent columns of rotating, rising air will top $400 million.

Recent data suggest that although we're not seeing more large and violent tornadoes, smaller tornadoes are becoming more numerous than ever. That may be the result of a subtle shift in America's climate, or it may just be the result of more people out in the field looking for them. The movie *Twister*, although somewhat exaggerated for Hollywood's purposes, has given birth to a new generation of the tornado-obsessed. When the watches are issued and the skies turn dark and brooding, many people head out with video cameras and cell phones, hoping to be the first breathless witness on the scene of a Texas-size, newscast-leading tornado.

In spite of an apparent increase in tornadoes in recent decades, the death toll has dropped steadily. That's a testament to improved technology from the National Weather Service and local TV stations that have invested millions of dollars in live Doppler radar systems. Warnings are getting out faster than ever, and most people know exactly what to do if a funnel whirls up in their backyard.

Tornadoes rarely drop out of the sky totally unannounced. Meteorologists have a pretty good idea when the witches' brew of ingredients is present, and

The St. Louis tornado of May 27, 1896, shot a shovel six inches into the trunk of a tree. According to the National Severe Storms Laboratory, this may have been the most damaging tornado in U.S. history. It was a violent tornado that stayed within populated areas on its entire path. If it were to take the same path through St. Louis today, it would leave behind more than $2 billion damage.

when thunderstorms might mutate into supercells, capable of spinning up a rare twister. If a watch is issued, severe storm or tornado, ask yourself where you would go and what you would do if a tornado was spotted nearby. Where would you ride out the storm?

What is a Tornado?

A tornado is a violently rotating column of air that is in contact with the ground. Tornadoes usually form underneath a cumulonimbus cloud, a thunderstorm. They do not descend from the cloud base, but rather twisting winds increase on the ground until debris is lifted into the air and the vortex becomes visible. A tornado is not an object, but rather a process.

Technically, a funnel cloud does not "touch down" in the classic sense. The entire spinning column of air becomes visible over time. For the circulating air to be called a tornado, the winds at the surface must be strong enough to produce some level of damage, and the vortex of spinning air must extend from the ground to the cloud base. A tornado is just the visible manifestation of a much larger circulation at the base of a severe, rotating thunderstorm. If you can see a funnel

Wall cloud and tornado. This eerie shot of a tornado forming over southern Minnesota shows the lowering cloud base, which usually comes at the tail-end of a severe, rotating thunderstorm. Melanie Metz from twistersisters.com captured this surreal sight near Mankato, Minnesota, on July 14, 2003.

forming, there's a good chance that tornado-force winds are swirling on the ground.

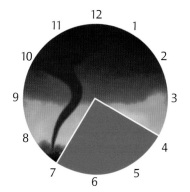

Tornadoes are most likely to strike late in the afternoon and evening, between 4:00 and 7:00, right after the period of maximum heating, the "high" for the day. It's around this time that the atmosphere is most unstable and capable of generating and sustaining the violent updrafts necessary to spin up a tornado.

That said, tornadoes are possible any time of the day. It's the twisters that strike late at night, when most people are sleeping, that produce a disproportionate number of injuries and fatalities.

Between 4:00 and 7:00 p.m. is the most likely time for tornadoes to strike.

The prime month for tornadoes along the Gulf Coast and Florida is January. The threat shifts northward with the rising sun and warming temperatures. May is the peak month for tornadoes across the entire United States. Tornadoes that hit earlier in the year tend to be more violent and intense, many of them over the southern part of the United States, where they can be wrapped in rain and harder to spot and track.

Surprisingly, it does not have to be hot and humid on the ground for a tornado to form. More critical are the dynamics overhead, the wind profile miles above the ground. On March 30, 1998, strong tornadoes ripped into southern Minnesota in spite of the fact that temperatures were in the low 50s! The weather was cool and damp, yet a major tornado outbreak took place—on such a chilly day!

A wall cloud is a lowering of the cloud base that usually precedes the formation of a tornado on the ground. It generally forms in an area of strong upward motion, a counterclockwise rotating updraft flowing into a severe thunderstorm. Wall clouds can be 1/2 mile to as much as 5 miles in diameter, and usually form on the south or southwest side of a storm, where warm, moist winds are blowing.

Not all wall clouds rotate, but rotation is usually visible a few minutes to an hour before a tornado develops. Wall clouds need to be monitored closely because of possible tornado formation.

Wall cloud. If you spot a rotating wall cloud, it's time to head for the basement or a small interior room, even if the sirens aren't sounding.

Dust Devils and Whirlwinds

A dust devil is a small, rapidly rotating wind that is made visible by the dust, dirt, or debris it picks up. Also called a whirlwind, it develops best on clear, dry, hot afternoons when the lower atmosphere is very unstable, with super-heated air near the ground, creating ideal conditions for these brief and spectacular swirls of dust and debris. Winds can top 50 mph, capable of stripping paint off cars and lifting small pets into the air, but they do not pose a significant threat of injury to people.

Tornado Ratings: From F-0 to F-5

No weather instrument has ever survived a direct strike from a tornado. Winds gusting to well over 100 mph in a matter of seconds will almost always rip off wind vanes and the cups on rapidly spinning anemometers, which measure wind speed.

In an effort to measure and classify tornadoes, the distinguished researcher Theodore "Ted" Fujita, working at the University of Chicago, devised a scale that measures the damage done by tornadoes. He examined tornadoes dating back to 1916 and flew over approximately 300 damage paths, from 1965 to 1991, to refine his system of ranking tornadoes.

His F-scale is used today, worldwide, to give scientists and the public a better understanding of the severity of the tornadoes that have been observed. An F-0 tornado is a minimal tornado, capable of only light damage and lasting a few minutes at most. An F-5 tornado is capable of enormous damage and can be as much as a mile wide.

Rare and deadly. Violent F-4 and F-5 tornadoes are rare, making up less than 2 percent of all twisters documented during a typical year. And yet this handful of tornadoes is responsible for 70 percent of all tornado-related deaths and injuries.

Ted Fujita. Tetsuya Theodore "Ted" Fujita studied not only tornado damage, but also microbursts, dangerous downdrafts which posed a special threat to aviation. He blamed a deadly 1975 airplane crash at Kennedy Airport on these phenomena, a discovery which would later lead to the installation of Doppler radars at major airports.

The Fujita Scale

	Est. Winds	Width	Length

F-0 under 73 mph   under 17 yards   less than 1 mile
Light damage. Some damage to chimneys, branches broken off trees, shallow-rooted trees blown over, sign boards damaged.

F-1 73–112 mph   18–55 yards   1–3 mile
Moderate damage. Rooftop surfaces damaged, mobile homes pushed off foundations or overturned, moving cars and trucks pushed off highways.

F-2 113–157 mph   56–175 yards   3–10 miles
Considerable damage. Roofs torn off frame houses, mobile homes demolished, large trees uprooted, cars lifted off the ground.

F-3 158–206 mph   176–556 yards   10–31 miles
Severe damage. Trains overturned, most trees in a forest uprooted, heavy cars lifted off the ground and thrown.

F-4 207–260 mph   .34–.9 mile   32–99 miles
Devastating damage. Homes are leveled, structures with weak foundations blown away for some distance, cars thrown and large missiles generated.

F-5 261–318 mph   1–3 miles   100–315 mles
Incredible damage. Strong frame homes leveled off their foundations and blown away, automobile-size missiles fly through the air for distances of at least 300 feet, bark peeled off trees.

F-6– 319–
F-12 734 mph
Inconceivable damage. A tornado with maximum wind speed in excess of F-5 has not officially occurred. If it did, consequences would be beyond comprehension.

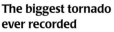

"Like whirlwinds sweeping through the southland, an invader comes from the desert, from a land of terror."
—Isaiah 21:1, one of 22 references in the Bible to tornado-like winds

The biggest tornado ever recorded
A typical, run-of-the-mill twister is about as wide as a football field, about 100 yards. So you can imagine how people living near the little town of Hallam, Nebraska, felt on May 22, 2004. The Omaha National Weather Service estimated that the tornado was 2 1/2 miles wide. This is probably close to the maximum size for tornadoes; but it is possible that larger, unrecorded ones have occurred.

White tornado. Since tornadoes usually occur at the tail-end of a severe thunderstorm, the sun often shines on the funnel, giving it a ghostly white appearance.

Waterspout. A tornado that forms over water is called a waterspout. Because temperature contrasts and jet-stream winds are somewhat lower over the Gulf of Mexico and the open waters of the Atlantic Ocean, winds within waterspouts are thought to be lighter, generally under 100 mph, still capable of damage to boats, docks, and coastal property.

Rope tornado. As tornado circulation weakens, usually because cool, wet air is being sucked into the warm updraft, the tornado becomes thinner and "ropes out" before dissipating altogether.

Wedge tornado. Some violent F-4–F-5 tornadoes are so large that they lose their funnel-like appearance and instead resemble a giant wedge or a thunderstorm that has lowered all the way to the ground. This can increase the danger. People don't realize that the approaching mass of churning black clouds is really a tornado, often until it's too late.

A lumpy "mammatus" cloud, sign of tornado? The smooth, rounded cloud bulges that form on the underside of a thunderhead anvil can be spectacular, especially when illuminated by a setting sun. They are evidence of hail and turbulence within the parent thunderhead, but they don't necessarily mean that a tornado is imminent.

Virga is not a tornado! The general public often mistakes "virga" for a tornado. Virga is simply snow or rain falling out of a cloud base, a streak of precipitation that evaporates before hitting the ground. But against a bright background it looks like a dangling dark cloud, similar to a tornado. The tip-off that it's not? Virga doesn't rotate, like a tornado or parent wall cloud. If there is no lightning or hail and the dangling cloud isn't rotating, chances are it is virga. No need to worry!

TORNADOES IN THE UNITED STATES							
	F-0	F-1	F-2	F-3	F-4	F-5	F-6
1990s	7,370	3,274	1,065	339	81	10	0
1980s	3,313	3,329	1,172	313	62	3	0
1970s	2,396	3,653	1,910	570	107	16	0
1960s	1,951	2,615	1,769	584	103	9	0
1950s	1,038	1,945	1,346	466	112	8	0

Good news and bad. Although the number of large and violent tornadoes has remained about the same or declined slightly, more weak tornadoes are being reported than ever before.

The Good Weather News

New technology is giving meteorologists and the public a potentially life-saving head start in protecting themselves against tornadoes. In roughly the last decade meteorologists have improved the lead time, the amount of time between when a tornado warning is issued and when the tornado touches down, from 6 to about 12 minutes. Every additional minute provides more time to reach a suitable shelter to ride out the storm. According to the National Weather Service, strong and violent tornadoes rarely strike without warning. This is true; however, the weaker tornadoes are harder to detect on Doppler radar and can strike with very little lead time. And these smaller tornadoes are still capable of inflicting serious damage and deadly force.

Where Is Tornado Alley?

Tornado Alley is the most likely real estate in America for tornado formation. It runs from Texas and Oklahoma north into Kansas, Missouri, and southern Iowa. It's here that the meteorological recipe for tornadoes is most often present: dry air aloft, moisture-rich air near the ground, powerful jet-stream winds blowing high overhead, and a "dry line" marking a sharp contrast between dry desert air to the west and sticky Gulf air to the east. This is where severe, long-lasting, rotating thunderstorms called supercells are most likely to form. Texas, by virtue of its size and location, gets top billing as the state with the most tornadoes every year, about 124.

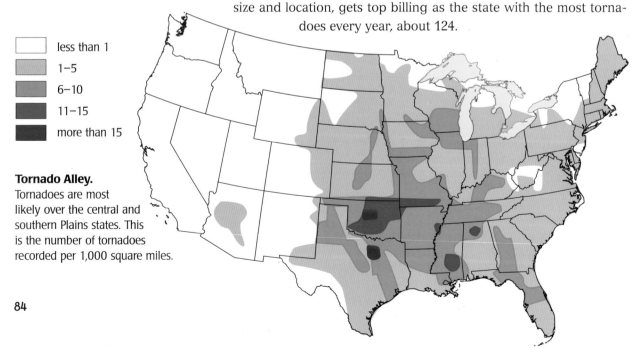

less than 1
1–5
6–10
11–15
more than 15

Tornado Alley. Tornadoes are most likely over the central and southern Plains states. This is the number of tornadoes recorded per 1,000 square miles.

Almost an F-6

A portable Doppler on Wheels, or DOW, used by meteorology students at the University of Oklahoma was deployed during the May 3, 1999, tornado that swept through Moore, Oklahoma, and the suburbs of Oklahoma City. Near Bridge Creek the radar measured sustained winds estimated at 318 mph, at the very upper end of the F-5 range of wind speeds.

The tornado was not officially upgraded to an F-6 for several reasons. The F-scale ratings are based on damage, not estimated wind speed, and the damage was consistent with an F-5 twister. The data gathered by the DOW team has been reviewed by other scientists, and there is some question as to whether the winds were as high as the estimate. But it seems fairly certain that winds did top 300 mph. In addition, the 318 mph wind was observed about 160 to 320 feet above the ground. Since wind speeds tend to increase the higher the wind is, it would be reasonable to assume that winds at ground level were not as high as 318. That said, the '99 tornado that swept through the Oklahoma City area set a new benchmark for large and violent tornadoes in the United States.

Bomb blast. The aftermath from an F-4 or F-5 tornado can look like something from a war zone.

What Does a Tornado Look Like?

Tornadoes often form in the southwestern region of a severe thunderstorm. People on the ground usually experience rain and then hail before sighting the tornado itself. Eyewitnesses say that skies brighten up as the tornado forms. Sometimes it's completely wrapped in rain or hail, and very hard to spot. If the tornado is to your north, there is a better chance of seeing the funnel on the ground. If the tornado is south of your location, chances are heavy rain and hail are obscuring your view, and this can lead to a false sense of security.

In spite of an apparent increase in tornadoes in recent decades, the death toll has dropped steadily.

In a study of 34 years of tornado tracks (over 22,800), it was found that the median tornado had a path length of 3/10ths of a mile and a width of 1/10th of a mile. But tracks of at least 31 miles were reported with 17 tornadoes, and 60 had tracks that were at least 1 mile wide!

> **THE MOST TORNADO-PRONE REGION OF THE UNITED STATES?**
>
> Based on National Weather Service data, the nation's tornado epicenter is located at latitude 40° 46' North and longitude 98° 07' West, which is approximately two miles east of the town of Giltner, Nebraska.

Predicting a Tornado

A tornado is the meteorological equivalent of a hiccup—short, brief, and random. This makes tornadoes notoriously hard to predict. Even with all the technological

Report From Inside a Tornado

At last, the great shaggy end of the funnel hung directly overhead. Everything was still as death. There was a strong gassy odor, and it seemed that I could not breathe. There was a screaming, hissing sound coming directly from the end of the funnel. I looked up, and, to my astonishment, I saw right up into the heart of the tornado. There was a circular opening in the center of the funnel, about 50 or 100 feet in diameter and extending straight upward for a distance of at least one-half mile, as best I could judge under the circumstances.

The walls of this opening were of rotating clouds and the whole was brilliantly visible by constant flashes of lightning, which zigzagged from side to side. Had it not been for the lightning, I could not have seen the opening, not any distance up into it anyway. Around the lower rim of the great vortex, small tornadoes were constantly forming and breaking away. These looked like tails as they writhed their way around the end of the funnel. It was these that made the hissing noise.

I noticed that the direction of rotation of the great whirl was anti-clockwise, but the small twisters rotated both ways—some one way and some another. The opening was entirely hollow except for something, which I could not exactly make out, but suppose that it was a detached wind cloud. This thing was in the center and was moving up and down. —Farmer Will Keller, telling his amazing story in a 1930 issue of *Monthly Weather Review*

Tornadoes have been observed on every continent of the planet except Antarctica. America experiences more tornadoes than any other country. Number two on the list: Bangladesh.

breakthroughs, there is no way to say exactly when or where a tornado will touch down. It is possible to highlight which days are ripe for tornado formation, but pinpointing which severe, rotating thunderstorms will go on to spawn a tornado is a very difficult task.

Researchers estimate that less than 20 percent of all rotating supercells spin up a tornado, but it's impossible to know exactly which spinning storms will mutate into tornado producers. As a result, meteorologists tend to overpredict tornadoes, issuing warnings while knowing that most of the warned counties won't experience a tornado. When it comes to protecting life and property, there is a desire to err on the side of safety.

But take any tornado watch seriously. A tornado watch is issued by the Storm Prediction Center in Norman, Oklahoma, when conditions are ripe for tornado formation. A watch covers an average of 25,000 square miles for a period of roughly six hours. The watch is upgraded to a warning if a tornado is observed by trained spot-

THE 10 DEADLIEST TORNADOES IN THE UNITED STATES

According to the Tornado Project about 200 tornadoes in America have claimed 18 lives or more, but the death toll has steadily dropped in recent years, thanks to improved detection and more efficient warnings.

Rank	State(s)	Date	Time	Dead	Injured	F-Scale	Town(s)
1	MO-IL-IN	March 18, 1925	1:01 p.m.	695	2027	F-5	Murphysboro,Gorham, DeSoto
2	LA-MS	May 7, 1840	1:45 p.m.	317	109	N/A	Natchez
3	MO-IL	May 27, 1896	6:30 p.m.	255	1000	F-4	St. Louis, East St. Louis
4	MS	April 5, 1936	8:55 p.m.	216	700	F-5	Tupelo
5	GA	April 6, 1936	8:27 a.m.	203	1600	F-4	Gainesville
6	TX-OK-KS	April 9, 1947	6:05 p.m.	181	970	F-5	Glazier, Higgins, Woodward
7	LA-MS	April 24, 1908	11:45 a.m.	143	770	F-4	Amite, Pine, Purvis
8	WI	June 12, 1899	5:40 p.m.	117	200	F-5	New Richmond
9	MI	June 8, 1953	8:30 p.m.	115	844	F-5	Flint
10	TX	May 11, 1953	4:10 p.m.	114	597	F-5	Waco

ters watching the skies or NWS meteorologists watching Doppler radar.

When a tornado watch is issued for your hometown, it does mean "watch out," stay alert, and keep an eye on the sky and on the local media for more updates. Make an effort to keep up with the weather, and make sure you can get the word by TV, radio, e-mail, or cell phone if a warning is issued for your specific county. Approximately 60 percent of tornado watches result in at least one confirmed tornado. That's up from 30 percent of watches in 1970. The science of tornado prediction continues to evolve . . . and improve with time.

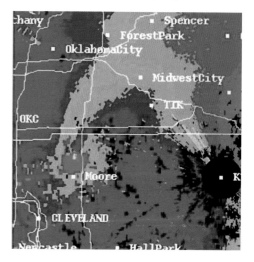

Doppler radar images of the F-5 tornado that swept away part of Moore, Oklahoma, in the Oklahoma City–area outbreak of May 3, 1999. The image on the left is a reflectivity display, showing rain and hail. The one below is a velocity image, showing the movement of air. It shows a "couplet": green means air is moving rapidly toward the radar site, red shows air moving away, so the radar is highlighting a rapidly rotating, and deadly, supercell storm.

Tornadoes and Doppler Radar

There actually was a man named Doppler. In 1842 Christian Doppler explained that when one stands near a railroad listening to the sound of a train passing, the train sounds differently as it approaches than it does after it recedes. This change is known as the Doppler effect. It occurs when the sound waves produced by an approaching object are compressed into a higher wave frequency (producing a higher pitch), while those of a receding object are lengthened, producing a lower wave frequency (and lower pitch). The same principle applies to the frequency of radio waves returning to a radar antenna.

Radar works by sending out a beam of energy as it rotates around. A tiny percentage of that energy is reflected back to the radar site after it bounces off a raindrop or hailstone. Based on how much energy returned and the time it took to do so, algorithms can compute the intensity of the rain or hail and just where it is located.

The ultrasensitive Doppler radar takes this one step further. Not only can the radar determine that there is a hailstone or raindrop, but also whether it is moving toward or away from the radar site, with movement parallel to the radar beam. Most tornadoes are too small and distant to be picked up by Doppler. However, it can highlight thunderstorms that are rotating or spinning—the supercell storms most likely to whirl up into a tornado.

Radial velocity display shows the true "Doppler effect." The radar can determine whether a raindrop or hailstone is moving toward or away from the radar site, and show the

relative velocity of the air up to 125 miles away. Using algorithms, the Doppler radar can then highlight which thunderstorms are rotating, and point out "couplets," where a strong inbound velocity is adjacent to a strong outbound velocity. It's here that the winds are twisting more violently and the potential for tornadoes is greatest. But here's the problem, in terms of prediction: Not all rotating thunderstorms go on to ultimately spawn a tornado. Knowing which ones will is currently the focus of much research.

Riding Out a Tornado

If this is an average year, about 80 to 100 Americans will die from tornado-related injuries. Many of these deaths are preventable if people in the path do the right thing within seconds of getting the warning or seeing the funnel.

At home: If a tornado warning is issued, refrain from running to the window to see if you can spot the funnel. Windows are the first thing to shatter in a tornado. Many people are injured or killed by windows imploding from a sudden drop in air pressure or flying debris.

You may have seconds to do the right thing: Go to the basement. Statistically the safest place to ride out the tornado is under the stairs, under a table or workbench, if possible. Do not get into your vehicle and try to drive away. Do not go out into the yard with a video camera or to warn the neighbors next door. The latter is a noble thought, but a tornado tracking at 40 to 50 mph will allow little time to react. Do err on the side of safety, and assume that this might be the day that a tornado does in fact come down your street.

No basement? If you don't have a basement, seek shelter in a small, windowless room on the ground floor. Two tips that may save your life:

DO ALL TORNADOES
SOUND LIKE FREIGHT TRAINS?

You've heard the description from breathless survivors: "It sounded like a freight train." The roar of a tornado is triggered by a combination of factors, including the sudden, sharp drop in atmospheric pressure, and the sound of thousands of pieces of debris colliding with each other and the ground. The result can be a sound like that of a jet aircraft, a low, loud rumble that you can feel throughout your entire body. Other tornado witnesses refer to an eerie noise that sounded like "a million buzzing bees." Every tornado is different and you can't rely on the sound to tip you off to trouble. Many tornadoes arrive with little or even no accompanying rumble.

The more walls you can get between you and a tornado, and the smaller the room, the better. Many people have survived by hiding in an interior closet, bathroom, or even a bathtub.

- The smaller the room, the better.
- The more walls you can get between you and the tornado, the better.

People have survived violent tornadoes by hiding in a closet or bathroom, even in the bathtub! Countless aerial pictures taken after major F-4 or F-5 tornadoes show nothing left of a house but the foundation and a bathtub, where terrified survivors rode out the storm. The reason? Pipes in the bathroom reinforce the bathtub, holding it down on the foundation. Take a blanket, or, better yet, a mattress, off the nearest bed, and use it to shield you as you lie in the bathtub. If you don't have a basement, this may be your best option.

At the office: Avoid outer walls and windows. If you have only seconds, dive under your desk or a heavy conference table. Another good option: interior bathrooms, near the center of the floor. Avoid elevators, but a concrete-reinforced stairwell may be another good option to ride out the storm.

At school: Tornado drills are a fact of life at most schools, and a good thing, because preparedness is critical. Most children are instructed to avoid windows, crouch down near lockers, and cover their heads. Avoiding gymnasiums and auditoriums is important. These larger rooms are often the first to have roofs collapse as winds gust over 100 mph. Ask your kids if they have routine drills, and what they would do if a tornado approached while they were in class. Take nothing for granted!

At the mall or store: Shopping centers can be especially dangerous. With their abundance of glass and high ceilings the threat of flying debris is high. If you can't reach a basement shelter, seek refuge in a public restroom or a concrete stairwell. Stay low to the ground, crouch down, and protect your head.

Salt Lake City, Utah, tornado. A rare twister hit on August 11, 1999, with no warning, carving a five-mile path of destruction through the city. One person was killed and 81 were injured.

91

TORNADO COUNTRY

These five states had the most tornadoes from 1950 to 1994.

1.	Texas	5,490 tornadoes
2.	Oklahoma	2,300 tornadoes
3.	Kansas	2,110 tornadoes
4.	Florida	2,009 tornadoes
5.	Nebraska	1,673 tornadoes

These five states had the most deaths from tornadoes during the same period.

1.	Texas	475 deaths
2.	Mississippi	386 deaths
3.	Arkansas	279 deaths
4.	Alabama	275 deaths
5.	Michigan	237 deaths

There are a disproportionate number of tornado deaths in the South. Because of milder weather, construction standards in the South are generally not as stringent as they are in the Plains states and in the northern U.S.

Cordell, Oklahoma, tornado.
There was a sinuous curl to the tornado that hit on May 22, 1981.

Outside: If you are close to home, make a mad dash indoors and don't look back. If you are unable to get home in time, run into the nearest building, such as a store, gas station, or house. If you can't get indoors, crouch up next to a house or garage, on the side of the building facing away from the storm, and get as flat on the ground as possible.

In your vehicle: In many cases you can drive away from a tornado, especially if you can drive away from the storm at a right angle. But some twisters have a forward speed of 30 to 50 mph, and it may be impossible to avoid the whirlwind. If no homes, stores, or other buildings are nearby, your safest course of action is to get out of the vehicle and get into a ditch. Do not hide in the car or under the car. Get out of the vehicle, even if rain or hail is falling.

> **MOBILE DEATHTRAPS**
>
> Lessons from the Wichita Falls tornado: On April 10, 1979, a multivortex tornado touched down on Wichita Falls, Texas, with F-4 strength winds over 250 mph. This was not your garden-variety funnel. This tornado was a wide, black, shapeless, horrific, mile-wide mass of churning debris, a "wedge" tornado that left a path of carnage nearly eight miles long. There was about a 35-minute warning that a tornado was on the way, but thousands of people got into their cars and tried to beat the tornado home. The result was a massive traffic jam just as the twister ripped into the city. Stunned commuters ran for ditches and nearby buildings; others braced themselves inside their cars and tried to ride out the storm. Of the 49 deaths in Wichita Falls that day, 25 were auto related, with many of the people crushed inside or underneath vehicles that were tossed around like toys.

The Wrong Message

There is an infamous video shot by a reporter and photographer on the day of the Andover, Kansas, tornado in April 1991. Unable to outrun the approaching tornado, the news crew, with camera rolling, hides under a concrete bridge overpass as the twister shrieks overhead. The group emerges after the tornado unharmed, and this video clip has been shown countless times, nationwide.

It sent the wrong message. The F-5 tornado that ripped through Moore, Oklahoma, in 1999 sent several people scurrying underneath bridge overpasses for shelter, and at least two people died doing so, hit by debris flying at 300 mph. Studies after the tornado suggested that unless you can seek refuge inside the girders of a bridge overpass made up of steel girders or concrete beams, literally climbing up inside the bridge, you should not use the bridge option. People hiding on the concrete slopes leading up to bridges have been swept to their deaths. The only way this makes sense is if no part of your body is protruding beneath the bottom of the bridge girders or beams.

A woman and her two children huddle under an overpass outside Newcastle, Oklahoma, as a half-mile tornado approaches.

The Tornado "Safe Room"

People living in tornado-prone areas experience anxiety and a loss of productivity unless a safe place is readily available. Researchers at the Wind Science and Engineering Research Center at Texas Tech have teamed up with the Federal

Safe room. Make sure your safe room has a three-day supply of water, nonperishable foods, blankets for each person, flashlights, and battery-powered radios.

Emergency Management Agency (FEMA) to encourage people to build special rooms within existing homes or small additions to be used when the sky turns threatening and violent.

A small windowless room, such as a closet or bathroom, readily accessible from all parts of the house, can provide protection. Such a shelter becomes the "in residence shelter" or "safe room." The concept is applicable to both existing residences and new construction. Post-storm inspections of hundreds of homes in more than 90 towns and cities struck by tornadoes revealed that in many instances a small room in the central portion of the house remained standing even when the house was severely damaged or nearly destroyed. The idea was then conceived that these interior rooms could economically be strengthened to provide a high degree of protection.

These special rooms have reinforced walls made of concrete, able to withstand a "missile" strike—a two-by-four hitting at 250 mph. Emergency ventilation, electricity, doors, and door frames are needed. Retrofitting an existing bathroom or closet can cost as little as $2,000 or as much as $6,000. This is a great option, especially for people living in or near Tornado Alley who do not have a basement. Financial incentives and special insurance programs are available in some states. Check with your local FEMA office to get more information.

Mobile Homes: A Special Vulnerability

It may seem that trailer homes act as a tornado magnet, but it's purely coincidence. Here is the harsh reality: When a tornado hits a mobile home park, the damage is almost complete, and there are usually more injuries and fatalities than when the same tornado hits homes that have foundations and basements. If you live in a mobile home, there should be a secure, underground shelter within a minute or two of your residence.

Statistics from the National Severe Storms Forecast Center in Kansas City, Missouri, show that from 1975 to 1991 nearly 36 percent of all tornado deaths occurred in mobile homes. There is no evidence that tornadoes hit mobile homes more often than conventional homes, but mobile homes are just that—mobile. They offer little or no protection in a tornado.

Here's a stark example of what can happen when a major tornado hits a

Data from the
Storm Prediction
Center show that
an average of
168 tornadoes hit
Texas every year.
Surprisingly,
Florida experiences
more tornadoes,
on average,
than Kansas.

Trailer parks can be
the site of nearly total
tornado destruction;
the odds of injury or
death here may be
10 to 15 times greater
than elsewhere. If
you live in one, make
sure an underground
shelter is nearby.

mobile home park. As previously mentioned, in April 1991 a violent tornado struck Andover, Kansas. Eighty-four frame homes and 14 businesses were destroyed or severely damaged. Then the tornado hit a mobile home park, destroying 223 trailers. Thirteen people were killed in Andover, all in the mobile home park. Two hundred residents of the mobile home park did survive in the park's storm shelter. Having an underground shelter nearby can save lives.

NOAA Weather Radio

The National Weather Service has established a network of transmitters that deliver weather and warning information 24 hours a day. A special radio is required to receive this information, but it's inexpensive and available at most electronic stores, costing from $25 to $80 for a high-end model.

Here's the advantage of NOAA Weather Radio: A special alert, a loud alarm, goes off when a warning is issued for your county, providing a wake-up call that trouble is lurking nearby. Remember that many deaths and injuries from tornadoes occur late at night when people are sleeping. The NOAA Weather Radio wakes up sleeping potential victims and often gives enough lead time for them to get to safety.

NOAA WEATHER RADIO FREQUENCIES

MHz	162.400
MHz	162.425
MHz	162.450
MHz	162.475
MHz	162.500
MHz	162.525
MHz	162.550

Cheap life insurance. NOAA Weather Radio is transmitted from 121 local National Weather Service offices providing an important source of severe-weather information 24 hours a day. In addition to potentially life-saving bulletins, NOAA Weather Radio provides real-time information about everything from earthquakes, chemical releases, and oil spills to Amber Alerts for child abductions.

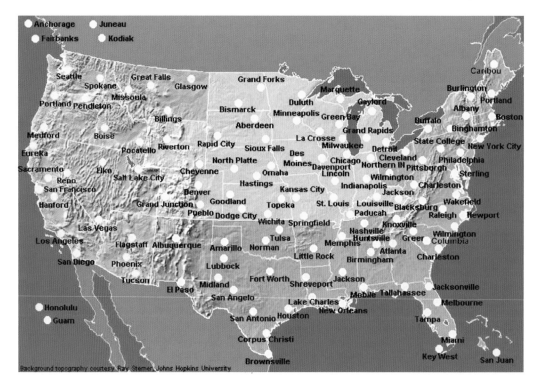

Background topography courtesy Ray Sterner, Johns Hopkins University

On April 4, 1997, at 4:52 p.m., the National Weather Service issued a tornado warning that included the small community of Shongaloo, Louisiana. The principal of the local high school was the only person in the school building at the time. He knew about the tornado because his weather radio had sounded an alarm for his parish. His wife also had a weather radio at home and called to tell him of the approaching storm. By the time the tornado hit Shongaloo at 5:00 p.m.—only eight minutes later—the principal had taken cover and was not injured.

On January 21, 1999, an NOAA Weather Radio alerted the superintendent of the Beebe, Arkansas, school district to monitor a strong line of thunderstorms heading toward his campus. When he later halted a regional basketball game and evacuated the 300–400 fans and players from the gymnasium, some people were upset. But when a tornado struck and completely destroyed the gymnasium a half hour later, no lives were lost.

Tornadoes in the City

It's often believed that tornadoes can't hit cities. Tell that to residents of St. Louis, Missouri. That city has been hit by 22 tornadoes in the last 45 years!

The urban heat island—warmer, drier air over

Troubling statistics. This school was devastated by a powerful tornado. Many schools around the United States do not use modern technology to get news of tornado warnings. Most rely on being able to hear outdoor emergency sirens while indoors, or local radio station warnings.

Emergency outdoor sirens were never meant to be heard indoors. They were designed to warn people who are outside that threatening weather is imminent. This means that school administrators may miss a critical tornado warning that could mean the difference between life and death for students and faculty.

		THE 10 WORST TORNADO-RELATED DISASTERS IN SCHOOLS			
Rank	Deaths	Date	Time	Location	F-Scale
1	33	March 18, 1925	unknown	DeSoto, IL	F-5
2	25	March 18, 1925	2:00 p.m.	Murphysboro, IL	F-5
3	17	February 1, 1955	2:20 p.m.	Commerce Landing, MS	F-3
4	16	January 4, 1917	11:00 a.m.	Vireton, OK	F-3
5	14	November 9, 1926	2:23 p.m.	La Plata, MD	F-3
6	13	April 21, 1967	3:50 p.m.	Belvidere, IL	F-4
7	13	May 2, 1929	12:55 p.m.	Rye Cove, VA	F-2
8	8	March 22, 1897	8:30 p.m.	Arlington, GA	F-2
9	8	January 11, 1918	1:40 p.m.	Dothan, AL	F-3
10	7	June 20, 1890	2:30 p.m.	Paw Paw, IL	F-4

Shower of glass. On March 28, 2000, a tornado tracked into downtown Fort Worth, Texas, ripping into high-rise office buildings. It struck at 6:15 p.m., after a majority of workers had already left for home. Five people were killed and over 100 were injured, with a damage toll for Fort Worth and the suburbs at close to half a billion dollars. Above, the Bank One building in downtown Fort Worth sits with many of the exterior windows broken out by the tornado.

the immediate downtown—may help to weaken the circulation of smaller tornadoes. But a larger tornado draws in warm, moist air from a 5- to 10-mile radius around the storm, and the presence of a few skyscrapers will have no effect on where the tornado goes or how intense it is. Consider that the tallest buildings in Fort Worth, Texas, were hit by a tornado on March 28, 2000, killing five people. The tornado struck after most people had already left their downtown offices for home, or the death toll would have certainly been much higher.

Oklahoma City: The Most Tornado-Prone City in America

Amazingly, the Oklahoma City metropolitan area has been struck by tornadoes at least 112 times since 1890. It is no coincidence that the National Severe Storms Laboratory is located in Norman, a suburb of Oklahoma City; this is where some of the world's most significant research into tornadoes and severe local storms is taking place. The Storm Prediction Center, where meteorologists monitor weather conditions and issue severe-storm and tornado watches for the entire nation, is also here.

DOWNTOWN TORNADOES
Selected tornadoes that have hit some part of the central business district of a major city.

City	Date	Deaths	Tornado Strength
St. Louis, MO	May 27, 1896	255	F-4
Waco, TX	May 11, 1953	114	F-5
Worcester, MA	June 9, 1953	94	F-4–5
St. Louis, MO	September 29, 1927	79	F-3
Louisville, KY	March 27, 1890	76	F-4
Oklahoma City, OK	May 3, 1999	40	F-5
Lubbock, TX	May 11, 1970	28	F-5
Charleston, SC	September 29, 1938	27	F-2
St. Louis, MO	February 10, 1959	21	F-4
Huntsville, AL	November 15, 1989	21	F-4
Nashville, TN	March 14, 1933	15	F-3
St. Louis, MO	March 8, 1871	9	F-3
Kansas City, MO	May 13, 1883	3	F-2
Little Rock, AR	January 21, 1999	3	F-3
Indianapolis, IN	May 18, 1927	2	F-3
Shreveport/ Bossier City, LA	December 3, 1978	2	F-4
Fort Worth, TX	March 28, 2000	2	F-2
Salt Lake City, UT	August 11, 1999	1	F-2
Nashville, TN	April 16, 1998	1	F-3
Dallas, TX	January 20, 1894	1	F-2
Washington, DC	September 16 1888	0	F-2
Shreveport, LA	April 17, 1978	0	F-2
Houston, TX	November 16, 1993	0	F-1
Miami, FL	May 12, 1997	0	F-1

On May 3, 1999, a violent F-5 tornado hit the city. The twister smashed through the suburbs of Bridge Creek, Moore, and Midwest City, snaking northeastward, nearly a mile wide at times. It was just one of 70 tornadoes that swept through central Oklahoma that day, killing 40 people and injuring another 675. The family of tornadoes damaged or destroyed nearly 8,000 homes and 1,000 apartments and over 125 businesses. When it was at its height, local meteorologist Gary England warned viewers that if they didn't have a basement, their best chance was to get in their cars and try to outrun it. It was that bad.

That Oklahoma tornado was the first billion-dollar tornado on record, the most expensive up to that time. It also carried the strongest winds ever recorded on the planet, 318 mph. But as bad as it was, it could have been worse.

The possibility of tornadoes in urban centers is one of the things that keep fed-

Trail of destruction. The aftermath of the May 3, 1999, F-4–F-5 tornado that ripped through the southern suburbs of Oklahoma City, visible as a brown swath from a helicopter surveying the scene.

eral, state, and local officials awake at night. Computer simulations have been run showing different scenarios for different radar tracks across metropolitan areas, coming at different times of the day.

Airborne missiles. It's not the tornado that will kill you; it's what's in the tornado that may cause death or injury. Most tornado fatalities are the result of blunt head trauma—being hit on the head by rocks, wood, bricks, glass, or other debris traveling at over 200 mph. Above, a golf club shaft embedded in a pantry door, a result of the Oklahoma City tornado.

New England Tornado Terror

On June 9, 1953, an F-4, or possibly F-5, tornado hit an unlikely place, the heart of New England, in Worcester, Massachusetts. When one thinks of tornadoes, New England is not a place that comes to mind. But weather records show 395 tornadoes in New England from 1950 to 1996.

That June morning in 1953, Buffalo meteorologists had warned of possible tornadoes, but the U.S. Weather Bureau in Boston did not use the word *tornado* in its outlook. Tornado warnings had been formally issued for only one year, and forecasters were concerned about inciting public panic by even mentioning the word.

By the time the tornado dissipated, it had

Uncatena Avenue, left, in Worcester, after the F-4 tornado swept through. Above, remains of a laundry truck.

traveled 46 miles over nearly an hour and a half, whipping up winds estimated at over 250 mph. The tornado left a horrible toll of death and destruction, killing 94 people, injuring 1,288, and leaving more than 10,000 people homeless.

The Multivortex Tornado

There is probably nothing quite as terrifying as the prospect of not one, but two, three, or even four tornadoes on the ground at once, all rotating around a common center. Although rare, these multivortex tornadoes do occur, especially over Tornado Alley.

The winds throughout most of a multivortex tornado may only be strong enough to do minor damage to a particular house. But one of the smaller embedded subvortices, perhaps only a few dozen feet across, may strike the house next door with winds from 150 to 250 mph, causing complete destruction. That's why one house can be relatively unscathed, while the house across the street is blown right off its foundation. Meteorologists have discovered suction vortices, cutting swaths of almost complete destruction within the tornado. Suction vortices can add over 100 mph to the ground-relative wind in a tornado circulation. As a result, they are responsible for most (if not all) cases in which narrow arcs of extreme destruction lie right next to weak damage within tornado paths. Tornado scientists now believe that most reports of several tornadoes at once, from news accounts and early twentieth century tornado tales, instead involved multivortex tornadoes.

Palm Sunday outbreak. Twin tornadoes devastate Dunlap, Indiana. On April 11, 1965, Palm Sunday, 51 tornadoes, many of them mile-wide F-4 and F-5 tornadoes, ripped into the nation's midsection, claiming 256 lives, the second-largest one-day loss of life from tornadoes on record. The monstrous pair of F-4 tornadoes seen above swept into Dunlap, where 36 people died. The citizens had no warning because high winds had knocked out power and the telephone grid.

Tornado Tales

Weather historian Snowden Flora reports a 1919 Minnesota tornado that "split open a tree, jammed in an automobile, and then clamped the tree shut again."

The F-5 tornado that swept into Xenia, Ohio, on April 3, 1974, demolished Victor Gregory's farmhouse, but left three fragile items totally intact: a mirror, a case of eggs, and a box of Christmas ornaments!

In 1917 an F-4 tornado in Connecticut picked up a jar of sweet pickles and dropped it, unbroken, in a ditch 25 miles away.

Tornado expert Tom Grazulis tells of a 9-year-old girl, Sharon Weron, and her horse during a South Dakota tornado. On July 1, 1955, she was riding her horse just 150 feet from her home when the tornado struck. The horse, with the girl astride, was lifted over a hill and carried across a valley. Apparently the girl's mother witnessed them both in the air, being carried over a second hill. Somehow the tornado dropped the girl gently, on her stomach; she landed "like an airplane" grabbing on to weeds to keep from being blown away again!

Canadian weather historian David Phillips tells of a close encounter in 1923 in Uren, Saskatchewan. A baby was sucked right out of a buggy by a tornado. After a frantic 10-hour search, the little girl was found, sleeping inside a shack two miles from where the buggy had been blown over!

An El Dorado, Kansas, tornado threw a woman 60 feet out of her house and safely deposited her next to a phonograph record of the song "Stormy Weather."

In 1996 a drive-in theater in Saint Catharines, Ontario, was struck by a tornado as it was showing the blockbuster tornado movie, *Twister*.

Weather may have provided a jolt to a young Bill Gates in 1962. Western Washington's first tornado hit Seattle's View Ridge neighborhood in that year, causing some damage but no loss of life. That's very fortunate on many levels, including that of America's economy and reputation for software innovation. For the tornado first struck the home at 7308 44th Ave. N.E. Inside were a frightened Mary Gates and her 6-year-old son, Bill, later of Microsoft fame.

Richard Morgan grew up in Tulsa, Oklahoma, and his family never treated tornado warnings lightly. That's because his father, Travis, had an unforgettable experience as a boy. Around the year 1900, a tornado hit the area and destroyed Travis's house. A few days later a friend, who lived 50 miles away, found a picture of Travis that had blown onto his street—courtesy of the twister!

Storm Spotters

Doppler radar has revolutionized the detection and tracking of severe storms, including tornadoes, but there are limitations. Because the earth curves, the radar beam, when 100 miles or more from the radar site, can be 2 or 3 miles above the ground, making it impossible to know exactly what's happening on the ground. This is where professional storm spotters are invaluable, providing ground truth—being able to look up and actually see a developing tornado.

Data strongly show that the most accurate and reliable tornado forecasts are made using a combination of Doppler radar and storm reports from ground level. Specially trained observers from police, fire, ambulance, and civil-defense go into action when a watch is issued, many of them communicating back to base using ham radio frequencies. These spotters risk their lives to be out on the front line, literally out in the field, making sure that the instant a tornado begins to form, critical information is relayed to the local National Weather Service, the local media, and the public, all within a matter of seconds.

The most dangerous conditions take place at night, when seeing the tornado can be difficult, even impossible. In most cases storm spotters have to rely on occasional lightning strikes to confirm the presence of a tornado funnel. The combination of darkness, rain, hail, and high winds can make storm spotting extremely treacherous.

There is also a volunteer group of storm spotters, members of Skywarn, who assist the National Weather Service by deploying to predetermined positions when a watch is issued. They report wind gusts, precipitation amounts, hail size, and the formation of wall clouds or funnel clouds, all possible precursors to a tornado.

Skywarn spotters are trained to provide accurate reports, and their observations are more trusted and valued than reports from the general public, who may mean well but whose reports are questionable. Unlike storm "chasers," who might drive for hundreds of miles a day in search of tornadoes, Skywarn spotters are dispatched locally and as a rule do not chase tornadoes once they form.

THE T-WORD

Weather forecasters in the United States were banned from saying the word *tornado* from 1886 to 1952. Government officials were concerned that a tornado forecast would incite panic among the general population. In their words, "the harm done by a tornado prediction would eventually be greater than that which results for the tornado itself." The ban was officially lifted on March 17, 1952, when the first "tornado watch" was issued.

Spotters risk their lives to be out on the front line making sure that the instant a tornado begins to form, critical information is relayed to the National Weather Service, the media, and the public, all within a matter of seconds.

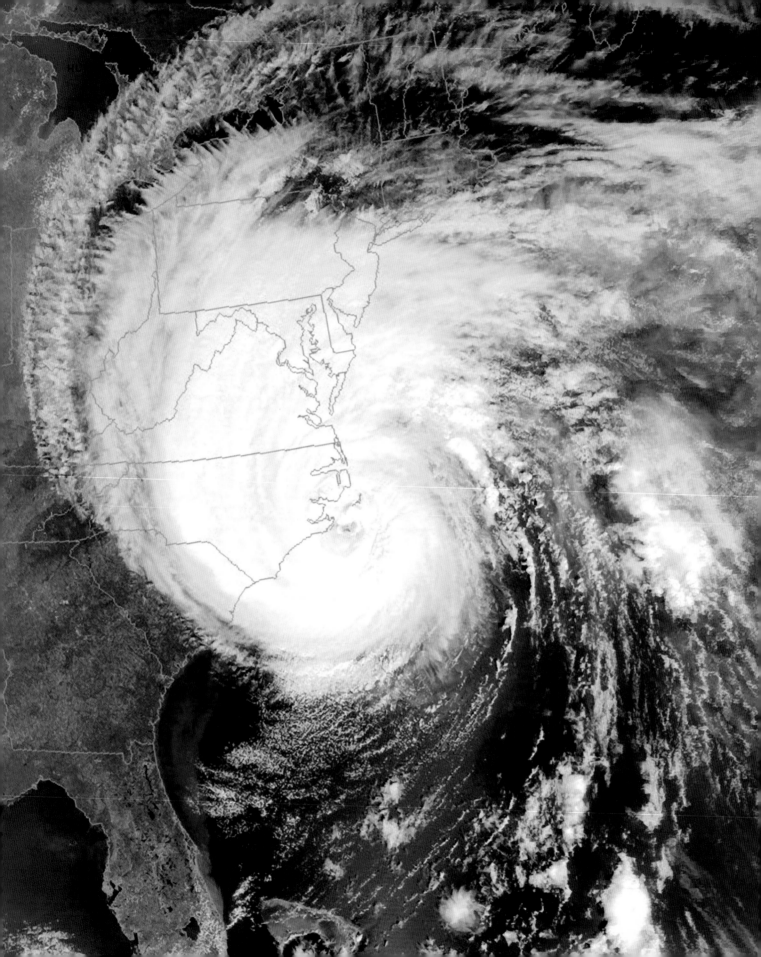

CHAPTER FOUR

Hurricanes
Superstorms From the Sea

"Hurricanes have their own agenda. We track them from space
every 7 minutes, but in spite of supercomputers and space-age technology,
their ultimate path is a mystery, and we remain at their mercy."— Paul Douglas

WHEN SUMMER HEAT begins to ease, and a tired sun sets noticeably earlier in the evening, and the first whisper of cool air trickles southward out of Canada, that's when they come. It happens slowly at first, catching some off guard. The sun gets tangled up in a strange-looking circular veil of cirrus clouds sneaking in from the south. The barometer begins to fall, slowly at first, and then tumbling right off the scale. Winds freshen from the east and northeast, and whitecaps froth and churn offshore. Foul gusts sweep in from the sea with blinding, drenching horizontal rains. The hurricane is coming ashore, transforming the sky into a runny blur. It's impossible to distinguish sea from sky. They are both one now. An impossible wind makes it difficult to stand up if you are unlucky enough to be outside. The storm surge is sweeping inland, a battering ram of foam and debris and brackish water.

Tornadoes are terrifying, yes, but nothing inspires as much wholesale dread, respect, and fear as a Texas-size hurricane grinding toward your home, a 500-mile-wide storm packing winds that rage 2 to 3 times the legal speed limit, shoving a two-story dome of water toward the coast. They are unstoppable weather monsters, their wind energy releasing the equivalent of three 10-megaton nuclear bomb blasts every hour. Unlike tornadoes, which may affect scores or hundreds of people and last 15 minutes or so, a typical hurricane lasts for days, even weeks, and may chase millions of people from their homes.

What keeps me up at night? The thought that Americans are too complacent about hurricanes. Hurricane experts believe we are headed into a very active period, one with more frequent and devastating hurricanes. The beach has an undeniable allure. There is something healing and wondrous about standing in the sand and contemplating the ocean. But there is a stark downside to having so

Opposite page:
Hurricane Isabel, looking like a vast 500-mile-wide sea monster, spreads tentacles of wind and waves up the East Coast of the United States in September 2003. Once an extreme category-5 storm, Isabel weakened before slamming into North Carolina with 105 mph winds, killing 27 people in seven eastern states, downing trees on the White House lawn, and spreading unusually high tides, resulting in severe flooding in Baltimore, Maryland.

Tropical storm Dennis
on August 25, 1999.

WEATHERFACT
Hurricanes were discovered by accident in the United States. In 1743 Benjamin Franklin noticed that a storm had obscured an eclipse of the moon in his hometown of Philadelphia. Oddly, the eclipse had been visible in Boston, 260 miles away. He put 2 and 2 together and deduced that storms actually move. At the time this was considered quite a bold theory.

A private citizen, Winthrop Redfield, documented a major storm in Connecticut back in 1821. He noted that trees 70 miles apart had fallen down in opposite directions, and he reached the conclusion that storms not only moved, as Mr. Franklin had suggested, but that they also rotated.

many people live so close to the water, millions of people hoping and praying that this isn't the year when a meteorological version of Russian roulette catches up with them, sweeping all their possessions into the next ZIP code.

The period from 1995 to 2001 saw the most intense hurricane activity in recorded history, with 27 major hurricanes whipping up ferocious winds of 111 mph or more. We may be headed into a still-more active period of hurricanes. Yet as a nation we are hopelessly and dangerously unprepared if a superstorm should come ashore. Nearly 100 million Americans live on or near the Atlantic or Gulf coast—85 percent of them have never lived through even a minimal hurricane, much less a monstrous category-5. Let's hope they never will.

What Is a Hurricane?

A hurricane is a large circular storm that develops over warm ocean water. These tropical cyclones develop when ocean water is at least 80 degrees, and winds are light. Hurricanes convert that warm water into wind energy. A storm can last for weeks, with peak winds approaching 200 mph in rare cases. Hurricanes create damage when they move ashore by whipping up punishing winds, raising tides by as much as 20 feet in a short period of time, and dumping as much as 20 inches of rain inland as they begin to weaken. Hurricanes can form in the Eastern Pacific and in the tropical Atlantic, the Caribbean, and the Gulf of Mexico.

Hurricanes inspire both fear and fascination. The Arawak tribes of the Caribbean called them *hurakan,* or "evil spirit." Living sacrifices were offered centuries ago to appease the ruthless god Yuracan, who came from the sea, rarely showing any mercy. The Japanese referred to them as divine winds, or *kamikaze.* The term *typhoon* is a derivative of the Cantonese *tai-fun,* which means "great wind."

A typical hurricane can be 300 to 700 miles wide, but usually the most damaging winds are found within about 100 miles of the storm's center. The relatively calm and sunny doughnut-shaped area of clearing at the center of a hurricane is called the eye. It can be anywhere from 5 to 50 miles in diameter, but a typical eye is about 20 miles across. Air in the hurricane's eye is descending and warming rapidly. It's here that the lowest barometric pressure is found.

The strongest winds in a hurricane occur in a band of rapidly rotating doughnut-rings of thunderstorms immediately outside the calm eye. It's here, in the eyewall, that sustained winds can reach 100 to 200 mph, whipping up mountainous 20- to 30-foot waves on the ocean floor below. The most wind damage occurs as the eyewall comes ashore.

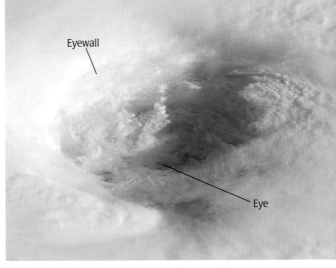

Eyewall

Eye

Unblinking eye. Around the relatively calm eye rages the doughnut-shaped eyewall, where sustained winds can top 150 mph, carving out waves three stories high on the ocean surface below.

Hurricanes begin as low-pressure systems that sweep off the coast of Africa. These areas of low pressure trigger clusters of thunderstorms in the tropical Atlantic, thousands of miles east of the Caribbean Islands. The vast majority of these storms fizzle out, but roughly half of them will continue to strengthen. Like a leaf caught in the current of a stream, they will meander westward. When ocean water is warmer than 80 to 82 degrees in the top 100 to 150 feet, these thunderstorms will continue to intensify, warming the air around them.

As the air warms, air pressure drops, and this low-pressure area becomes a partial vacuum. More moisture is funneled into the center of the storm, which fuels more thunderstorms, which warm the air even more, dropping the pressure, and so on.

This cycle continues, unabated, unless the hurricane passes over land or cooler water, or unless it encounters strong jet-stream winds 4 to 7 miles overhead,

An angry homeowner sums it up best.

The amount of heat energy released by an average hurricane unleashes the power of three Hiroshima-size bombs going off every minute,

which can shred the storm's circulation and cause it to slowly weaken over time. Strong winds aloft can decapitate the thunderheads and cause a hurricane to sputter and dissipate, so forecasters analyze upper-level wind profiles when determining whether a hurricane will strengthen or weaken.

A hurricane is, in a sense, a runaway chain reaction triggered by warm water and thunderstorms, being swept along by a continuous conveyor belt, an ocean-wide cycle that moves Atlantic waters in a clockwise, circular manner around the Atlantic Ocean.

The force of the energy released is almost unfathomable. The amount of heat energy released by an average hurricane unleashes the power of three Hiroshima-size bombs going off every minute, roughly equivalent to the amount of electric energy produced by the United States in one entire year!

Hurricanes seem to serve a purpose in nature. These spinning energy monsters are the atmosphere's automatic pressure-relief valves, similar to a built-in thermostat. Hurricanes carry excess moisture and heat away from the equator toward the poles. There have been many instances in the last century of hurricanes providing critical rains during the late summer. These drought-busters are capable of dumping 3 to 4 months' worth of rain in a few days, replenishing water supplies and soil moisture.

Many people mistake the eye for the end of the storm and head outside to inspect their homes, only to be surprised when the second half of the storm arrives and high winds whip up from the opposite direction, creating life-threatening conditions in a matter of seconds.

A Hurricane's Progress

Hurricanes grow in three separate stages:

Tropical depression: This is an area of low pressure with an organized, counterclockwise wind flow around a cluster of thunderstorms. Sustained winds are less than 39 mph.

Tropical storm: Sustained winds reach at least 39 mph. The area of low pressure is given a name.

Hurricane: Sustained winds top 74 mph. As the hurricane gets closer to land, special Air Force "Hurricane Hunter" aircraft are dispatched to fly into the storms to gather more information used to predict the track and intensity of the storm.

From 1900 to 1996 a total of 158 hurricanes slammed into the U.S. mainland; that's an average of 2 major hurricanes, with winds over 111 mph, every three years. Thankfully, records show that an intense hurricane will hit America, on average, only once every seven years.

One of the most destructive aspects of a hurricane is the storm surge. A combination of low barometric pressure, high winds, and the slope of the land offshore creates a dome of water that is pushed ashore ahead of the hurricane's eye. Tides can rise by 5 to 20 feet in a matter of minutes, cutting off escape routes and flooding many first- and even second-story dwellings along the coast. This is the way many people perish, drowning as a wall of water, foam, and debris is swept ashore.

> **WEATHERFACT**
> National Hurricane Center statistics show an average of about 10 named tropical storms every year in the Atlantic basin. Of these, roughly 6 will become hurricanes—with sustained winds over 74 mph—and 2 or 3 will become major hurricanes. On average, 1 or 2 hurricanes will hit the United States in any given year.

How Severe Is that Hurricane?

There is a system, the Saffir-Simpson scale, which uses a rating from 1 to 5 to measure the damage potential of a hurricane. The scale uses the speed of sustained winds to estimate the severity of damage and flooding.

Category-1 hurricane:

Winds 74 to 95 mph. Storm surge generally 4 to 5 feet above normal. No real damage to building structures. Damage is primarily to unanchored mobile homes, shrubbery, and trees. Also some coastal road flooding and minor pier damage.

Category-2 hurricane:

Winds 96 to 110 mph. Storm surge generally 6 to 8 feet above normal. Considerable damage to shrubbery and trees, with some trees blown down. Coastal and low-lying escape routes flood 2 to 4 hours before arrival of the hurricane center. Small craft in unprotected anchorages break moorings.

> **WEATHERFACT**
> In a hurricane, or any other storm, the wind force is proportional to the square of the wind speed. What does this really mean? When the wind speed doubles, the force exerted on windows, walls, and rooftops quadruples! Said another way, a hurricane with 150 mph winds has four times the power of a minimal, 75 mph hurricane.

A piece of plywood driven through the trunk of a royal palm by the category-5 Hurricane Andrew.

Horizontal rains. Just remaining upright during a hurricane can be difficult, and dangerous. Hurricane Andrew's approach to Miami in 1992 whipped up gale-force gusts hundreds of miles away from the eye. Much as in a tornado, the danger is not being blown over, but being hit by flying debris.

Category-3 hurricane:

Winds 111 to 130 mph. Storm surge generally 9 to 12 feet above normal. The National Hurricane Center characterizes this level a "major hurricane." Some structural damage to small residences with a minor amount of exterior wall failures. Large trees blown down. Low-lying escape routes are cut off by rising water 3 to 5 hours before arrival of the center of the hurricane.

Category-4 hurricane:

Winds 131 to 155 mph. Storm surge generally 13 to 18 feet above normal. This is a severe hurricane. Some complete roof structure failures on small residences. Shrubs, trees, and all signs are blown down. Complete destruction of mobile homes. Extensive damage to doors and windows of houses and other buildings. Low-lying escape routes may be cut off by rising water 3 to 5 hours before arrival of the center of the hurricane.

Category-5 hurricane:

Winds greater than 155 mph. Storm surge generally greater than 18 feet above normal. This is an extreme hurricane. Complete roof failure on many residences and industrial buildings. Some complete building failures with small utility buildings blown over or away. All shrubs, trees, and signs blown down. Low-lying escape routes are cut off by rising water 3 to 5 hours before arrival of the center of the hurricane.

Like tornadoes, a small percentage of hurricanes are responsible for most of the deaths and injuries. Hurricane expert William Gray's research shows that the "intense" hurricanes, making up only 20 percent of land-falling hurricanes, cause 80 percent of the damage. This Colorado State University professor issues a hurricane forecast every year, and so far he has had remarkably consistent skill in predicting the number of tropical storms and hurricanes that will affect the Atlantic seaboard. His research shows that between 1900 and 2000 a total of 218 major hurricanes whipped up in the Atlantic. Of these, only 73, roughly 1 out of 3, actually came ashore in the United States.

Naming the Hurricane

For several hundred years, hurricanes in the West Indies were often named after the particular saint's day on which the hurricane occurred. For example, Hurricane San Felipe struck Puerto Rico on September 13, 1876. Another storm struck Puerto Rico on the same day in 1928, and this storm was named Hurricane San Felipe the Second.

The modern system of naming hurricanes started during World War II. Lonely American pilots tracking typhoons in the western Pacific started naming these massive storms after their wives and girlfriends. The first pilot to find the storm had the honor of picking its name. The names made it easier to remember and track the storms, especially when there were a few hurricanes spinning up at the same time.

In 1953 America's weather services officially began using female names for storms. Many women complained that this practice was sexist, and in 1979 it was replaced with a system of alternating masculine and feminine names.

TROPICAL- STORM AND HURRICANE NAMES ATLANTIC OCEAN

2004	2005	2006	2007	2008	2009
Alex	Arlene	Alberto	Andrea	Arthur	Ana
Bonnie	Bret	Beryl	Barry	Bertha	Bill
Charley	Cindy	Chris	Chantal	Cristobal	Claudette
Danielle	Dennis	Debby	Dean	Dolly	Danny
Earl	Emily	Ernesto	Erin	Edouard	Erika
Frances	Franklin	Florence	Felix	Fay	Fred
Gaston	Gert	Gordon	Gabrielle	Gustav	Grace
Hermine	Harvey	Helene	Humberto	Hanna	Henri
Ivan	Irene	Isaac	Ingrid	Ike	Ida
Jeanne	Jose	Joyce	Jerry	Josephine	Joaquin
Karl	Katrina	Kirk	Karen	Kyle	Kate
Lisa	Lee	Leslie	Lorenzo	Laura	Larry
Matthew	Maria	Michael	Melissa	Marco	Mindy
Nicole	Nate	Nadine	Noel	Nana	Nicholas
Otto	Ophelia	Oscar	Olga	Omar	Odette
Paula	Philippe	Patty	Pablo	Paloma	Peter
Richard	Rita	Rafael	Rebekah	Rene	Rose
Shary	Stan	Sandy	Sebastien	Sally	Sam
Tomas	Tammy	Tony	Tanya	Teddy	Teresa
Virginie	Vince	Valerie	Van	Vicky	Victor
Walter	Wilma	William	Wendy	Wilfred	Wanda

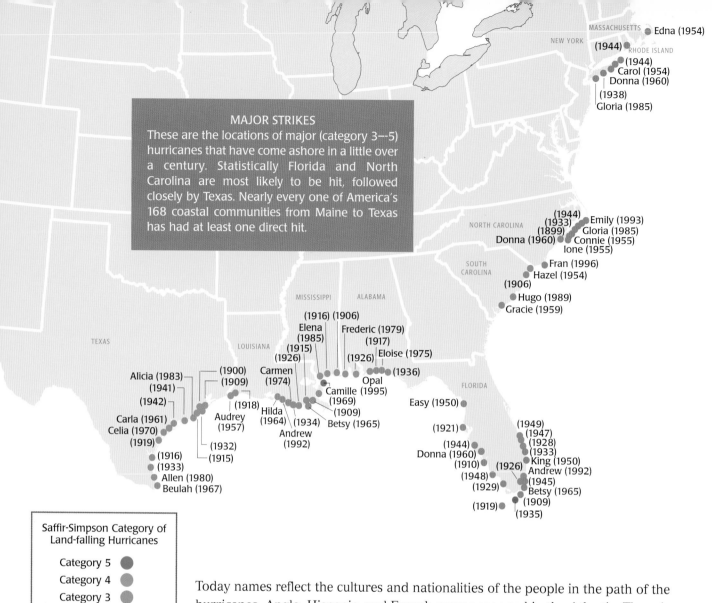

MAJOR STRIKES
These are the locations of major (category 3–5) hurricanes that have come ashore in a little over a century. Statistically Florida and North Carolina are most likely to be hit, followed closely by Texas. Nearly every one of America's 168 coastal communities from Maine to Texas has had at least one direct hit.

Edna (1954)
MASSACHUSETTS
NEW YORK
(1944)
RHODE ISLAND
(1944)
Carol (1954)
Donna (1960)
(1938)
Gloria (1985)

NORTH CAROLINA
(1944)
(1933)
(1899)
Donna (1960)
Emily (1993)
Gloria (1985)
Connie (1955)
Ione (1955)

SOUTH CAROLINA
Fran (1996)
Hazel (1954)
(1906)
Hugo (1989)
Gracie (1959)

MISSISSIPPI   ALABAMA
(1916) (1906)
Elena (1985)
Frederic (1979)
(1917)
(1915)
(1926)
(1926)
Eloise (1975)
(1936)
TEXAS
LOUISIANA
Carmen (1974)
Opal (1995)
Camille (1969)
(1909)
Betsy (1965)

Alicia (1983)
(1941)
(1942)
Carla (1961)
Celia (1970)
(1919)
(1900)
(1909)
(1918)
Audrey (1957)
Hilda (1964)
(1934)
Andrew (1992)
(1932)
(1915)
(1916)
(1933)
Allen (1980)
Beulah (1967)

FLORIDA
Easy (1950)
(1921)
(1944)
Donna (1960)
(1910)
(1948)
(1929)
(1919)
(1926)
(1949)
(1947)
(1928)
(1933)
King (1950)
Andrew (1992)
(1945)
Betsy (1965)
(1909)
(1935)

Saffir-Simpson Category of Land-falling Hurricanes

Category 5 ●
Category 4 ●
Category 3 ●

Today names reflect the cultures and nationalities of the people in the path of the hurricanes. Anglo, Hispanic, and French names are used in the Atlantic. There is a separate list of names for the East Pacific. The name lists have an international flavor because hurricanes are tracked by the weather services of many countries.

Lists of names rotate every six years. There are no hurricane names for the letters Q, U, X, Y, and Z. At the end of that six-year run the names are repeated, unless a name has been retired. Some storms named were so deadly or costly that the future use of that name would be inappropriate for reasons of sensitivity. There will, for example, never be another Hurricane Andrew, Agnes, Floyd, Hugo, Mitch, Camille, or Gloria. Approximately 50 hurricane names for the Atlantic basin have been retired since 1954.

Tracking the Wild Hurricane

Predicting the track of a hurricane is still as much an art form as a science, but the National Hurricane Center (NHC) in Miami, Florida, has made significant improvements in forecasting where a hurricane will go. The NHC issues 72-hour tropical-cyclone track and intensity forecasts four times per day for all storms in the North Atlantic and the North Pacific east of 140 degrees west. The NHC uses nine different models to predict the track of a tropical storm, and another four models to get a better handle on changes in the intensity of the storm: will it strengthen or weaken? These computer simulations of how the hurricane should behave work better in certain conditions than others.

Hurricane researchers admit that predicting the track of a hurricane is easier than predicting its intensity. Forecasters can now predict the tracks of tropical cyclones about 35 percent more accurately than they did prior to 2000. Weather experts believe that improved computer models and better data from the centers of hurricanes are allowing them to make five-day forecasts that are just as reliable as a three-day forecast was 15 years ago. But they warn that people should not be focused on the precise strike zone in any one area, because destructive winds swirl concentrically more than 200 miles from the hurricane's eye. The margin for error is now about plus or minus 90 miles of coastline when a storm is still 24 hours away, which is a significant improvement. By comparison, in 1965 the average error between predicted path and actual path was 155 miles, 24 hours in advance.

NOAA's weather models in Washington, D.C., can now integrate real-time weather data from dropsondes, the parachute-borne instrument packages deployed by NOAA's high-altitude Gulfstream IV aircraft. Introduced in the mid-1990s, these enhanced dropsondes yield far greater detail than was previously available on winds in and near hurricanes, including high-altitude steering currents, helping to create more accurate track predictions.

In contrast, meteorologists have made little progress in predicting the future intensity of hurricanes, and this is the focus of

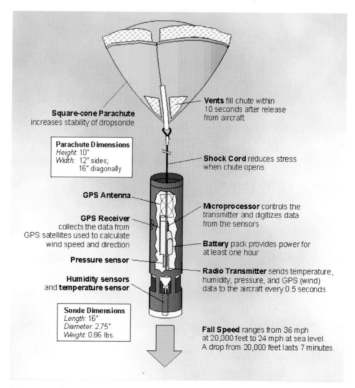

Square-cone Parachute increases stability of dropsonde

Parachute Dimensions
Height: 10"
Width: 12" sides;
       16" diagonally

GPS Antenna

GPS Receiver collects the data from GPS satellites used to calculate wind speed and direction

Pressure sensor

Humidity sensors and **temperature sensor**

Sonde Dimensions
Length: 16"
Diameter: 2.75"
Weight: 0.86 lbs.

Vents fill chute within 10 seconds after release from aircraft

Shock Cord reduces stress when chute opens

Microprocessor controls the transmitter and digitizes data from the sensors

Battery pack provides power for at least one hour

Radio Transmitter sends temperature, humidity, pressure, and GPS (wind) data to the aircraft every 0.5 seconds

Fall Speed ranges from 36 mph at 20,000 feet to 24 mph at sea level. A drop from 20,000 feet lasts 7 minutes.

Dropsonde. These instruments parachute down through the relatively calm eye of a hurricane, sending back detailed meteorological information, data that helps hurricane forecasters predict a storm's future track and intensity.

increased research in the scientific community. In October 1995 Hurricane Opal's near-disastrous strengthening from a category 2 to a category 5 in one night sounded the alarm. The simple truth is that we don't yet understand what controls a hurricane's intensity.

Hurricanes' Biggest Threats

When a hurricane forms, considerable attention is paid to the sustained winds raging near the calm eye of the storm. But surprisingly, winds don't cause the most damage.

Hurricanes wreak havoc in many ways, but recent research shows that the deadliest weather posed by hurricanes is heavy rain and the resultant flash flooding well inland from the coast, in some cases days after the hurricane comes ashore. According to the National Hurricane Center, the most dangerous elements of a hurricane, in order, are:

1. Flash flooding inland
2. The storm surge
3. High winds
4. Tornadoes

Yes, tornadoes. Thunderstorms embedded in the spiral bands of a hurricane can turn horizontal wind shear, a radical change in wind speed, into vertical rotating and twisting capable of spinning up weak tornadoes. By one estimate Hurricane Beulah whipped up 141 tornadoes as it came ashore over Texas and Mexico in 1967!

One of the biggest hurricane myths is that only coastal residents should be concerned. It is true that storm surge along the coast is historically the biggest killer during hurricane landfall. But far more people have died inland in the past three decades as a result of flash flooding triggered by heavy rains associated with hurricanes. In one study of U.S. hurricanes from 1970 to 1999, drowning accounted for 82 percent of the 600 deaths, and more than half the deaths occurred in inland counties or parishes, sometimes hundreds of miles from the coast. By comparison, high winds killed 71 and the storm surge accounted for only 6 deaths during this period. Researchers also found that the greatest inland flood threat seems to come from the earliest storms of the season, forming when winds aloft are still relatively light in August or early September.

> ### A DRAMATIC DROP
> Tthe death toll from hurricanes has dropped significantly from thousands or tens of thousands of lives lost every year, to under a hundred hurricane fatalities in recent times. Improved warnings, better building codes, more accurate computer forecasts, and weather satellites are all thought to be responsible for the dramatic drop in hurricane fatalities.

Hurricane risk.
Surprisingly, since the 1970s, the biggest danger from hurricanes has come from inland flooding, in some cases days after the hurricane or tropical storm comes ashore.

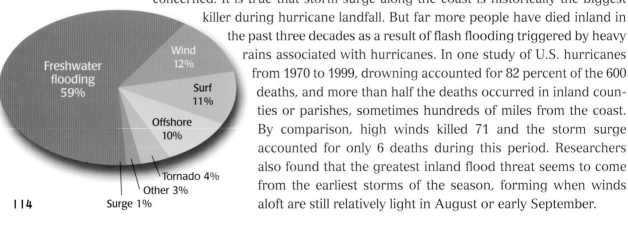

Freshwater flooding 59%
Wind 12%
Surf 11%
Offshore 10%
Tornado 4%
Other 3%
Surge 1%

Hurricanes Are Costly Storms

Moving people away from potentially deadly hurricanes is expensive. Today a typical hurricane warning costs about $192 million, the result of preparation, evacuation, and lost commerce. And that's before the storm ever reaches land. As coastal communities continue to grow, evacuation orders need to be given sooner. But in some cases there are so many people that more than 48 hours would be required to get everyone to safety inland, and predicting the exact place a hurricane will strike, in that lead time, is a stretch for our present forecasting ability.

Adjusting for inflation, hurricanes have triggered an average of $5 billion in damage every year in the United States. Hardest hit: Florida. Here are the five states reporting the most hurricane-related damage during the twentieth century:

Florida	$239 billion
Texas	$100 billion
North Carolina	$34 billion
Louisiana	$34 billion
New York	$18 billion

HURRICANE ALLEY

The following U.S. cities get "brushed" by more tropical storms and hurricanes than any other cities in America, with the center of the storm passing within 60 miles of the downtown. (The data is from 1871 to 2002.)

	City	How often (on average)
1.	Hollywood, FL	every 2.64 years
2.	Florida City, FL	every 2.69 years
3.	Grand Isle, LA	every 2.69 years
4.	Cape Hatteras, NC	every 2.69 years
5.	Deerfield Beach, FL	every 2.69 years
6.	Delray Beach, FL	every 2.69 years
7.	Miami, FL	every 2.75 years
8.	Fort Pierce, FL	every 2.75 years
9.	Boca Raton, FL	every 2.75 years
10.	Key West, FL	every 2.8 years
11.	Fort Lauderdale, FL	every 2.8 years
12.	Stuart, FL	every 2.87 years
13.	Lake Worth, FL	every 2.93 years
14.	Elizabeth City, NC	every 2.93 years
15.	Morgan City, LA	every 3 years

By comparison:

Cape May, NJ	every 4.55 years
Long Island, NY	every 5.5 years
Providence, RI	every 7.76 years
Boston, MA	every 6.28 years

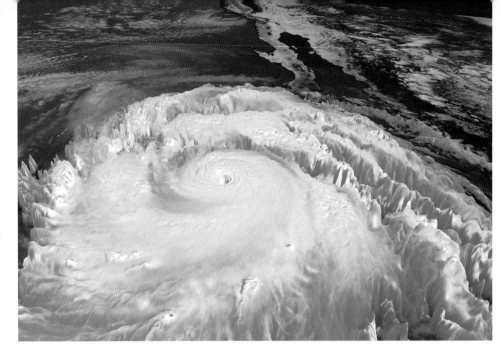

Close call. Hurricane Linda, packing sustained winds of 185 mph, the most powerful eastern Pacific hurricane ever observed. Ocean water warmed by El Niño could have guided the storm directly into San Diego and Los Angeles.

El Niño's warm waters caused Linda to grow explosively into a large howling hurricane, with sustained winds up to 185 mph, and gusts over 200.

El Niño and Hurricanes

Residents of the West Coast can thank a phenomenon known as upwelling for a lack of serious hurricanes most years. A persistent westerly wind pulls deeper, colder ocean water up to the surface, keeping surf temperatures mostly in the 50s, much too chilly for hurricane formation. On rare occasions a hurricane that forms off the west coast of Mexico can spread heavy rain into Southern California. On August 23, 1838, a hurricane with 100 mph winds leveled what was then the small town of Los Angeles.

However, Southern California was threatened by a massive hurricane in the recent past. El Niño produced unusually warm ocean water off the west coast of Central America and Mexico in 1997. On September 9, 1997, Hurricane Linda formed about 700 miles southwest of the Baja peninsula. As the storm slowly moved north along the Mexican coastline, El Niño's warm waters caused Linda to grow explosively into a large howling hurricane, with sustained winds up to 185 mph, and gusts over 200 mph. Linda had become the most powerful East Pacific hurricane in the history of weather records, big enough to cause some scientists to propose a new category, 6—for super hurricanes!

As the storm swirled and strengthened, growing even larger and deadlier, meteorologists were stunned as they pored over the forecasts coming out of the computer models. The extreme hurricane would most likely slam the coast somewhere between San Diego and Los Angeles. El Niño had slowed the prevailing westerly winds, allowing warm, 80-degree water to linger, thereby providing a fertile breeding ground for a hurricane to churn due north toward Southern California. It was a perfect storm of warm water and raging winds. Los Angeles seemed to be in Linda's crosshairs.

At almost the last moment, an upper-level trough—a stormy wrinkle of cold, windy air aloft—moved erratically, and Hurricane Linda veered out to sea.

As an El Niño, especially a strong one, progresses, residents of Southern

California seem to become increasingly vulnerable to nature's worst storm. For a fleeting moment in 1997, Los Angeles came terrifyingly close to experiencing a direct hit from one of the most powerful East Pacific hurricanes in history.

Satellites and Hurricane Hunters

Before we had weather satellites, hurricanes often slammed into the United States with almost no warning at all.

The "Long Island Express" that hit New England in 1938 (see page 25) carried winds possibly as high as 180 mph as it slammed into Long Island. Residents along the coast knew a storm was coming but had little idea of its intensity. When the hurricane finally came ashore, the storm surge was so large that it didn't even look like an ordinary wave. At first people thought it was a tall fog bank rolling in from the south. As it got closer, horrified onlookers realized that it wasn't fog, but water. A ledge of water, maybe 30 feet high, was being pushed ashore by what were described as screaming winds. The eyewitnesses found it difficult to turn away from the spectacle. One man told his children that it was a fog bank approaching, but even the young kids knew. The wave was coming straight at them.

HAWAIIAN NIGHTMARE

On September 11, 1992, a little more than a month after Andrew had smashed into South Florida and Louisiana, an unusually powerful hurricane, named Iniki, smashed into the Hawaiian Island chain, hitting Kauai especially hard.

Hurricanes are rare in Hawaii; only four storms have grazed the islands since 1950. Two hurricanes, Dot in 1957, and Ewa in 1982, were just a stiff blow compared to the incredible power of Iniki.

A $2 billion storm, Hurricane Iniki is now thought to be America's fifth-costliest weather disaster, with much of that damage taking place in one hour! Had the storm hit Honolulu, the damage could have topped $30 billion.

Until the low-altitude, polar-orbiting Tiros-1 satellite sent back the first grainy black-and-white pictures from space on April 1, 1960, meteorologists were shooting in the dark when it came to hurricane forecasting. They relied on sporadic reports from ships caught up in a hurricane's circulation, or observations from weather stations in the path of these fickle storms. That often meant very little warning, with some hurricanes going virtually undetected.

Satellites revolutionized the tracking and prediction of hurricanes. Meteorologists were unprepared for the comprehensive look they now had at storms and fronts from this unique platform in space. Tiros-1 provided 22,000 images before it went dark 89 days later. The meteorological world would never quite be the same.

But there is still no substitute for flying into the throbbing, turbulent hearts of these shrieking weather beasts to gather critical data. America is the only country

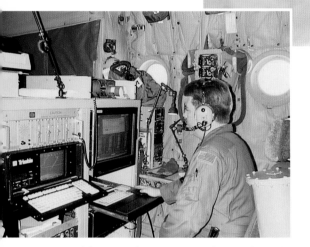

Inside a Hurricane Hunter. The crew keeps continuous watch on weather conditions, which are transmitted, in realtime, back to the National Hurricane Center.

that sends manned reconnaissance flights into the raging core of hurricanes to help forecasters by pinpointing a storm's exact location, strength, and movement. The combination of weather satellites and reconnaissance flights results in the most accurate information about a storm's intensity—whether it is strengthening or weakening.

The Air Force Reserve at Keesler Air Force Base in Mississippi has the sole responsibility for hurricane reconnaissance. The men and women of the 53rd Weather Reconnaissance Squadron, the "Hurricane Hunters," fly directly into the heart of a storm packing 100 to 200 mph winds. That may sound nearly as crazy as "tornado-chasing," but it's an integral part of the process that keeps Americans safer when hurricanes threaten.

The Air Force uses 10 WC-130 airplanes to accomplish these weather missions. (The WC-130 is a specially equipped version of the C-130 Hercules, a very sturdy turboprop plane.) With the highly sensitive weather equipment installed on the WC-130, the team can cover up to five storm missions per day, anywhere from the mid-Atlantic to Hawaii. Six people make up a typical crew: aircraft commander, copilot, flight engineer, navigator, weather officer, and a dropsonde system operator. The weather officer collects flight-level data at 30-second intervals, including position, temperature, dew point, and pressure.

A dropsonde is a parachute-borne weather-sensing canister, which, as it falls to the surface of the ocean, radios back to the weather aircraft the temperature, humidity, pressure, and winds inside the storm. The dropsonde system operator makes periodic releases from the aircraft to probe for the most accurate meteorological information. Of particular importance are the data from the eye of the storm, which give the National Hurricane Center the best measurement of the storm's location and intensity.

The tops of a hurricane's clouds near the eye may reach up to 50,000 feet, so the aircraft do not fly over the storm but go right through the thick of the weather to collect their information. The Alpha Pattern flown through the storm looks like an X. The crews fly at least 105 miles in each corner of the storm to map the extent of the damaging winds, and pass through the eye every two hours, continuing the pattern until the next aircraft is ready to take its place in the around-the-clock surveillance of the storm.

The tops of a hurricane's clouds near the eye may reach up to 50,000 feet, so the aircraft do not fly over the storm but go right through the thick of the weather to collect their information.

Since 1997, forecasters have used Global Positioning System dropwindsondes, the measuring devices dropped from high-altitude research jets, into the eyewall, the windiest part of the hurricane. The dropwindsonde system measures temperature, barometric pressure, water vapor, and wind data every 15 feet on its way down. This new method gives meteorologists an important glimpse into the true strength of these devastating storms.

Hurricane Hunter aircraft encounter slowly building winds as they fly toward the center of a hurricane. But the gradual building of wind speed allows the pilots to adjust for the violent headwinds. (Going from light winds to 150 mph winds in a few seconds would result in catastrophic failure, with possible ripping off of the wings and the control surfaces.)

That's not to say that there is no risk involved. On September 26, 1955, a Navy P-2V-5F disappeared in Hurricane Janet over the Caribbean Sea with nine Navy men and two Canadian journalists aboard. It was a tragic loss, but considering the thousands of flights into hurricanes since 1944, the record is one of amazing safety. In all a total of 34 researchers have died over the years.

And the data gathered has proven invaluable both for scientists and for nervous residents in the path of these monster storms. Studies have shown that the high-accuracy data from our Air Force Reserve and NOAA aircraft have improved forecast accuracy by about 25 percent.

The next time you encounter light turbulence on a commercial airline, imagine the white-knuckle ride the Hurricane Hunter scientists endure as they're thrown around the cabin by a hurricane's wild winds!

FLYING INTO A HURRICANE

It all started with one brave and daring man, and a hunch.

On the morning of July 27, 1943, Colonel Joseph Duckworth set out to prove his theory that hurricanes could be penetrated with specially equipped aircraft. A former pilot for Eastern Airlines, Duckworth was convinced that a pilot could fly into almost any kind of weather relying on instruments alone.

He and a crew of two took off in his single-engine AT-6 trainer with no special equipment to speak of. They encountered blinding, horizontal rains and severe turbulence as they flew through the stormy skies. But they persevered, penetrating the calm eye to get an exact fix on the center of the storm. Duckworth and his crew were able to keep their composure and fly back through the raging hurricane one more time before returning to Bryan Field, Texas, a little bruised and battered, and grateful to be safely on the ground. Some of his superiors thought that Duckworth was a barnstorming hot dog looking for praise and attention, but others recognized the significance of that first flight for the science of meteorology and hurricane tracking. He earned the U.S. Air Medal for his courage and bravery.

HURRICANE HUNTER TRIVIA

Highest wind speed recorded: 233 mph, Hurricane Allen, 1980

Most eye penetrations on a single flight: 21, Hurricane Claudette, 1991

As many as 4 lightning strikes occur per storm penetration. Usually the only damage is small burn holes

A P-3 aircraft measured the lowest surface air pressure ever recorded in the Western Hemisphere, 26.22 inches of mercury for Hurricane Gilbert in 1988.

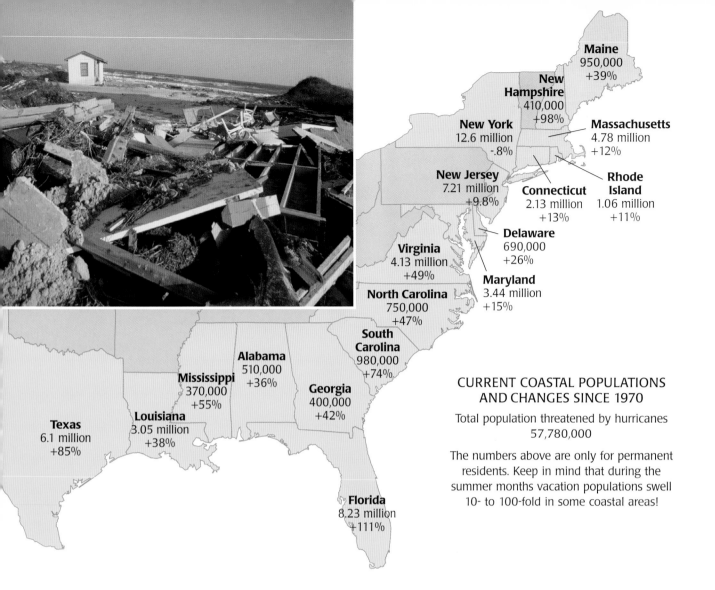

CURRENT COASTAL POPULATIONS AND CHANGES SINCE 1970

Total population threatened by hurricanes 57,780,000

The numbers above are only for permanent residents. Keep in mind that during the summer months vacation populations swell 10- to 100-fold in some coastal areas!

Maine 950,000 +39%

New Hampshire 410,000 +98%

New York 12.6 million -.8%

Massachusetts 4.78 million +12%

New Jersey 7.21 million +9.8%

Connecticut 2.13 million +13%

Rhode Island 1.06 million +11%

Delaware 690,000 +26%

Virginia 4.13 million +49%

Maryland 3.44 million +15%

North Carolina 750,000 +47%

South Carolina 980,000 +74%

Alabama 510,000 +36%

Mississippi 370,000 +55%

Georgia 400,000 +42%

Texas 6.1 million +85%

Louisiana 3.05 million +38%

Florida 8.23 million +111%

Coastal America: The Special Dangers

More Americans than ever are moving to our nation's coasts. Who wouldn't want to live near the ocean? But there is a downside to that beautiful panorama of sand and whitecaps. People who buy or build in coastal areas are rolling the dice every late summer and fall. Here is why federal, state, and local officials are so worried. At the same time the coastal population is mushrooming, the potential for major hurricanes is increasing. Hurricane landfalls were common along the East Coast from the 1940s through the mid-1960s. Then in the 1970s and '80s, landfalls decreased. Hurricane researchers believe that activity has now returned to pre–World War II levels, meaning a greater potential for "major hurricanes," category-3 strength or higher, which means storms capable of widespread damage and loss of life.

The probability of a U.S. landfall is high because of warm water that results from a phenomenon called the thermohaline circulation system. This ocean current moves warm, salty water from the tropics to the North Atlantic and is asso-

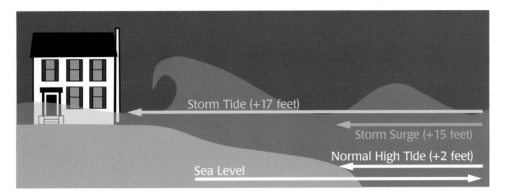

Storm Tide (+17 feet)

Storm Surge (+15 feet)

Normal High Tide (+2 feet)

Sea Level

Storm surge. The combined effect of high winds and unusually low pressure can push a "dome" of water ashore ahead of the eye, with a sudden 5- to 20-foot rise in sea level.

ciated with increased hurricane land strikes. This circulation first appeared in 1995, and meteorologists say there is no sign of it vanishing. Historically this circulation has resulted in higher probabilities of major hurricane landfalls along the East Coast and the Florida peninsula, and more weak cyclones striking the Gulf Coast.

Scientists are just now beginning to understand the fluctuations in ocean water temperatures that take place over the span of decades, shifts between warm and cool phases that can last 20 to 40 years. This Atlantic multidecadal mode, as the NOAA calls it, is now entering a more active period, and many researchers are concerned that the next 15 years may bring more frequent and intense hurricanes.

Combine this with Americans' love affair with the beach and you have a recipe for potential disaster. More people and more cars mean that inland-bound roads quickly become gridlocked during evacuations.

The key to safe and timely evacuations is a combination of better forecasts, efficient warnings, and public response.

If a major hurricane approaches, will people evacuate in time? Will roads and bridges even be able to handle a mad crush of traffic as people flee inland? How many people will decide to stay and ride out the hurricane?

Some Big Ones
Hurricanes have resulted in major loss of life in recent years.

Mitch
One sobering wake-up call was Hurricane Mitch, in the fall of 1998. Not since the 1780 hurricane that struck Martinique, Saint Eustatius, and Barbados, killing between 20,000 and 22,000 people, has the Atlantic hurricane basin seen such storm-related fatalities. Wire services attribute some 11,000 deaths to this storm,

Ticking time bomb.
Literally overnight, on the night of October 3, 1995, Hurricane Opal strengthened from a category-2 to a very strong category-4 hurricane, with sustained winds of 150 mph.

with thousands more missing. A category-5 hurricane, Mitch registered average sustained winds near 180 mph on October 25, with gusts well over 200 mph. Mitch was the strongest hurricane ever observed in the month of October. The storm stalled for nearly three days over Central America, drenching parts of Honduras and Nicaragua with an estimated 50 inches of rain, resulting in catastrophic flash floods and deadly mudslides.

Opal

Hurricanes are by nature erratic and fickle, capable of confounding even the most seasoned forecasters at the National Hurricane Center in Miami. Case in point: Hurricane Opal.

In early October 1995 Hurricane Opal had grown into a weak hurricane in the Gulf of Mexico, one that forecasters weren't paying much attention to. But literally overnight it became a meteorological "bomb," undergoing explosive intensification. In one night the winds near the core of Opal strengthened, causing the hurricane to go from category-2 to near category-5, with sustained winds close to 150 mph. It also started to speed up and veer toward the coast. The sudden shift in speed and strength caught hurricane forecasters in Miami by surprise.

Most residents in the path of the storm had stayed home, determined to ride out what they thought would be a relatively minor category-2 storm. But now that it was nearly a category-5, government forecasters were faced with an extremely dangerous situation. Urgent warnings were issued, but a combination of late bulletins and roads under construction turned what should have been an orderly evacuation of Pensacola, Florida, into something out of a horror movie. An estimated 10,000 frantic motorists became stranded on the highways and interstates, listening to increasingly dire broadcasts on their radios. Some of them abandoned their vehicles altogether and set off on foot, scrambling to reach higher ground.

Opal weakened before coming ashore and a catastrophe was narrowly averted, but the storm was a wake-up call for meteorologists at the National Hurricane Center. Rapid intensification of a hurricane just before landfall, as the storm moves over a deep pool of warmer water, can pose a grave threat to human life and to property. The computers still don't do a good enough job of catching these occasional last-minute spikes in a hurricane's strength.

Floyd

In mid-September 1999 Hurricane Floyd triggered something close to widespread panic along the Eastern Seaboard. It quickly strengthened into a category-5 storm, with winds over 155 mph off the Bahamas, prompting the largest peacetime evacuation in our nation's history, nearly 3 million Americans. The storm weakened to category-2 strength with 105 mph winds, before coming ashore near the aptly named Cape Fear, North Carolina.

Hurricane Floyd resulted in 30 deaths and billions of dollars in damage, but it may be remembered primarily for pointing out the difficulty of trying to move millions of people across often-antiquated highway systems and bridges leading away from the coast. Traffic jams hundreds of miles long snaked inland from coastal Savannah, Georgia, to Wilmington, North Carolina.

Camille

Researchers are learning more about how a hurricane can tap into a warm eddy, an unusually deep layer of warm ocean water capable of giving the storm a sudden jolt of energy. This last-minute strengthening may have been a factor in category-5 Hurricane Camille, which decimated the coast of Mississippi in 1969.

Perfect Storm

On October 30, 1991, there was a convergence of meteorological events that created what was described by some as the perfect storm. A dying hurricane named Grace weakened into a tropical storm east of Florida, as a cold front approached from the west and a storm stalled over southern Canada, producing conditions ripe for rapid intensification. At the last moment the weak tropical storm passed over warm Gulf Stream waters and intensified explosively, carving out monstrous 100-foot waves and winds over 80 mph, hurricane force. It is now referred to as the "Unnamed Hurricane of 1991." It left behind a very real Halloween nightmare for mariners in the Atlantic, and was the basis for Sebastian Junger's book *The Perfect Storm.*

Record surge.
Hurricane Camille produced the biggest storm surge ever recorded from a storm hitting the United States. A 25-foot rise in water levels pushed freighters half a mile inland from the Gulf of Mexico.

123

On August 27, 1999, rain drenched New York City, flooding major highways and closing down subway systems.

America's Most Vulnerable Cities

Researchers and insurance experts say the greatest losses from a direct strike of an extreme hurricane would occur in heavily populated coastal cities and surrounding communities. The worst place in the United States for an extreme hurricane to strike is the Miami–Fort Lauderdale area, according to AIR Worldwide Corp., a catastrophe-modeling and weather-risk management company. A severe hurricane striking this heavily populated region, just north of where Andrew struck in 1992, could produce insured losses of more than $60 billion, and total economic losses could exceed $122 million.

TOP 10 MOST EXPENSIVE PLACES FOR AN EXTREME HURRICANE TO HIT

Rank	City	Insured Losses	Total Losses
1.	Miami/Ft. Lauderdale	$61.3 billion	$122.6 billion
2.	New York City	$26.5 billion	$53 billion
3.	Tampa/St. Petersburg	$25.1 billion	$50 billion
4.	Houston/Galveston	$16.8 billion	$33.6 billion
5.	New Orleans	$8.4 billion	$16.8 billion
6.	Mobile, AL	$ 6 billion	$12 billion
7.	Boston	$5.1 billion	$10.2 billion
8.	Biloxi/Gulfport, MS	$5.1 billion	$10.2 billion
9.	Myrtle Beach, SC	$4.3 billion	$8.6 billion
10.	Norfolk, VA	$3.9 billion	$7.8 billion

Tropical Storms: Just As Dangerous

Agnes was an erratic tropical storm that stalled over Pennsylvania in June 1972, dumping nearly 15 inches of rain in less than a day. Agnes was only a category-1 hurricane when it came ashore, and it weakened to a tropical storm as it traveled inland. Nobody predicted that this dying storm would do a loop over Pennsylvania, prolonging the rains and triggering a horrific flood of the Susquehanna River, the worst since 1784, that inundated the town of Wilkes-Barre and even flooded the Governor's Mansion in Harrisburg.

Agnes became America's costliest natural disaster at the time, with damage from flooding estimated at over $3 billion, more than twice that of deadly category-5 Hurricane Camille. Flooding ravaged at least 12 Eastern states, and at least 117 people died from this relatively weak storm. The inland rains more than made up for coastal storm surges and high winds.

Allison

Residents of Houston, Texas, knew that Tropical Storm Allison was headed into Texas in June 2001, but they were thoroughly unprepared for the scope of the damage caused by Allison's intense rains. The city was broadsided by up to 36 inches of rain, much more than the amount called for in flood warnings. More than 40 people died as Allison tracked from Houston to Philadelphia, leaving damages amounting to more than $4 billion.

Flying Glass, a Hurricane Hazard

Another hazard for residents of large cities is flying glass. Even a category-3 hurricane with winds over 111 mph could dislodge windows and result in horizontal showers of deadly, splintered glass shards, a nightmare scenario for people on the streets below.

One case in point: A New York City landmark, the uniquely shaped 59-story Citicorp Center. Built in the 1970s, the tower, as it later turned out, was constructed improperly, leaving it vulnerable to the howling winds of a hurricane. An extreme storm might even have brought down the whole thing, killing 200,000 people, according to a Red Cross estimate. New York City officials, informed of the flaw, were very concerned about the building and had a secret plan to evacuate hundreds of thousands of people living and working in Midtown Manhattan. It is an amazing story.

The renowned and beautiful Citicorp Center required major post-construction strengthening if it was to withstand a rare but possible combination of storm and winds.

The building's supporting framework had been designed by distinguished structural engineer William LeMessurier. The graceful, towering structure was supported on high, arching legs, with the building cantilevered over a church on one side and a plaza on the other. The whole appearance was of a silver tower floating in midair.

One day, years after the tower had been completed, an architectural student brought some fateful calculations to LeMessurier. The student's questions concerned the placement of those graceful columns. His figures showed that they were in the wrong place, at the center of the building rather than at the corners. With that placement, high winds, blowing from a specific direction—something called a cross-corner wind blowing in at a 45-degree angle—would put too much pressure on the columns supporting the building, threatening its structural integrity. Such winds could be expected once every 16 years, according to the Sandia National Laboratories in New Mexico.

LeMessurier assured the student that the columns were placed correctly and gave him the data to support it.

But there was another problem. During construction the steel braces inside

Skyscraper in downtown Houston with its windows blown out from the force of Hurricane Allison.

the building, the braces that helped it to resist winds, had been bolted together. Le Messurier's design called for the braces to be welded. The change had been made for economy, naturally, and at the time was thought to be a safe and acceptable modification of the original design. It also conformed to New York City's building code, which provides for some kinds of winds, but not others. LeMessurier had not been consulted about the change, but even when informed of it later, he continued to think the building was safe as built.

And yet, he couldn't put the whole issue out of his mind. He went back and looked at the initial design, re-did his calculations factoring in now the combination of bolted braces and high cross-corner winds, and realized, to his horror, that the change in brace construction had created a potentially fatal flaw. Faced with certain wind conditions, the building could weaken and collapse.

Frantic, LeMessurier contacted Citigroup and explained the small but unacceptable risk of the entire building coming down. Stunned, Citigroup agreed to reinforce the tower, and quickly. Work was carried out late at night, in secret. Halfway through the project a hurricane formed in the Atlantic and roared up the coast, heading right for New York City. The Red Cross was activated, ready to evacuate thousands of residents, if necessary.

Luckily, the storm veered out to sea at the last moment, and construction crews were able to finish their work without the media, or even any employees, finding out.

Citicorp Center is now prepared for a major hurricane, which is a true worst-case scenario.

But this drama raises more unsettling questions. How many other high-rise buildings, from Miami to Boston, would be unable to withstand whirling 115 to 150 mph winds from a major hurricane? The truth: Nobody really knows.

Can Man Weaken Hurricanes?

The question comes up every year: Can we weaken hurricanes before they hit the United States?

The answer is, we tried. From 1962 to 1983 an ambitious research program into hurricane modification was carried out. American researchers attempted to tame hurricanes by dumping a chemical called silver iodide into the tallest clouds surrounding each eye. The goal was to widen this doughnut-shaped ring of heavy weather, where the strongest winds are found, and drop wind speeds in the process. Cloud seeding was carried out on four hurricanes over eight days. On

10 THINGS YOU CAN DO TO LOWER YOUR FAMILY'S RISK DURING A HURRICANE WARNING

When a warning is posted and evacuation orders are issued, don't wait! Don't get stranded on a barrier island or coastal highway. Once inland, remember that now the threat has shifted from storm surge and coastal flooding to flash flooding.

1. Stay alert and listen to the media. Is it a watch or really a warning? Know the difference!

2. Fill up bathtubs and other containers with fresh water in case you stay in your home.

3. Fill up your car with gasoline in advance. Be ready to go at a moment's notice.

4. Get more cash than you think you'll need for 3 to 6 days. Remember that after a hurricane many banks and ATMs may be temporarily closed.

5. A warning is issued: Enact your family disaster plan, the drill is now a reality!

6. Map out your route. Use travel routes specified by local authorities. Do not get out on the road without a place to go.

7. Bring prepared food and a disaster supply kit, including all important documents, such as birth certificates, passports, mortgages, bank and investment documents.

8. Secure your home before leaving. Board up windows and glass doors, anchor loose yard objects or bring them inside, and be sure to lock your doors.

9. Notify family and friends of your plans.

10. When evacuating: if possible, go to the home of either friends or family in a non-vulnerable area within your own county. If that isn't possible try a motel or hotel. Go to a public shelter only as a last resort. Shelters are not designed for comfort and often don't accept pets.

four of these days, the winds decreased between 10 and 30 percent. The lack of response on the other days was interpreted to be the result of faulty execution of the seeding.

In 1969 Hurricane Debby's winds dropped by about 30 percent after seeding. Scientists couldn't determine if the drop in wind speed was from the silver iodide or just a coincidence—that Debby would have weakened on her own.

However, when word got out that some hurricanes were being manipulated, Japan and China cried foul. Those nations, and others, didn't want America tinkering with potential storms, fearing that we were robbing them of much-needed rains. No more experimentation on hurricanes has been done since, and studies after the fact suggest that there is too much natural ice in hurricanes for cloud seeding to be effective in weakening a hurricane's potential. So the odds of successfully taming or weakening a hurricane are probably slim to nil.

CHAPTER FIVE

Thunderstorms
Lightning, Hail, and High Water

"There is no terror in a bang, only in the anticipation of it . . ."—Alfred Hitchcock

A S YOU READ THIS, somewhere over America an angry sky is growling. Thunder and lightning are as inevitable as the setting sun. Showers arrive with a fanfare, welcome dowsings of rain for gardens, thirsty lawns, and farmers' fields. But the lightning . . . tell me why that's necessary again? We nervously tolerate the flickers of lightning dancing above our heads, and count out the seconds until the shock wave of thunder shakes the skies. "How far away was that one? Wow!" We whistle under our breath. "That was close."

Despite all of our technological breakthroughs, there is not a thing we can do about the weather and that black line of storms bearing down on our homes. Meteorologists can tell you where it is with neighborhood-level precision, but, like it or not, it's still coming. There is something egalitarian and democratic about a thunderstorm. It pounds wealthy neighborhoods as hard as it does low-income projects. Everyone has to deal with a bad-hair day, the well-coiffed C.E.O.'s as well as the construction crew working hard outdoors. A storm, any storm, reminds us just how small, meek, and powerless we are in the world, and on some level that has to be a bit reassuring.

Don't wait for the sirens to take cover in a bad thunderstorm. The emergency sirens are sounded only for tornado warnings, or when dangerous straight-line winds of 75 mph or more have been observed.

This year researchers estimate that about a hundred thousand thunderstorms will mushroom over America, unloading their precious cargo of rain, flattening crops with hail, and jabbing farms, suburbs, villages, and cities with 20 million lightning strikes.

Unless you live in northern Alaska, there is an excellent chance you'll be stalked by at least one nasty thunderstorm this year. Hopefully, you'll develop a healthy respect for those roiling cumulonimbus clouds, giving them a wide berth whenever possible. Admire them from a distance; there are few things in life more awe-inspiring and majestic than a 10-mile tower of water spitting lightning, hemorrhaging hail, and capped with an anvil hat, their rumble sounding like the booming footsteps of some dreadful weather monster. But they should be admired from a respectful distance, as one of nature's most astonishing spectacles.

When Thunderstorms Turn Severe

Out of 100 thunderstorms, fewer than 10 will ever mutate into something severe, a storm capable of wind or hail damage. Severe thunderstorms take many different forms, but there are usually some telltale signs on radar, and on the ground, that this is no ordinary thunderstorm.

The National Weather Service defines a severe thunderstorm as one that has winds of at least 58 mph and/or 3/4-inch hail. All thunderstorms are capable of deadly lightning, even storms that are not producing hail or high winds.

In a severe thunderstorm, powerful rain and hail-cooled downdrafts touch the earth and spread out, often reaching speeds of over 100 mph. On radar these surges of violent wind can cause a line of thunderstorms to bulge, resembling a horseshoe or a backward letter C. Meteorologists refer to these as bow echoes. Severe winds are most likely just to the north of where the line bends the most.

Lines of intense thunderstorms often form 100 to 250

SEVERE THUNDERSTORM WATCH: Tells you when and where severe thunderstorms are more likely to occur. Watch the sky and stay tuned to know when warnings are issued.

SEVERE THUNDERSTORM WARNING: Issued when severe weather has been reported by spotters or indicated by radar. Warnings indicate imminent danger to life and property to those in the path of the storm!

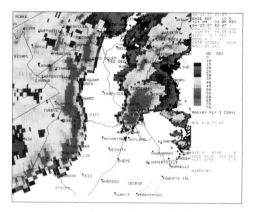

Bow echo. National Weather Service Doppler radar from Wilmington, North Carolina, shows severe thunderstorms over South Carolina on April 22, 1997. The bow echo to the left sparked severe wind damage as it swept across the state.

miles ahead of the main cold front, out in the warm, humid air found in a storm's "warm sector." It's here that the environment for storm formation is best. These linear squall lines usually form well south of the main area of low pressure, and can travel for hundreds of miles before dissipating. They spark those swift and furious straight-line winds and, on rare occasions, tornadoes.

Downbursts, Microbursts, and Derechos

That violent storm breaking over your head could fall into one of these categories:

Downbursts. Tornadoes are violent updrafts, but downbursts are extreme surges of wind energy diving down toward the ground at speeds sometimes exceeding 100 to 125 mph. Downbursts can be strong enough to topple trees and peel rooftops off homes. They have the wind energy of a tornado, but spread out over thousands of square miles. In fact, they're often mistaken for tornadoes because their damage can be so extensive. Rain and hail-cooled air are suspended in the upper reaches of a thunderstorm, until they become so massive and heavy that the warm updraft can't support them, and the chilled air comes crashing toward the ground with a violent force.

Microbursts are similar to downbursts, but smaller, usually lasting less than 5 or 10 minutes and measuring less than 2 1/2 miles wide. But they are not to be

NORTH WOODS TERROR

On July 4, 1999, the 1:27 p.m. Doppler radar scan from the National Weather Service in Duluth showed a clearly visible bow echo tracking across northeastern Minnesota. On the ground, winds were howling at over 130 mph, eventually leveling an estimated 172,000 acres, knocking over as many as 25 million trees in only a couple of hours. The 2,500 campers in the Boundary Waters Canoe Area had no warning. Canoes capsized. Campers were thrown through the air, and many were trapped under trees for hours until they could be rescued. Miraculously, no deaths were reported. On the day this wall of wind and water, called a derecho, struck, the temperature was in the 90s and the dew point temperature was near 80, unbearably humid. The result was a storm of awesome ferocity. It continued eastward across Ontario and Quebec, reaching Maine during the wee hours of the next day before finally weakening over the colder waters of the Atlantic Ocean.

Lake Superior

Ominous clouds.
If a thunderstorm cell is tilting over to one side, or if smooth, symmetric clouds are radiating out from the storm's rain and hail-cooled downdraft, there is a good chance that the storm will be severe. A rotating wall cloud lowering toward the ground may produce large hail and even a tornado.

Shelf cloud. This ominous ledge of advancing clouds, sometimes called an arc cloud, usually marks the leading edge of a gust front with high winds, torrential rain, and possible hail.

Anvil. As violent updrafts of warm moist air reach the stable stratosphere, where temperatures begin to warm with altitude, they spread out into an easily recognizable cap, sometimes streaking hundreds of miles downwind of the actual storm. The flat tops of thunderstorms can extend 40,000 to 60,000 feet into the atmosphere.

Cell merger. When two thunderstorms merge or collide, the result can be an even stronger cell, with a higher probability of hail and violent winds.

133

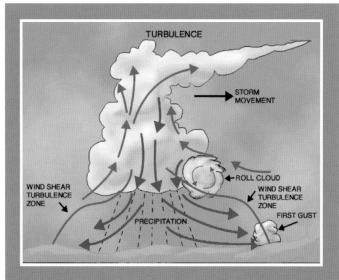

CLASSIC THUNDERSTORM

For a thunderstorm to grow, a rising bubble of warm air, a thermal, breaks through a stable layer and accelerates, moving straight up at 50 to 100 mph. This violent updraft gives rise to a strong downward-moving rush of rain and hail-cooled air, the downdraft. As this cool air reaches the ground, it spreads out, forming the gust of damp air that usually precedes a thunderstorm. This rush of wet air can create a shelf cloud, evidence of severe turbulence along the leading edge of the storm.

Cauliflower cloud.

The crisp, sharp outline of a rapidly expanding thunderhead, opposite, is evidence of a vigorous updraft and further strengthening within the storm. As a storm weakens, warm air is choked off by a cold downdraft, and the clouds appear fuzzy and blurry from a distance.

ignored. Microbursts pose a very real risk to aircraft. Pilots steer clear of thunderstorms, not because of lightning, but because an encounter with a downburst or microburst can trigger rapid changes in wind direction and speed, resulting in a sudden and potentially catastrophic loss of lift on the plane's wings. The leading edge of this downward rush of rain and wind is called the gust front. Winds can gust as high as 150 mph, capable of tornadolike damage.

A **Derecho** is a long-lived squall line of intense thunderstorms, a convergence of downburst winds that can last 24 hours or more, covering hundreds of miles in the span of an afternoon and night. They are most likely to form on warm, muggy evenings of late June and early July in the Midwest. But these swarms of storms can and do spread into New England and the northeast. They are capable of moving very quickly, reaching forward speeds of 40 to 70 mph, leaving little time for people to take cover. Winds within the storms can top 100 mph. To be characterized as a derecho, a bow echo showing up on radar must be producing damage over an area roughly 250 to 300 miles.

What is Lightning?

Lightning is a brief surge of negatively charged particles that travels from a cumulonimbus cloud to the ground along a narrow, pencil-thin channel of air molecules that have been ionized, literally ripped apart.

Meteorologists still have competing theories as to how charged particles become separated in a thunderstorm. The prevailing wisdom is that warm updrafts sweep positively charged particles into the upper reaches of a thunderhead, while negatively charged particles collect near the bottom of the ground. The attraction between the base of the cloud and the ground creates the actual lightning bolt, a massive spark.

It happens in stages. An electrical impulse, called the stepped leader, reaches downward from the cloud base in steps, each step jerking downward about 150 feet, zigzagging on the way. When the leader nears the ground, streamers rise up to meet it, and the circuit is complete. A bright flash of electricity, the stroke of

Monster spark.
Weather satellites detect more than 3 million lightning flashes around the world every day; that's an average of 30 strikes every second.

The sound of thunder can be deafening, with an intensity approaching 120 decibels. That's about 10 times louder than a chain saw or pneumatic drill.

lightning, ascends along the same path the leader took. Additional strokes follow in rapid succession. The entire sequence is blindingly quick. The step leader travels at 136,000 mph. The main return stroke moves at over 61,000 mph, and all subsequent strokes, as many as 40, happen so fast that the eye sees only a single flickering lightning bolt.

Lightning does not always flow from the cloud base to the ground. If contrasting charges accumulate within the same thunderhead, or even nearby storms, a lightning bolt can form within the same cloud, or arc from cloud to cloud.

What triggers the rumble and rattle of thunder that follows the lightning bolt? For a few milliseconds a channel of air no thicker than your finger is heated to 50,000 degrees. This explosive heating of the air creates a shock wave, a blast of superheated air moving away from the lightning strike at approximately the speed of sound. The deep rumble of rapidly expanding air is what we call thunder.

It's rare to hear thunder from a storm more than 15 miles away, although it is possible to see lightning from a thunderstorm hundreds of miles away.

The sound of thunder can be deafening, with an intensity approaching 120 decibels. That's about 10 times louder than a chain saw or pneumatic drill!

Meteorologists are fascinated by lightning found in tornadic storms, supercell thunderstorms that go on to spin up tornadoes. Research suggests that there are more cloud-to-ground lightning strikes in thunderstorms where tornadoes are forming. A new generation of NASA weather satellites may help forecasters at the

Storm Prediction Center use lightning within a thunderhead as another tip-off that a storm may be about to whip up nature's most violent wind.

The Perils of Lightning

One in 86,000 lightning bolts hits someone, and one in 345,000 bolts kills someone. Americans are twice as likely to die from lightning as they are from a tornado or hurricane. Of weather-related deaths, only flash flooding and extreme heat will claim more lives this year.

An estimated 600 to 1,000 Americans will be injured by lightning every year. Most of them will survive the initial strike, but many will have lifelong disabilities as a result of being in the wrong place at the wrong time. Burns are common, usually occurring at the strike's entrance and exit points of the body. Many lightning victims suffer additional injuries, such as broken bones, from being thrown by the strike. In some cases the blast is so severe that people's clothes are blown right off their bodies. The leading cause of lightning-related death is cardiac or cardiopulmonary arrest, a massive heart attack.

"Thunder is good, thunder is impressive; but it is the lightning that does the work." —Mark Twain

And yet there is an upside to lightning. It does serve a purpose in nature. Lightning produces an invaluable form of fertilizer that helps to keep lawns and gardens green, and America's farm fields lush. Lightning causes oxygen and nitrogen in the earth's atmosphere to combine, forming nitrogen oxide. It can take days for the nitrogen oxide formed in thunderstorms to wash all the way to the ground, but when it gets there it adds vital nutrients to the soil. Worldwide, as much as 10 million metric tons of nitrogen oxide are created by lightning every year.

GOOD ODDS

The one-year odds of being struck and killed by lightning are 1 in 6.5 million.

The lifetime odds of being struck and killed by lightning are 1 in 30,000.

The lifetime odds of being killed by extreme heat are 1 in 12,310.

The lifetime odds of being killed by extreme cold are 1 in 6,165.

So you are about 13 times more likely to be killed by a cold front than you are by lightning!

Men Are Struck by Lightning More Often Than Women

Lightning appears to discriminate. According to a study by the National Severe Storms Laboratory and the National Weather Service, men are struck by lightning four times as often as women, accounting for 84 percent of lightning fatalities and 82 percent of injuries. It's important to note that most of the people struck are engaged in outdoor recreation, such as hunting, fishing, and boating, or in work-related activities outside. Men have no genetic predisposition to being hit by light-

State-by-State Lightning Casualties 1959–1994

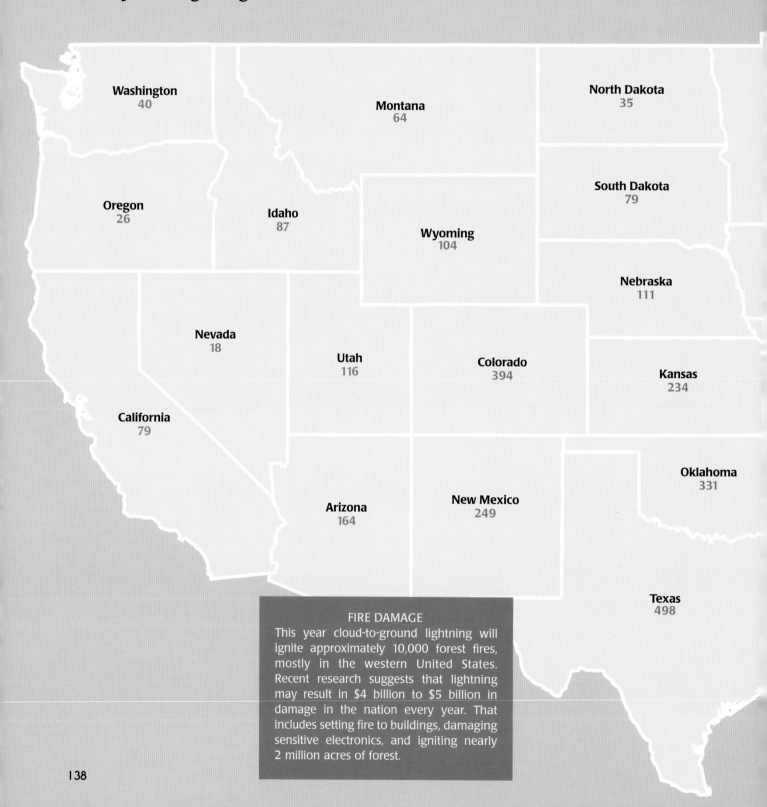

Washington
40

Montana
64

North Dakota
35

Oregon
26

Idaho
87

South Dakota
79

Wyoming
104

Nebraska
111

Nevada
18

Utah
116

Colorado
394

Kansas
234

California
79

Arizona
164

New Mexico
249

Oklahoma
331

Texas
498

FIRE DAMAGE
This year cloud-to-ground lightning will ignite approximately 10,000 forest fires, mostly in the western United States. Recent research suggests that lightning may result in $4 billion to $5 billion in damage in the nation every year. That includes setting fire to buildings, damaging sensitive electronics, and igniting nearly 2 million acres of forest.

LIGHTNING CASUALTIES
Data from 1959 to 1994 show that most lightning deaths and injuries take place in the South and the East. Florida is the lightning capital of the United States. The region from Tampa to Orlando routinely sees over 100 days with lightning and thunder every year.

Minnesota 169
Wisconsin 241
Michigan 732
Iowa 227
Illinois 360
Indiana 238
Ohio 545
Missouri 176
West Virginia 108
Kentucky 278
Tennessee 473
Arkansas 355
Mississippi 295
Alabama 296
Georgia 410
Louisiana 347
South Carolina 306
North Carolina 629
Virginia 235
Florida 1523
New Hampshire 76
Vermont 30
Maine 126
New York 577
Massachusetts 355
Pennsylvania 644
New Jersey 185
Connecticut 88
Rhode Island 49
Delaware 42
Maryland 250

LIGHTNING-PRONE CITIES
The following metropolitan areas experience the most lightning strikes during an average year, in this order:

1. Tampa/St. Petersburg, FL
2. Denver, CO
3. Orlando, FL

ning. Testosterone does not, in and of itself, attract bolts from the sky. But men generally spend more time working and playing outside than women, leaving themselves more vulnerable to lightning-related injury and death.

A disproportionate number of men and women are injured and killed every year while playing golf. PGA pros take no chances. Whenever they play, a mobile, on-site weather service tracks lightning strikes. By the time storms actually move in, the golfers have long since left the greens and fairways for a safe shelter.

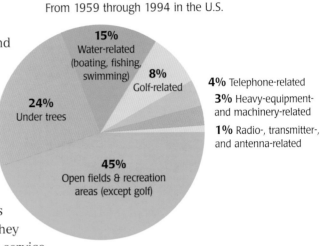

Lightning Fatalities
From 1959 through 1994 in the U.S.

- **15%** Water-related (boating, fishing, swimming)
- **8%** Golf-related
- **4%** Telephone-related
- **3%** Heavy-equipment- and machinery-related
- **1%** Radio-, transmitter-, and antenna-related
- **24%** Under trees
- **45%** Open fields & recreation areas (except golf)

ROY "DOOMS" SULLIVAN: THE HUMAN LIGHTNING ROD

Roy Sullivan was a park ranger who spent a considerable amount of time outdoors, at the mercy of the elements. And for some reason, Mother Nature was not kind to Roy, who picked up the nickname "Dooms." He was called that because the man had an uncanny knack for attracting lightning. During his 41-year life span he was struck a total of seven times, burning his chest and eyebrows, knocking off a toenail, even setting his hair on fire—a stunned friend standing nearby had to dump water over Roy's head to extinguish the flames. According to the *Guinness Book of World Records*, Sullivan has the distinction of being the most lightning-prone person ever to walk the earth.

The 30-30 Rule for Safety

Many lightning deaths and injuries could be prevented if people would remember a simple precaution known as the 30-30 rule. If you count to a number only up to 30 between "seeing the flash and hearing the bang," the storm is six or fewer miles away, and it's time to head indoors. Also, wait at least 30 minutes after hearing the last clap of thunder before heading back outside. Just because the heavy rain is over doesn't mean that the lightning risk has passed. People are most likely to be struck at the very end of a thunderstorm, after the rain has ended and skies have begun to clear. National Weather Service statistics show that more than 50 percent of all lightning-caused deaths occur after the thunderstorm has passed.

The Safest Places to Be When Lightning Threatens

Much as with other catastrophes, meteorologists and public officials are haunted by the possibility of lightning striking a large crowd of people assembled for an outdoor event, like a concert or sporting event. There is every reason to be concerned. During a Frisbee tournament on April 10, 1994, in Nashville, Tennessee, lightning hit nearby and spread out on the ground, as is often the case. One person was killed and 18 were injured. On June 13, 1991, one spectator was killed and five others injured while taking shelter under a tree during the U.S. Open Golf Tournament near Minneapolis. In July 1991 at least 22 people were injured when lightning struck a crowded beach in Potterville, Michigan. None of the victims were in the water at the time.

Statistically, just about the safest place to ride out a lightning storm is in your house or some other indoor shelter. So if a storm is nearby, head inside. Go about your normal activities, but avoid standing near windows or outer walls. If you want to talk on a cell phone or cordless phone, fine,

PRIME TIMES FOR LIGHTNING

• June   21%
• July   30%
• August 22%

3 p.m. is the most dangerous time of day for lightning. For example, it's five times more likely to strike at 3 p.m. than at 9 a.m.

LIGHTNING FACTS
• The United States is struck by an estimated 22 million lightning bolts every year.
• For a few milliseconds, lightning heats a pencil-thin channel of air to a temperature five times hotter than the surface of the sun, about 50,000 degrees.
• Lightning does strike the same place twice. The Empire State Building in New York City can be struck 15 or more times a day, more than 100 times every year!
• Lightning can cook potatoes growing in the fields and melt the nails in buildings.
• The average lightning bolt is about 3–5 miles long. A single strike can travel 10 miles before ever reaching the ground.
• Power failures triggered by lightning strikes cost utility companies as much as $1 billion every year, charges eventually passed on to consumers.

but avoid talking on a landline that is wired to the wall. People have been struck by nearby lightning while chatting on the phone. Also avoid taking a bath or shower until the storm has ended; on rare occasions lightning has struck plumbing and delivered a nasty shock.

A vehicle is one of the safer places to be during an electrical storm. A direct lightning strike may flatten your tires and short-circuit the electronics in your vehicle, but chances are you'll live to tell your grandkids about it someday. One word of caution: Do not touch anything metallic within the car or truck if you're riding out the storm in a vehicle. To do so increases the chance of getting an unpleasant electrical jolt.

For extra safety, consider installing a lighting rod for your home or business to lower the risk of a damaging strike. Lightning rods are usually made of copper or another good conductor of electricity. They are often placed on rooftops, steeples, and masts to protect people from lightning strikes.

If You Are Caught Outside

Remember that lightning is lazy; it wants the easiest path from the cloud base to the ground. So you do not want to be the tallest object in the area. If you are caught outdoors during a thunderstorm with no shelter nearby, find a low spot away from trees, fences, and poles. Make sure the area is not prone to flooding. If you feel your skin tingle or your hair stand on end, squat low to the ground on the balls of your feet. Place your hands over your ears and keep your head as low as possible. The goal is to make yourself the smallest target possible and minimize your contact with the ground. Do not lie flat on the ground; this only increases your exposure to lighting.

Avoid direct contact with other people (do not hold hands or hug each other!). Get into a ditch or shallow depression, if possible; crouch down with your feet close together. Remove or drop objects containing any metal, such as belts and golf clubs.

Do not get under a tree or any other isolated tall object. Many people hide under trees because they don't want to get wet. It's far better to get soaked to the bone and live another day.

Avoid all outdoor metal objects like flagpoles, fences, gates, tall utility poles, bleachers, golf carts, and machinery.

In short: Avoid trees. Avoid water. Avoid fences and poles. Avoid open fields. Avoid high ground.

Many survivors of lightning strikes report that immediately before being struck their hair was standing on end and they had a metallic taste in their mouth. Others told of a loud "clicking sound" before the lightning struck. If you experience any of these potential symptoms, drop to the ground immediately.

STRUCK BY LIGHTNING

"One bolt of lightning was so close that there was no time at all between the flash and thunder. I heard a loud splitting sound and saw a bright flash, then a slamming boom of thunder that I could feel in my chest and stomach. Within 10 seconds, there was another close call: I saw a blinding flash come off the top of a telephone pole just two blocks ahead of me, and heard an instant explosion of thunder. I was running down a sidewalk toward home in fear of my life, as fast as I could. Around the corner from my block, while I was running under a big pecan tree, I blacked out. When I woke up, I was lying in the wet grass under the tree, next to the sidewalk. My head hurt; and my ears were ringing. It was still raining hard, with loud thunder; but I was too dizzy to get up and run right away. I had only been out for a minute or less; but I felt like a stiff, sore zombie."

—Roger, sixth-grader, who was hit by lightning on May 2, 1979, while walking home from school

If Lightning Strikes

If someone is struck by lightning, there is no danger in initiating chest massage and mouth-to-mouth resuscitation to revive the victim. The basic rule to follow if several people are struck by lightning is to "save the dead first." That may sound odd, but often lightning victims who appear dead are in cardiac arrest. The immediate application of CPR may revive them. Usually the people who are in the most obvious pain and distress are not the ones in most danger.

There remains to this day a dangerous myth that anyone struck by lightning is still electrically charged and dangerous to the touch. That's not true at all. More than half of lightning victims who appear to be dead can be successfully revived by prompt and effective CPR.

Lightning Phobias

Keraunophobia is an irrational fear of lightning. An overwhelming fear of thunder is called brontophobia.

According to National Weather Service statistics, Floridians may have the most lightning-related phobias, and for good reason. Florida, surrounded by warm water, is a haven for anyone who loves boating, golf, and sunbathing. But this abundance of water, coupled with strong heating of the land, increases the probability of afternoon

THE LIGHTNING ROD

Benjamin Franklin invented the lightning rod as part of his groundbreaking research into electricity. He speculated on what he could accomplish with an iron rod, sharpened to a point at the end: "The electrical fire would, I think, be drawn out of the cloud silently, before it could come near enough to strike."

His famous kite experiment in June of 1752 (which should never be repeated) reportedly took place because he was tired of waiting for Christ Church in Philadelphia to be completed so he could place a lightning rod on top of it. Franklin didn't profit from any of his inventions, including the lightning rod, but gave them to the world freely, to benefit everyone.

thunderstorms, which usually mushroom into existence like clockwork every day. The average square mile of Florida real estate is hit by cloud-to-ground lightning 25 times every year. The entire state is struck by an estimated 1.35 million lightning strikes annually. From the Tampa Bay area to Orlando, lightning flickers overhead almost one-third of the year.

Strange but True Lightning Stories

A car traveling on I-35 near Des Moines, Iowa, was struck directly by a bolt of lightning. The car was stopped dead in its tracks, but the startled driver was uninjured. The car had major electrical damage, many small holes in its body, and all its tires eventually went flat. The roadway beneath the car had a yard-wide, several-inch-deep crater.

Two Michigan motorists were in a road accident during a rainstorm. While huddled under an umbrella watching the tow truck hoist their wrecked car, lightning struck the umbrella, shocked the motorists, and then jumped over and shocked the tow truck driver. None were seriously hurt, but it was a bad ending to what had already turned into a very unpleasant day.

On October 24, 1991, a lucky resident of Chicago Heights, Illinois, was comfortably sleeping in bed when . . . KABOOM! Lightning struck, traveled through a cable television line into the house, and struck the bed, which then caught fire. The person was dazed, but uninjured.

A 75-year-old German grandmother was being attacked by a street burglar. As the assailant raised a crowbar to her, he was struck dead by a bolt of lightning.

A Greenwood, South Carolina, electrician (go figure) survived a direct strike by lightning over 30 years ago. But since then he has never been cold. He can stay outside wearing summer clothing in subzero temperatures for hours without any discomfort, a true medical oddity!

Lightning once struck a house in Minnesota, setting it afire. This bolt from the blue then crossed the street, striking a fire alarm box. The sudden power surge resulted in an alarm being sounded, and the fire department responded promptly and put out the house fire.

A cowboy in Utah was literally blown out of his saddle when struck by a lightning bolt in August 1993. He found a hole in his felt hat, his hair had melted in several spots, and he had numerous burn marks on his torso. He was OK otherwise; his faithful steed, however, didn't survive.

Lightning in your genes? A Midwest woman was struck by lightning in 1995. Nothing odd there, you say. But her nephew had recently been struck and had suffered temporary blindness. Her cousin was dazed in the 1970s when lightning struck her unfolded umbrella. The same woman had been struck once before, back in 1965. Her grandfather was killed by lightning while working on his farm in 1921. And his brother was killed while standing in the doorway of his house in the 1920s. Spooky, but apparently true!

On July 17, 1988, lightning struck near a house in upstate New York. Tires on cars parked in the driveway were flattened by the heavenly jolt, and some hubcaps were blown off. Oddly enough, the home owner's contact lens also popped out of his eye.

A Safe Distance

Airplanes are designed to withstand lightning strikes; in fact, most commercial aircraft are struck once or twice a year. Aircraft often trigger lightning strikes as they fly through cumulonimbus clouds with strongly charged particles. But modern fuel tanks are designed to prevent entry of electrical charges and the lightning strike is redirected around the outer metallic fuselage of the aircraft. Flying in the vicinity of a thunderstorm can be a white-knuckle experience, but you shouldn't be concerned about lightning.

The worst aviation-related lightning disaster occurred over Elkton, Maryland, on December 8, 1963. Lightning ignited vapors in the fuel tank, sending the plane into a fiery crash which killed all 82 passengers aboard. The crash prompted the redesign of fuel tanks to prevent such an accident from ever happening again, and in the last 40 years there has not been another major lightning tragedy in the air.

Some Mysterious Lightning

Ball lightning. This is a mysterious phenomenon that has been seen and described by thousands of eyewitnesses, a bizarre atmospheric discharge that seems to defy some of the laws of nature. Scientists believe that ball lightning may be a new form of charged, energized plasma that can take on different forms, but there is little question that ball lightning is a baffling occurrence, one that doesn't usually linger long enough to be captured by photographers.

Ball lightning. One of the few images ever captured of the elusive and rare phenomenon known as ball lightning, in this photograph shot from a moving train window in Japan.

In many cases spherical balls of light and energy fall from the sky and then travel horizontally, floating silently while giving off a slight hum. They tend to last a few seconds, although sometimes these spheres of light linger for several minutes. They are usually the size of grapefruits, but can be as small as peas or as large as buses. These phantom balls of light have been seen bouncing off the ground and walls and rolling or spinning down fences and power lines. They have slipped through narrow cracks in doors and windows, only to reform into the original shape on the other side.

Ball lightning is rare, but it's most likely right after a thunderstorm, in the wake of a lightning strike. There are currently no theories as to how or why ball lightning forms but some link to high-energy electrical fields is probable.

Meia Wozniak, living in Worcester, Massachusetts, during the summer of 1995, witnessed something beyond her comprehension. Here is her account of the terror she experienced witnessing what was probably ball lightning:

"There was a big thunderstorm going by and I decided to go on our front porch and watch as I usually do. Towards the middle of the storm, I saw a bright round ball of white fire. It was rolling up the middle of our street, and it looked about 4 feet in diameter. A quarter of the way up our street the lightning split in 3's. Then halfway up the street, it split to 6's. Three-quarters up the street it connected to 3's again. All the while I was hearing a low rumbling sound like thunder and a sharp crackling-hissing sound, a lot like frying food. During this event small tendrils of the lightning would reach out to cars, telephone poles, anything close by. As this happened our power went out, and was out for 2 1/2 hours. I remember it to this day."

In January 1984, ball lightning entered a Russian passenger aircraft, and, according to a Russian news release, "flew above the heads of the stunned passengers," subsequently leaving through the tail section. The ball lightning left two holes in the plane.

For over a decade researchers have been fascinated by a new generation of electrical phenomena visible above thunderstorms. Airline pilots have described mysterious flashes of colored light visible above thunderheads in the distance, and new data confirms that they were not mere hallucinations.

Red sprites are reddish, angel-shaped apparitions visible in the upper atmosphere, corresponding with strong lightning strikes below. They occur within a fraction of a second after a cloud-to-ground strike, soaring as much as 60 miles into the stratosphere.

Red sprite. These 40-mile long lightning flashes, looking like red jellyfish, sometimes appear above a severe thunderstorm, startling airline pilots.

Why would lightning shoot straight up? Just as the solid earth is electrically conducting and attracting lightning, so is the ionosphere, the layer of the atmosphere that lies above the stratosphere. When a large stroke of ordinary lightning occurs, it triggers a wave of electromagnetic disturbance, a kind of recoil. That wave hits the energetic ionosphere, ripping loose electrons and exciting the thin air to the degree that it emits light. Its colors tell us that nitrogen, the most abundant gas in the air, is mostly responsible for the ghostly red glow of "sprite light."

Blue jets are even more mysterious. From airplanes they appear as bluish, cone-shaped beacons of dim light that start out near the flat, anvil top of a thunderhead and

Blue jet captured by NASA researchers on July 24, 1995, over Carrizozo, New Mexico, colorized from its original black-and-white image.

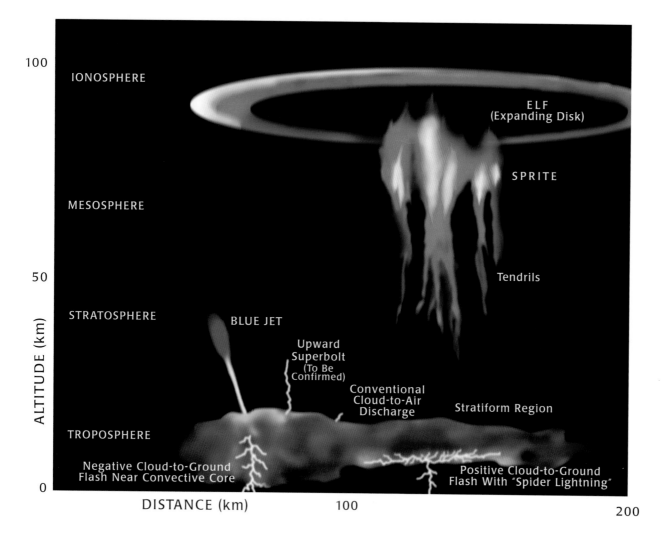

then extend upward about 30 miles into the atmosphere, like a quick puff of smoke. Blue jets occur at lower altitudes than red sprites and are harder to observe and study.

Elves are extremely brief, flat disks of dim light that appear to form about 60 miles above the earth's surface. Strong lightning strikes as far as 30 miles away can send a pulse of electromagnetic energy into the upper atmosphere, triggering these brief wisps of light.

Trolls, short for Transient Red Optical Luminous Lineament, seem to occur after an especially strong sprite, a downward cascade of light. Each event seems to start in the red glow of a sprite's "tendril," or tail, and then drains downward toward the ground.

10 Thunderstorm and Lightning Safety Tips

• If you are caught in the open during a lightning strike and the hair on your head or neck begins to stand on end, go inside the nearest building. If no shelter is available, crouch down immediately in the lowest possible spot and roll up in a

ball with your feet on the ground. Do not lie down; to do so only increases the risk of electrocution.

- When a thunderstorm threatens, get inside a home, a large building, or an all-metal (not convertible) automobile. Any enclosed shelter will offer some protection.
- During a thunderstorm, do not use the telephone except for emergencies. Cell phones and cordless phones are OK. Stay out of the shower or bathtub until the storm passes.
- If you are caught outside, do not stand underneath a tall isolated tree or a telephone pole. Avoid projecting yourself above the landscape. For example, don't stand on a hilltop, in a field, or on a golf fairway. In a forest, seek shelter in a low area under a thick growth of small trees. In open areas, go to a low place, such as a ravine or valley.
- Get away from open water and get off of tractors or other metal farm equipment or small metal vehicles such as motorcycles, bicycles, and golf carts.
- Put down golf clubs and take off golf shoes.
- Stay away from wire fences, clotheslines, metal pipes, and rails.
- Make sure your children can recite the 30-30 rule (see page 140). Remind them that the time people most frequently get struck by lightning is at the tail end of a thunderstorm. They need to wait at least 30 minutes after hearing the last thunder-clap before heading outside to play.
- The first time you hear thunder, get out of the pool, get off

> ### LIGHTNING MYTHS AND THE REALITY
> #### THE MYTHS
>
> 1. If it isn't raining, then there is no danger from lightning.
>
> 2. Rubber soles of shoes or rubber tires on a car will protect you from being struck by lightning.
>
> #### THE FACTS
>
> 1. Lightning often strikes outside of heavy rain and may occur as far as 10 miles from any rainfall.
>
> 2. Rubber soles and rubber tires provide no protection from lightning. The steel frame of a hard-topped car does provide increased protection if you aren't touching metal.

the beach, head for the clubhouse. Remember that lightning can reach almost 10 miles from the thunderhead, striking even with clear skies overhead. Don't tempt having a close encounter with a bolt from the sky.

• Stay informed and use common sense. Tune in to the local media and keep a watchful eye on the sky. Remember that most lightning strikes occur during the mid and late afternoon. If possible, schedule your events for earlier in the day to cut down on the lightning risk.

Hail: A Storm's Dangerous Fruit

Thunderstorms produce precious rains that make lawns and gardens green and that coax hearty plants and vegetables out of farmers' fields. But sometimes the storms mutate, producing a toxic brew of icy pellets that can threaten people, animals, and crops.

Hail is most likely in April, May, and June, when the air a few miles above the ground is still relatively cold. It forms in a thunderstorm's warm and violent updraft. A tiny pellet of ice is coated with supercooled water within the cumulonimbus cloud. As the pellet falls to the ground, it may be swept up in the updraft many times. Each time it's coated with another layer of ice, until it becomes so heavy that gravity pulls it to the ground.

Heaviest hailstone.
NCAR scientist Nancy Knight holds the amazing hailstone that hit Coffeyville, Kansas, on September 3, 1970. It weighs 1.67 pounds and spans 5.7 inches, almost grapefruit size! The hailstone hit the earth at speeds estimated at up to 120 mph.

Cross sections of hailstones show concentric rings, much like the layers of an onion. The spikes sometimes found on the outside of big hailstones are the result of smaller stones sticking onto larger stones as they take their wild ride through the thunderhead. An updraft of 55 mph can suspend a golf-ball-size hailstone, but a 90 mph updraft is needed to keep a baseball-size stone in the air.

The larger the hailstone, the harder it eventually hits the ground. Baseball-size chunks of ice can hit at close to 100 mph, hard enough to cause serious injury or even death. Even penny-size hail is said to be severe.

Every year in the United States, hail results in an estimated $1 billion in damage, dinging car hoods and flattening crops that took months to grow in a few horrific seconds. Swaths of damage can be 10 to 20 miles wide and up to 100 miles long, with hail falling so hard that it accumulates on the ground in spite of air temperatures in the 60s and 70s!

Over the years people have tried to control hail, with much fanfare but little luck. In the 14th century, people in Europe attempted to ward off hail by ringing church bells and firing cannons. After World War II, scientists across the world experimented with cloud seeding as a means of reducing hail size. In Soviet Georgia, scientists fired silver iodide into thunderclouds from ground level. Such

Aftermath. Softball-size hail, nearly 4 inches in diameter, can hit the earth at over 100 mph. It's capable of causing serious damage to cars, homes, and people.

methods were supposed to stimulate the formation of large numbers of small hailstones that would melt before they reached the ground, but comparable experiments performed in Switzerland and the United States did not confirm Soviet theory.

Today the fact remains that there is probably little that can be done to thwart the formation of hail in a thunderstorm. Although computer models suggest that cloud seeding may be able to reduce the size and quantity of hailstones in a thunderstorm, the American Meteorological Society remains cautious. It points out that the current understanding of hailstorms is not sufficient to allow confident prediction of the effects of seeding individual storms. Done improperly, cloud seeding could increase hail. Research into hail modification continues, and it's likely that in our lifetime hail modification will become more predictable, with satisfactory outcomes from cloud seeding.

Hailstone Country

Hail can fall anywhere in the United States, turning a routine thunderstorm into a painful affair as people make a mad dash to get out of the way of these stinging stones. But there is a Hail Alley, a 600-square-mile area where Colorado, Nebraska, and Wyoming meet. Hail falls in this area an average of 9 or 10 days every year. That's a far cry from the world's hail capital: Kericho, Kenya, about 50 miles south of the equator, at an elevation of 6,500 feet, where hail falls about 132 days a year.

Hailstorms can cause big trouble. In Orient, Iowa, in August 1980, hail drifts were reported to be six feet deep. The snow plows had to be called out. On July 11, 1990, softball-size hail in Denver, Colorado, caused $625 million in property damage, mostly to automobiles and rooftops. It was America's costliest hailstorm. Forty-seven people at an amusement park were seriously injured when a power failure trapped them on a Ferris wheel and they were battered by softball-size hail. Another massive hailstorm hit the Denver area in 2001, smashing windows, punching holes in rooftops, and damaging at least 60 airplanes.

THE MAN WHO RODE THUNDER

There have been some harrowing encounters with thunderstorms and hail. In 1959, Marine Colonel William Rankin penetrated a thunderstorm while flying his jet fighter. At 48,000 feet, he lost control of the disabled aircraft, bailed out, and deployed his parachute inside the storm. For over 30 minutes he was swept around by the winds within the thunderstorm, going up with updrafts and down with downdrafts. He survived his ordeal and documented his experience in the book *The Man Who Rode the Thunder.*

"The temperature outside was close to 70 below zero," he recalled. "I had on only a summer-weight flying suit, gloves, helmet and marine flying shoes. . . . I could feel my abdomen distending, stretching, until I thought it would burst. My eyes felt as though they were being ripped from their sockets, my head as if it were splitting into several parts, my ears bursting inside, my entire body racked by cramps. . . . A massive blast of air jarred me from head to toe."

Towering trouble.
Generally the taller the thunderhead, the higher the probability of hail and severe winds. Thunderheads routinely grow to 50,000 feet. On rare occasions the flat, anvil tops spread out 70,000 feet, rising into the stratosphere!

Call out the plows. Slow-moving summer thunderstorms can unleash several inches of hail, enough to require snowplows to clear icy streets!

There have been only three deaths in the United States directly linked to hail. The first occurred on May 13, 1930, during a hailstorm just outside of Lubbock, Texas. An unfortunate farmer was caught unprotected in a wide field when the storm broke. On July 30, 1979, a second tragedy occurred when a storm bombarded Fort Collins, Colorado, with hailstones said to be as large as softballs in certain neighborhoods. Over two dozen people were injured, and a three-month-old infant was killed. On March 28, 2000, in Fort Worth, Texas, the third fatality took place. Five people lost their lives that day from a storm—two from tornadoes, two from floods, and one who was struck by a baseball-size hailstone.

Considering the sheer number of hailstorms during a typical year, the United States has been relatively lucky. Other countries haven't been as fortunate. An estimated 200 people died when a summer hailstorm hit China in 1932, and many other countries report multiple deaths from similar occurrences.

Hail signature. National Weather Service NEXRAD Doppler radar shows a three-body-scatter strike over Dallas County, Alabama, on February 21, 2003. This storm produced nickel-size hail, which damaged roofs and trees. Meteorologists look for these spikes as a tip-off that a thunderstorm cell may produce large and damaging hail.

Warning Signs of Hail

New Doppler radars can detect hail forming in the upper reaches of a thunderstorm, allowing meteorologists to warn the public—in some cases 10 to 20 minutes before the largest hailstones start to hit the ground. Forecasters look for the telltale sign of hail within a storm, a "three-body-scatter strike," a spike extending outward, away from the radar beam, evidence that the Doppler's energy is reflecting off

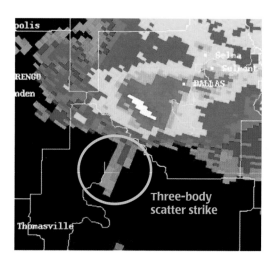

Three-body scatter strike

hailstones and painting a "false echo" on the radar display.

Remember that hail forms in a thunderstorm, so after that first clap of distant thunder you should already be indoors. Stay away from windows. A sharp gust of wind may hurl hailstones through your window, raising the specter of injury from flying glass. Close drapes, blinds, or shades to prevent debris from blowing inside. Avoid areas with skylights and doors during a storm.

As with lightning, you're relatively safe in your vehicle: In the worst case you'll get a good scare and your windshield will get cracked or dented, but most insurance policies will pick up the tab.

Flash Floods

Floods claim more lives in America than tornadoes, hurricanes, or lightning, and most of those fatalities are the result of flash flooding. That is America's number-one storm-related killer, with an average of 140 deaths every year. There has been a steady drop in the death toll from tornadoes and lightning, but technology has not produced a similar improvement in flash-flood forecasting. It's possible to know when a flash flood will occur, but predicting the magnitude of the event is still very difficult for meteorologists. Most weather forecasters fail to predict the extreme rainfall amounts that can result in life-threatening floods.

Tempting fate. Two feet of rapidly moving water can float your vehicle with potentially tragic consequences. This is how most flash flood victims die, trying to cross a flooded road, especially at night, when it's impossible to estimate water depth.

Unlike river flooding, which usually builds gradually, allowing days for preparation, flash flooding happens so quickly that there is little time to reach higher ground. A wall of muddy water and debris can turn streams into raging rivers in a matter of seconds. Water levels can rise as much as 40 feet, rolling boulders, tearing out trees, smashing bridges, and leveling buildings in the path of the flood.

On June 9, 1972, in the Black Hills near Rapid City, South Dakota, 15 inches of rain fell in five hours, producing a raging 40-foot wall of water and debris that killed 238 residents and campers. On June 14, 1990, in Shadyside, Ohio, 4 inches of rain fell in less than two hours, creating a 30-foot wall of water, which left 26 people dead.

Most thunderstorms have a natural life span of about 45 minutes. Usually a cold downdraft within the storm will choke off the warm updraft, and then the cumulonimbus cloud begins to dissipate, and the heaviest rains taper off.

In rare situations, when winds aloft are light or a frontal boundary stalls, thunderstorms can stall overhead, pouring out copious rains. Meteorologists describe

Campers beware.
Camping next to streams and rivers during the summer months brings the threat of flash flooding, from storms as far as 30 miles away. When storms are in the forecast consider finding a camping site on higher ground.

a phenomenon known as a train echo effect, in which thunderstorms repeatedly pass over the same county, much like the cars of a train pass over the same section of track. The result can be 6, 10, or even 20 inches of rain falling in a short period of time. The result is a flash flood.

The intensity and duration of heavy rain are critical; so are the topography, soil conditions, and ground cover. If the ground is already saturated from previous rains, the threat of flash flooding is much higher. Urban areas have seen an increase in flash flooding in recent years. As land is converted from fields and woods to roads and parking lots, it loses its ability to absorb rainwater. Urbanization increases runoff by 2 to 6 times over what would occur on natural terrain. Water rapidly runs off into streets and storm sewers, producing life-threatening conditions.

There is another kind of massive rainstorm that tends to form during the summer months, especially over the Plains states. A mesoscale convective system, or MCS, is a swarm of severe thunderstorms that usually flares up at night and weakens during the morning hours. This line of storms can produce 5 to 10 inches of rain that affect hundreds of counties, resulting in the potential for serious flash flooding.

The greatest danger of flash floods: washed-out or flooded roads. Too many people lose their lives in flash floods while behind the wheel, trying frantically to get out of a window, wishing up until the last moment that they had turned around and tried another way to get home.

Remember that only six inches of moving water can knock you off your feet. Two feet of moving water can turn your vehicle into a boat and float you downstream, with tragic consequences. Estimating water depth, especially at night, is nearly impossible. If you come across a flooded road, do not drive into that muddy water. Don't tempt fate. If your vehicle stalls, leave it immediately and seek higher ground. Don't park near streams, and think twice about camping near even a small stream during summer thunderstorm season.

A word here about SUVs. Sitting up high behind the wheel of that four-by-four gives many drivers a misplaced feeling of invincibility. But as secure as they may seem, SUVs cannot invalidate the laws of nature. All it takes is two feet of rapidly moving water to turn that big plush ride into a rudderless boat, careening helplessly in the surging water.

Even if you're not caught up in rapidly rising water from a flash flood, any heavy rainstorm raises the possibility of hydroplaning in your vehicle. At speeds greater than about 25 mph, a thin layer of water can build up between the highway and your tires. The tires may temporarily leave the roadway surface, leaving you with little or no control over steering and breaking. To avoid going out of control, slow down, pump your brakes gently, and try to avoid driving in the well-worn grooves of the highway surface, where excess rainwater is most likely to collect.

The amount of water generated by late-afternoon thunderstorms is staggering. A typical cluster of late-day storms may affect a 100-square-mile area. Just one inch of rain falling on that area would weigh over 7 million tons!

Here are some clues to protect yourself from flash flooding:

- Watch for distant thunder and nearly continuous lightning nearby, telltale signs of a strong thunderstorm that can produce flooding rains at your location.
- In your vehicle, watch for dips in the highway surface, bridge overpasses, and low areas, all susceptible to rapidly rising water.
- If your vehicle stalls, leave it immediately and head for higher ground. It's better to be wet than dead.
- Remind your kids not to play around high water or storm drains.

Even if you're not caught up in rapidly rising water from a flash flood, any heavy rainstorm raises the possibility of hydroplaning in your vehicle.

More than half of all flash-flood fatalities are the result of people driving into what seems to be a safe level of water, and being swept to their death. In the words of NOAA, "turn around—don't drown."

CHAPTER SIX

Forecast 2020
A Warm and Stormy Future

Climate change is truly a global issue,
one that may prove to be humanity's greatest challenge.
—*Science*, December 5, 2003, "State of the Planet" issue

GLOBAL WARMING. Is it really happening? And if it is, should we really care? I live in Minnesota, where a statistically significant percentage of the population believes that global warming has a nice ring to it and should be encouraged. "What's all the fuss about?" some people ask. "Why should I get worked up over a few degrees?"

Good question. Here's the problem: if you warm up the atmosphere, even slightly, there could be some unpleasant side effects and complications, things that we can't even predict in advance. Greenhouse gases—the warming gases trapped in the atmosphere about us—have been increasing from the combustion of fossil fuels and other chemicals. There is no scientific debate on this point. Carbon dioxide in the atmosphere has increased by 31 percent since preindustrial times, and more than 80 percent of that increase occurred since 1900. The amount of carbon floating over our heads is now higher than it has been at any time in the last 500,000 years, and the levels may double by the end of this century. Massive quantities of carbon, which took billions of years to form into oil, gas, and coal, have been released into the sky in the last 250 years, a geological blink of an eye. We are conducting a vast experiment on our atmosphere, one with unforeseen consequences. We are entering uncharted territory.

How convincing is the science? Is there a critical mass of incontrovertible evidence that supports the claim that man is having an impact on weather and climate above and beyond what is considered "normal weather"? Can we see man's thumbprint amid the white noise of everyday weather extremes?

My answer is a cautious yes. Am I 100 percent certain? Of course not. The only thing I am completely certain of is sunrise and sunset. But if you look at the data objectively, just let the numbers do the talking, a case can be made that the atmos-

Smog capital.
Californians like to joke that they don't trust air they can't see. California's air has gotten cleaner in recent decades, but the Golden State is still home to nine counties and six metropolitan areas with the worst air in the nation. That's based on EPA data from 1999 to 2001. The American Lung Association estimates that half of all Americans are living in counties with unhealthy smog levels. EPA standards were strengthened in 1997 after research showed that smog can harm human health at levels much lower than previously thought.

phere is warming, and there's a significant probability that man is accelerating that warming trend.

If I told you that there was a 40 percent probability of an afternoon thunderstorm, you might consider taking an umbrella. So it goes with climate change. If there's a 40 percent, or even a 30 percent, probability, do we collectively take small steps today to minimize the impact farther down the road? There is a temptation to look away. There are, after all, so many other distractions and legitimate concerns. The economy. Our own comfort and convenience. And the atmosphere is impossibly complex. Perhaps some natural checks and balances will kick in and cool us back down.

Perhaps. But I just can't escape the trends in the data and a mounting body of evidence. There is a growing consensus among meteorologists, climatologists, oceanographers, and physicists worldwide, the vast majority of whom are free from political demagoguery and the influence of energy-industry lobbyists, that global warming has gone from theory to reality.

The United States is responsible for about a quarter of all the carbon being released into the atmosphere, more than any other nation on the planet. There is a moral imperative here. We have an obligation to future generations to take constructive steps to minimize the potential impacts of global warming and climate change. In this area there is no right wing or liberal wing or Green Party. In the end we are all stewards, all with an obligation to the generations that follow. When it comes to the air we breathe, the pond in which we live, all of us are environmentalists.

Measuring Global Climate Change

Scientists have a number of tools at their disposal to examine previous weather and longer-term climate. We can look back centuries, even millennia, to determine trends in moisture and temperature. Severe storms or droughts or a particularly strong El Niño can cost billions of dollars, so the ability to predict the frequency of destructive events can help to save money and lives. And by looking at historical data, researchers can gain clues that will help us plan for future climate change.

But there's a problem here. Satellite records go back just over 20 years. Other measurements from rain gauges and thermometers cover less than 150 years, too short a time to examine the full range of climatic variability. To get an accurate picture, it's necessary to examine climate change going back hundreds, even thousands, of years.

To do this scientists use paleoclimatic records—material from trees, corals, ice cores from glaciers, and sediment samples from lake bottoms—to reconstruct what the weather was like eons ago.

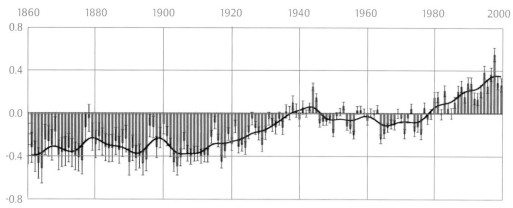

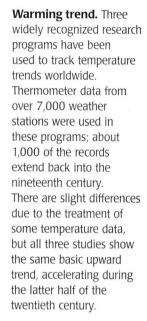

Warming trend. Three widely recognized research programs have been used to track temperature trends worldwide. Thermometer data from over 7,000 weather stations were used in these programs; about 1,000 of the records extend back into the nineteenth century. There are slight differences due to the treatment of some temperature data, but all three studies show the same basic upward trend, accelerating during the latter half of the twentieth century.

Paleoclimatic data have been helpful in showing that the earth's weather system can be amazingly erratic, shifting dramatically in the span of decades or just a few years. Understanding these climate shifts and surprises is critical if we are to avoid disruptive and expensive changes in our weather and in our longer-term climate.

In the last 150 years of accurate temperature records, the earth's global average temperature has increased by about 1 degree, but 3- to 5-degree increases have been noted at northerly latitudes in Canada and Alaska. Scientists are trying to determine how much of that can be explained by natural forces, such as subtle fluctuations in the amount of solar energy reaching the earth or slight shifts or wobbles in the earth's orbit, and how much is the result of greenhouse gases being released into the atmosphere.

Tracking Global Weather From 1850 to Now

Satellite-derived temperature records have been used to reconstruct global atmospheric temperatures for the past 21 years. Current NOAA calculations show the lower atmosphere to be warming at the rate of .12 degrees per decade. Satellite observations showing slightly less warming since 1979 may have been biased by stratospheric cooling, a byproduct of global warming, according to scientists at NOAA and the University of Wisconsin.

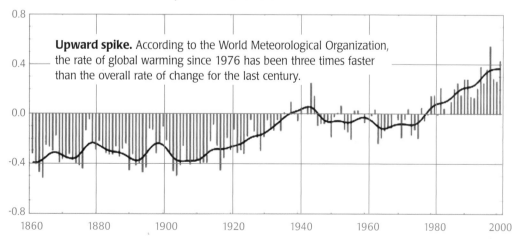

Upward spike. According to the World Meteorological Organization, the rate of global warming since 1976 has been three times faster than the overall rate of change for the last century.

The Last 1,000 Years of Weather

Looking back beyond 150 years requires scientific detective work, the examination of "proxy data" to determine what the weather was like hundreds of years ago. Historical documents, such as ship and farm logs, can provide accurate data about past weather, but there are other clues from the earth itself.

Corals build their hard skeletons from calcium carbonate, a mineral extracted from sea water. The carbonate contains isotopes of oxygen that can be used to estimate the water temperatures in which the coral grew. Those temperature recordings can then be used to reconstruct what temperatures were like at the time in the air overhead.

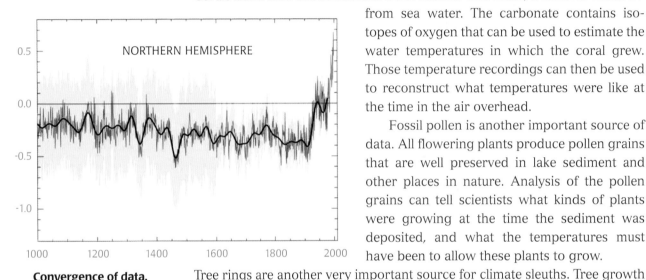

Convergence of data. A combination of thermometer, tree-ring, coral, and ice-core data that reflects back to 1000 A.D. shows a sudden upward jump in temperature in the latter half of the twentieth century. Temperatures are in degrees Celsius.

Fossil pollen is another important source of data. All flowering plants produce pollen grains that are well preserved in lake sediment and other places in nature. Analysis of the pollen grains can tell scientists what kinds of plants were growing at the time the sediment was deposited, and what the temperatures must have been to allow these plants to grow.

Tree rings are another very important source for climate sleuths. Tree growth is directly affected by climatic conditions, that is, the temperature and amount of moisture. In most regions where there is a distinct growing season, trees generally produce one ring a year. Subtle changes in the width, density, and isotopic compositions of those tree rings can allow researchers to determine what the climate was like hundreds or even thousands of years ago.

Sediment accumulates by the tons at the bottoms of lakes and oceans every year. Instead of drilling into ice, scientists can drill down into these layers of sediment below the water, looking for tiny fossils and chemicals that can be used to interpret past climates.

Troubling Weather Trends

After looking at the data, a consensus of scientists around the world believe that either the warming witnessed in the last 30 years is the Mother of All Coincidences, or some very distinct and troubling trends are emerging. Since 1980 the earth has experienced 19 of its 20 hottest years on record. Ten of the warmest years have occurred since 1990, including each year since 1997. Globally 1998 was the warmest year ever observed. The years 2002 and 2003 were the second and third warmest, according to the World Meteorological Society.

The twentieth century was warmer than any century during the last 1,000 years in the Northern Hemisphere. Alaska is as much as 5 degrees warmer than it was at the turn of the twentieth century. The permafrost there is melting into the soil, killing trees and affecting home construction. Fifty million acres of Alaskan forest are under attack by spruce budworms, which thrive in warmer weather.

From the Rockies to the Alps to the Andes, glaciers are disappearing at an alarming rate. In Glacier National Park the number of glaciers has fallen from 150 to 50 since 1850. The world's oceans are experiencing widespread death of coral reefs, the result of rapidly warming water. And a 6- to 10-inch rise in ocean water since 1900 is consistent with the concept that warming air causes volumetric increases in the water below.

Scientists disagree about the causes of global warming and how much can be attributed to man, but there now seems to be little doubt that the sky above us is growing hotter. Of course, the atmosphere is amazingly complex. Many factors

Troubling trend.
Hawaii's Mauna Loa Observatory, at an altitude of nearly 11,000 feet, routinely measures some of the cleanest air in the world. NOAA's Climate Monitoring and Diagnostics Laboratory has been measuring a steady increase in the amount of carbon dioxide in the Mauna Loa air since 1958. Carbon levels there reached a record high in March 2004.

can affect the rate of warming, everything from dust to volcanic eruptions to minor fluctuations in the sun's energy to subtle changes in how heat energy is transferred from oceans to the atmosphere.

The best estimate is that most of the observed global warming of the last century can be attributed to increases in man-made greenhouse gases. At this rate, computer models, simulations of future weather and climate, suggest that global temperatures may be as much as 2 to 10 degrees warmer as we enter the twenty-second century, a warming trend beyond the scope of anything our atmosphere has ever experienced before.

The Greenhouse Effect

First, an important disclaimer: Without greenhouse warming—the trapping of warm air in our atmosphere—there would be no life on earth. Think of our existence here as a Goldilocks syndrome of sorts. Conditions have to be just right or we fall victim to the fates of other planets in our solar system. Too much warming produces a runaway effect similar to that found on Venus, where the temperature is a blazing 730 degrees in the shade. Not enough warming and you're left with a barren, lifeless planet like Mars, where temperatures can fall below minus 100 degrees.

What makes earth different? Life-giving amounts of our sun's energy are absorbed by land and water. A warming earth radiates some of this infrared radiation back into the sky. However, a significant percentage is absorbed by water vapor, carbon dioxide, and other "greenhouse gases" in the atmosphere. These molecules in the air radiate the sun's energy in all directions, warming up the atmosphere and the planet below.

When you step into your car on a cold winter day and notice that the temperature inside is 10 to 20 degrees warmer than it is outside, you're getting a sample of how the greenhouse effect works. Greenhouse gases act as a kind of warm blanket, keeping the warmth below where our bodies and the world around us need it. But too many greenhouse gases can accelerate this warming and turn up the earth's natural thermostat to uncomfortable or potentially dangerous levels.

Milder winters. NASA satellite imagery from February 2002. Scientists confirm that across the Northern Hemisphere spring "green-up" now comes about one week earlier and lingers an extra week, into late autumn. One possible benefit of global warming would be milder winters with a lower risk of frostbite, hypothermia, and traffic accidents triggered by snow and ice. On the other hand, more than 75 percent of water for human consumption in the western United States comes from snowmelt. Global warming increases the potential for water shortage and drought.

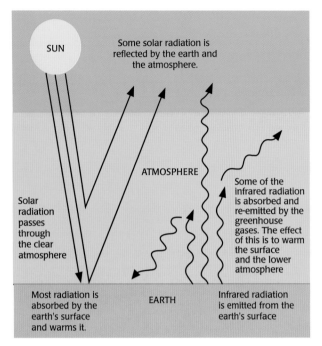

SUN

Some solar radiation is reflected by the earth and the atmosphere.

ATMOSPHERE

Solar radiation passes through the clear atmosphere

Some of the infrared radiation is absorbed and re-emitted by the greenhouse gases. The effect of this is to warm the surface and the lower atmosphere

Most radiation is absorbed by the earth's surface and warms it.

EARTH

Infrared radiation is emitted from the earth's surface

The Difference a Degree Makes

Why quibble over a couple of degrees anyway? Well, there are several things to consider. A warmer atmosphere holds more water vapor, increasing the potential for violent storms. National Weather Service statistics show a 20 percent increase in flooding in the last 100 years. And our rain is not falling as gently as it did in our grandparents' era. Reports of damaging hail and tornadoes are on the rise worldwide.

The tempo of El Niño events in the Pacific Ocean is increasing, lashing California with bigger storms and spinning up more nighttime tornadoes over the Deep South. Rivers are flooding more often, with a 1-in-500-year flood in 1993 and a 1-in-1,000-year epic flooding of the Red River in Grand Forks only four years later. Coincidence? Perhaps. But the United States has been clobbered by over 190 weather-related disasters, with more than $100 million in damage, since 1949, and the tempo of weather mayhem seems to be getting quicker.

So what? you might ask. It warms up a few degrees, and we may have a few more storms. We've had bad storms before. The earth will still spin on its axis. The sun will rise in the east. Life goes on. We'll adapt. We always have.

It's true that the atmosphere's thermostat has maintained a delicate balance for many millennia, but the industrial revolution, exponential increases in standards of living worldwide, and a thirst for the fuel to power this spike in productivity and wealth is straining the system. Instead of occurring every 20 years, severe drought may grip portions of America once every 4 or 5 years. Increase the background temperature only slightly and the *severity* and *frequency* of heat and drought rise dramatically. In July 1995 nearly 800 people in Chicago died in only two days, the result of a sudden overpowering heat "storm." The temperature felt like 130 degrees in the shade. Residents described walking outside and immediately having trouble breathing and speaking, a feeling similar to that of being punched in the stomach. The heat was overwhelming, and those who couldn't cool themselves were doomed.

Here's a paradox. Summer heat hasn't increased dramatically in recent years, but across much of America winter temperatures are substantially warmer, especially nighttime temperatures, and especially at northerly latitudes from Boston to Detroit to St. Paul.

164

SOME POTENTIAL PROBLEMS POSED BY GLOBAL WARMING

If you live in a northern city, the concept of global warming may have a certain allure. But we're not talking about year-round shorts, sandals, and palm trees. Experts on climate suggest that warming earth's atmosphere by only a couple of degrees may eventually lead to:

• More frequent drought, especially in the far western and central Plains states. The kind of crops grown and the location of farmlands may be impacted, even in our lifetime.

• A potential for more numerous heat storms in major cities, where a combination of heat and humidity could trigger heat indexes as high as 130 degrees.

• Water woes. Heavier showers and storms in a warmer world may result in more flash flooding and soil erosion.

• The warmer the air, the more water vapor it can contain. The result could be more hurricanes and thunderstorms, hail and tornadoes.

• Reduced water quality in America's rivers and lakes because of increased algae blooms and less oxygen in warmer waters.

• More troublesome pests and dangerous diseases, including West Nile and malaria.

• Extinction of some animal and plant species by 2050. A recent study in the journal *Nature* found at least 279 species of plants and animals responding to global warming. Some will be able to migrate and survive; others may not be able to adapt.

• Shifts in the locations of grasslands and forests.

• More wildfires, dust, asthma, smog, and respiratory problems.

• The loss of beaches along the East Coast of the United States, some within 25 years, according to the Intergovernmental Panel on Climate Change. The current rate of sea level risings is three times the historical average and appears to be accelerating. Scientists predict an additional rise of 19 to 37 inches by the end of this century, posing a threat to coastal cities. Banks and insurance companies are growing increasingly concerned. An estimated $2 trillion in insured property along the Eastern Seaboard is at risk.

Similar heat storms may increase in the years ahead as we go from warm fronts to hot fronts. Some projections show a doubling or even tripling of 90-degree days. Highs over 100 degrees may become commonplace across much of the Midwest from June through August.

If current emissions of greenhouse gases continue, the world may face the fastest rate of climate change in at least the past 10,000 years, altering everything from daily weather to ocean currents. Even a slight warming and drying may have a profound effect on what grows on our farms. Many species of trees, plants, and crops are exquisitely sensitive to temperature and moisture. America's heaviest rains and most fertile farmland may shift north, where soils are not favorable for growing the corn, soybeans, and other cash crops our farmers depend on. Agriculture may have to try new strains more resistant to heat and drought.

More hail, tornadoes, and hurricanes may affect where we build our homes and businesses, and how we design these dwellings to better withstand volatile swings in weather. A drop in water levels may affect development, starting in the Southwest, where water is already being rationed. Water, not oil, may prove to be America's most precious natural resource in the next generation.

A warmer world would increase the potential for diseases like West Nile virus and malaria, and millions of people might be displaced, searching for reliable water and food supplies. That in turn could heighten political instability and regional conflict. Already the fight for clean drinking water has reached a fever pitch from the Middle East into much of Africa.

In this case that tired cliché "There is no free lunch" may be dead on. Production of our biggest, proudest export, the American Dream—the rolling economic miracle that is now being duplicated from India to China to Brazil—has required massive amounts of power and fuel, and that has released a steady torrent of carbon into the atmosphere. Global warming is real. We can argue about who or what is responsible, and to what degree, but there is little argument that the warming is a reality.

The debate now is shifting to just how warm it's going to get, what the impact on natural resources will be, and whether earth's species, including man, will be able to adapt fast enough to a warming planet. The long-range forecast is still clouded in uncertainty, but a majority of atmospheric scientists are confident that man-made greenhouse gases are overpowering natural forces. They are predicting an increase in extreme weather events, like flooding, but also in more frequent heat waves, droughts, wildfires, vegetation stress, and a continued slow and steady rise in sea levels that will threaten coastal cities, especially during major storms.

What do we do now? There are no simple answers. Addressing this issue will take time, resolve, and innovation, from negotiated global action to grass-roots, community-level initiatives. Breaking our addiction to fossil fuels and other pollutants won't come easily or overnight, but America can reclaim the high ground, launch new renewable-energy initiatives, and set an example for the rest of the industrialized world.

UNLIKELY THUNDER

At 11:00 p.m. on June 19, 2000, thunder rumbled over the sleepy little town of Barrow, Alaska. Barrow is at the northerly tip of the United States, on the edge of the Arctic Ocean. According to the National Weather Service, this was only the third time since 1978 that a thunderstorm had been observed there.

Computer model confidence. How reliable are computer models in predicting global rises in temperature this century? Researchers used five of the most reliable computer models to see how they would have predicted warming in the twentieth century. The model was run four times under slightly different conditions. The experiment found an impressive agreement between what was predicted (in gray) and what actually happened (plotted in red).

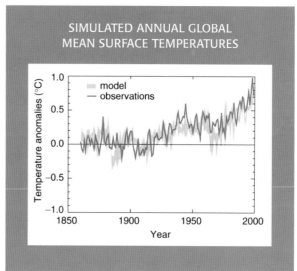

SIMULATED ANNUAL GLOBAL MEAN SURFACE TEMPERATURES

Volcano weather. This spectacular image, taken from the International Space Station Alpha, shows a plume of ash from the Popocatepetl, or Popo, volcano, about 30 miles southeast of Mexico City, on January 23, 2001. Volcanic ash can have a temporary cooling effect hundreds or even thousands of miles downwind, masking warming from greenhouse gases.

A Silver Lining to a Warmer World?

Some researchers believe that smog—caused by man-made aerosols resulting from the burning of fossil fuels, crop waste, and rainforests—may be blocking some of the sunlight reaching the earth, counteracting the effects of global warming. They argue that without the man-made blanket of haze and smog the warming measured in recent decades might have been far worse. If temperatures and greenhouse gases continue to rise, there might even be a few benefits:

- Some northern latitudes would have less snow and ice, translating into fewer traffic accidents and the attendant injuries and deaths. Warmer winters might also result in fewer deaths from influenza and pneumonia.

- Warmer winters would mean lower heating bills.

- Some crops, plants, and vegetables would thrive in a carbon-rich environment where the growing season is longer, but changes in rainfall patterns and availability of water would ultimately determine the impact on agriculture. (Unfortunately, increased CO_2 and photosynthesis would also increase weed growth.)

Melting ice. A computer simulation from the Geophysical Fluid Dynamics Laboratory shows a gradual shrinking in the polar ice cap. By 2050 there may be little more than half the arctic ice observed in 1950.

167

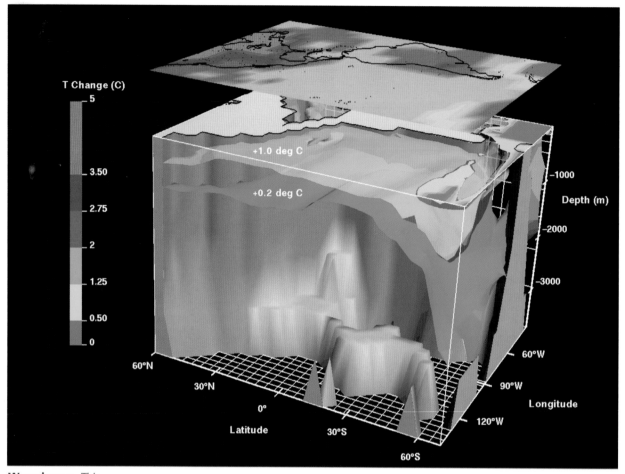

Warming up. This sophisticated "coupled" computer forecast takes into account ocean water temperatures responding to global warming in the middle of the twenty-first century. As with other computer predictions, warming would be most pronounced, by more than 10 degrees, over the northern-tier states of America and over Canada.

- A warmer atmosphere would evaporate more moisture from the oceans, possibly triggering more cloud cover, which would reflect more of the sun's energy into space, putting the brakes on any long-term warming.
- Some forests would thrive and expand as carbon levels and temperatures rose, soaking up additional CO_2 in the process.

Ozone: The Good and the Bad

Much has changed since the first Earth Day in 1970. That was the year President Nixon warned that without big changes the nation's air would soon be unfit to breathe. At that time the Environmental Protection Agency (EPA) didn't exist and America's cities were submerged under a foul stew of pollutants. Since then legislation and an environmentally friendly mind-set on the part of industry and consumers have helped to clean up the air. The EPA reports that six major air pollutants have declined by nearly 50 percent in the last 35 years.

But problems remain, especially with ozone levels. In the stratosphere, the upper atmosphere 6 to 30 miles above the ground, ozone is a naturally occurring gas, which shields the earth from harmful ultraviolet radiation. This is the "good ozone." It's a protective layer high in the skies that makes life possible on the earth.

But near the ground, too much ozone can be harmful. This is the "bad ozone," which can combine with sunshine and man-made pollutants to produce smog.

The term *smog* is derived from the words *smoke* and *fog* but is used to describe a pervasive noxious cloud of pollutants generated by vehicles and industry. Most smog is produced by nitrogen oxides and organic compounds emitted by cars and trucks, gasoline vapors, and chemical solvents. A photochemical reaction with the sun creates ozone at ground level, which can drop visibilities, damage plants, reduce crop and forest yields, and increase susceptibility to pests and disease. Half a billion dollars in reduced crop yields can be attributed to city smog reaching surrounding farms. Ozone can also irritate the eyes, trigger respiratory distress and chest pain, and aggravate emphysema and bronchitis. It can even lead to permanent lung damage.

SMOGGY SKIES

The following is the American Lung Association's ranking of the smoggiest metropolitan areas and counties in America.

Smoggiest Metropolitan Areas

1. Los Angeles, CA
2. Visalia-Porterville, CA
3. Bakersfield, CA
4. Fresno, CA
5. Houston, TX
6. Merced, CA
7. Sacramento, CA
8. Hanford, CA
9. Knoxville, TN
10. Dallas-Fort Worth, TX

Smoggiest Counties

1. San Bernardino, CA
2. Fresno, CA
3. Kern, CA
4. Tulare, CA
5. Riverside, CA
6. Harris, TX
7. Los Angeles, CA
8. El Dorado, CA
9. Merced, CA
10. Kings, CA
11. Fulton, GA
12. Sevier, TN
13. Nevada, CA
14. Sacramento, CA
15. Ventura, CA
16. Rowan, NC
17. Placer, CA
18. Anne Arundel, MD
19. Mecklenburg, NC
20. Tarrant, TX

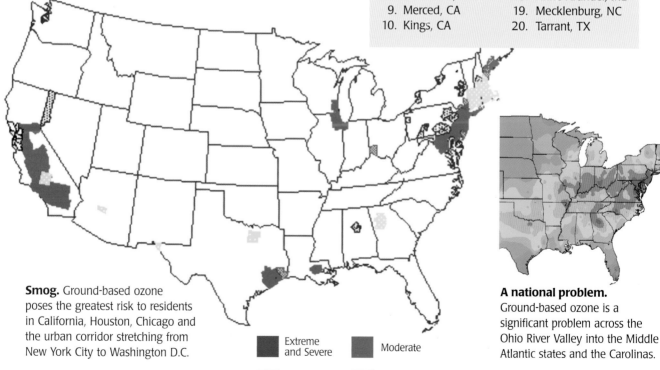

Smog. Ground-based ozone poses the greatest risk to residents in California, Houston, Chicago and the urban corridor stretching from New York City to Washington D.C.

Extreme and Severe

Serious

Moderate

Marginal

A national problem. Ground-based ozone is a significant problem across the Ohio River Valley into the Middle Atlantic states and the Carolinas.

AQI. The EPA's Air Quality Index is a scale that reports levels of ozone and other potentially harmful pollutants. The higher the number, the greater the risk, especially for children, athletes, outdoor workers, and people with respiratory problems. Visit www.epa/gov/airnow to get information for your metropolitan area.

AIR QUALITY INDEX

Index Values	Descriptors	Cautionary Statements for Ozone
0 to 50	Good	None.
51 to 100	Moderate	Unusually sensitive people should consider limiting prolonged outdoor exertion.
101 to 150	Unhealthy for sensitive groups	Active children and adults, and people with respiratory disease, such as asthma, should limit prolonged outdoor exertion.
151 to 200	Unhealthy	Active children and adults, and people with respiratory disease, such as asthma, should avoid prolonged outdoor exertion; everyone else, especially children, should limit prolonged outdoor exertion.
201 to 300	Very unhealthy	Active children and adults, and people with respiratory disease, such as asthma, should avoid all outdoor exertion; everyone else, especially children, should limit outdoor exertion.

Protecting Yourself From Bad Ozone

Even healthy people can experience difficulty breathing when ozone concentrations are high. Most vulnerable are kids who play outside on hot summer days, as well as people who exercise and work outside. Here are some steps you can take to reduce ozone-based smog in your city, and stay healthier in the process:

- Check the air quality forecast in your area. During times when the air quality index (AQI) indicates an unhealthy environment, limit physical exertion outdoors. In many places, ozone peaks mid-afternoon to early evening. Consider cutting down on intense, outdoor workouts when ozone levels are high.

- Conserve energy at home and the office. Set your thermostat a few degrees higher in the summer. Start participating in your local utilities' load-sharing and energy-conservation programs.

- Reduce air pollution from cars, trucks, gas-powered lawn and garden equipment, boats, and other engines by keeping your equipment properly tuned and maintained. During the summer, fill your gas tank during the cooler evening hours and be careful not to spill gasoline. Limit driving if you can; use public transportation, walk, or bicycle to work or school.

- Carpooling can really make a dent in air-pollution and ozone problems. A 2001 report in *JAMA: The Journal of the American Medical Association* found that during the 1996 Summer Olympics in Atlanta ozone pollution was reduced by 28 percent because of carpooling and increased use of mass transit. The journal also

WEATHERFACT

Air pollution from motor vehicles in the United States may be responsible for $40 billion to $50 billion in annual healthcare expenditures and as many as 120,000 unnecessary or premature deaths, according to studies by the American Lung Association.

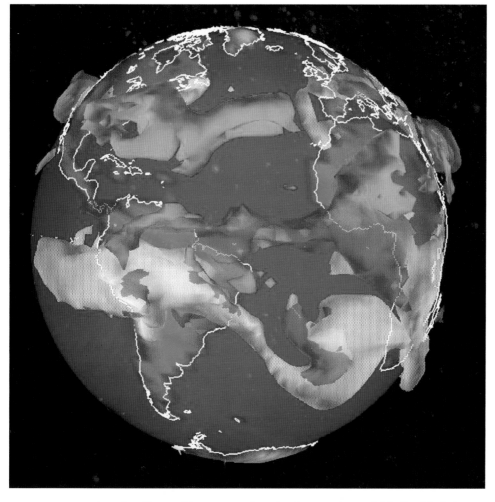

Global problem.
This global chemical computer model for the earth shows ozone and other chemicals spreading thousands of miles downwind.

reported a significant 44 percent drop in the number of Medicaid claims of treatment of childhood asthma.

- Use household and garden chemicals wisely.

The Ozone Hole

In recent years, the "good ozone" in our atmosphere has been depleted by a dangerous brew of man-made chemicals drifting into the upper atmosphere. Chlorofluorocarbons (CFCs) and hydrochlorofluorocarbons (HCFCs), halons, methyl bromide, and other chemicals used in air-conditioning systems, as well as solvents and pesticides, can remain in the upper air for up to a century, combining with ozone to create oxygen and then reducing the ozone level overall. Less ozone in the upper atmosphere means that more harmful UV rays can reach the earth, threatening plant life and increasing the potential for impaired immune systems in humans, along with skin cancer and cataracts. Worldwide a 3 percent thinning of stratospheric ozone has been observed since 1969, meaning that 6 percent more UV radiation is reaching our beaches and lakes.

171

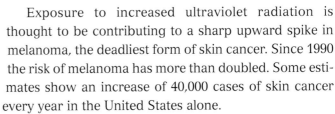

Exposure to increased ultraviolet radiation is thought to be contributing to a sharp upward spike in melanoma, the deadliest form of skin cancer. Since 1990 the risk of melanoma has more than doubled. Some estimates show an increase of 40,000 cases of skin cancer every year in the United States alone.

Although many of these potentially harmful chemicals have been reduced or eliminated, a gaping lack of stratospheric ozone, an ozone "hole," routinely shows up in satellite-based observations, especially over polar regions. The good news: Recent research indicates that the depletion of the "good ozone" is slowing worldwide.

The United States, along with over 180 other countries, has recognized the ongoing threat posed by the reduction of stratospheric ozone. In 1987 the industrialized nations of the world adopted a treaty called the Montreal Protocol, which would phase out the use of ozone-depleting substances. In accordance with the protocol, the EPA has established stringent regulations to phase out ozone-depleting chemicals in the United States. Warning labels must now be placed on all products containing CFCs or similar substances, and nonessential uses of ozone-depleting products are prohibited. Releases into the air of harmful refrigerants used in car and home air-conditioning units and appliances are prohibited. Some substitutes for ozone-depleting products have been produced and others are being developed. If the United States and other countries stop producing ozone-depleting substances, natural forces are expected to return the ozone layer to normal levels by about 2050. With any luck our children will see a day when there will be no need to make reference to an ozone hole.

There Is No Such Thing As a Healthy Tan

A tan is the skin's response to injury. Madison Avenue may celebrate a dark, "healthy" glow, but excess sun will eventually leave your skin wrinkled and leathery and increase your potential for skin cancer.

Here are things you can do to protect your skin from the sun's harmful rays:

- Avoid sunburn, and make sure your children wear sunscreen with a high SPF factor. Just three blistering sunburns before the age of 8 can increase your child's risk of developing melanoma later in life by 50 percent.
- Avoid the midday sun whenever possible; wear a hat and lightweight, light-colored cotton clothing to protect your body, even on hot days.
- Beware of tanning beds; many emit potentially harmful UVA rays. Recent research suggests that tanning beds may double your risk of skin cancer.
- Wear UV-protected sunglasses.

Ozone hole.
Using a mapping spectrometer, NASA's Goddard Space Flight Center rendered this 3-D image of the hole in the ozone layer above Antarctica. Scientists discovered the hole in the 1980s, and every spring in the Southern Hemisphere the phenomenon reappears. When chlorofluorocarbons first entered international consumerism, people hailed them as wonder compounds. Nobody expected they would rise into the upper atmosphere and destroy the ozone that protects the earth from harmful ultraviolet radiation.

UV INDEX

Too much exposure to sunlight can be dangerous. The National Weather Service and the EPA developed a scale for harmful ultraviolet radiation from sunlight. The higher the UV index number, the higher the risk of sunburn and other sun-related ailments. Calculated each day for many cities across the United States, the index takes into account predicted cloud cover and local factors. The national map is updated at 1:30 p.m. each day, with a prediction for the following day. You can find it at www.cpc.ncep.noaa.gov/products/stratosphere/uv_index/uv_current_map.html.

UV INDEX NUMBER
Exposure Level

0 to 2	Minimal
3 to 4	Low
5 to 6	Moderate
7 to 9	High
10+	Very High

Acid Rain

Acid rain is formed when airborne moisture combines with sulfur dioxide and nitrogen oxide to produce sulfuric and nitric acid. Some of this occurs naturally in nature, but we have definitely accelerated the process with our polluting ways. These acidic raindrops and snowflakes can fall into our lawns, fields, and lakes.

Ironically, the construction of taller smokestacks has transformed air pollution from a local problem into a global one. Taller stacks, many from coal-fired power plants in the Midwest and Ohio Valley, have helped clear the air in some towns. But because sulfur and nitrogen are being pumped higher into the atmosphere, these gases can travel hundreds, even thousands, of miles downwind, giving them more time to combine with cloud droplets to form acid rain.

Lakes and forests, especially in New England, are vulnerable to long-term damage triggered by acid rain. A major federal study published in 1996 concluded that without additional reductions in air pollution, the number of acid-damaged lakes in the Adirondacks of New York—now estimated at 17 percent—would increase by almost 40 percent by 2040. A 2001 report from the New Hampshire–based Hubbard Brook Research Foundation showed that 41 percent of the lakes in the Adirondacks and 15 percent of the lakes in New England have become acidic. Roughly a quarter of the Adirondacks' 1,469 lakes are too acidic to support fish populations.

While the Adirondack Mountains region is often portrayed as suffering especially acute acid rain damage, there is now evidence that acid rain also has a harmful impact in such diverse locations as New England, Virginia, Tennessee, California, and Colorado.

There is good news. Some lakes across New England show signs of recovering. The tougher amendments to the Clean Air Act, designed to reduce industry emissions, are working, albeit slowly. There has been a steady decline in sulfuric

ACID RAIN

The slow degradation of lakes, soil, and trees continues, in spite of emission cuts mandated by the 1990 Clean Air Act. Recent studies blame acid rain for a decline in red spruce trees across the Eastern United States and sugar maples in central and western Pennsylvania. Since the 1960s roughly half the canopy of red spruce trees in New York's Adirondack Mountains and Vermont's Green Mountains has died, and damage is clear in New Hampshire's White Mountains.

173

acid in rain since the 1970s. Nitrous oxide produced by vehicles is a tougher problem, and so acid rain will continue to pose a risk to our forests and lakes through the twenty-first century.

Are We Changing Our Local Weather?

The urban heat island—a term scientists use—is one example of how we are accidentally modifying our weather every day. Urban asphalt and concrete retain some of the sun's heat energy, releasing it slowly at night, keeping temperatures as much as 10 degrees warmer than the outlying suburbs, especially when skies are clear and winds are light. That's why meteorologists often give a range of 5 to 10 degrees when predicting nighttime low temperatures; there can be that much variation within just 20 to 30 miles.

Cities tend to be not only warmer but drier, because there is less soil moisture available to evaporate into the atmosphere. As a result small tornadoes may be less likely over major downtowns, but paving over our metropolitan areas has significantly increased the potential for flash flooding when hard rains fall. There is simply nowhere for rainwater to go. It can't drain into the soil, so it runs off into streets and storm sewers, flushing chemicals, pesticides, and fertilizers into area lakes and rivers.

Cities may also trigger heavier showers downwind, over the suburbs. In 2001 data from NASA satellites confirmed a 28 percent increase in rainfall rates 18 to 36 miles downwind of major cities including Atlanta, Dallas, Nashville, and San Antonio. Because cities tend to be 1 to 10 degrees warmer than surrounding suburbs and rural areas, the added heat can destabilize the air and change the way it circulates. Rising warm air may help produce clouds that result in more rainfall around urban areas. The satellite data confirmed what scientists have suspected for decades: that urban heat islands can impact local rainfall around cities.

Other man-made impacts on our daily weather are more subtle. Studies show that jet contrails from high-flying aircraft can spread out into a thin canopy of cirrus clouds about 25,000 feet above the ground, keeping daytime temperatures 3 to 5 degrees cooler and nighttime readings as much as 5 degrees milder. Power-plant cooling towers release moisture into the lower atmosphere, increasing relative humidity levels and the potential for dense fog nearby.

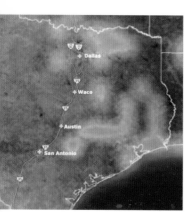

Man-made showers. NASA's Tropical Rainfall Measuring Mission satellite has a built-in radar system that has detected higher rainfall rates just downwind of major cities along the I-35 corridor in Texas. The eastern suburbs of many major U.S. cities may be getting wetter due to a steady release of heat and pollutants over our downtowns. In other words, cities are sparking more rain over the suburbs.

Man-made clouds. Ice crystals in jet contrails can persist for hours, spreading out into a cellophane-thin layer of cirrus clouds that can keep temperatures warmer at night and cooler during the day.

Global Cooling: A Possibility?

Could the sudden climate shift shown in the movie *The Day After Tomorrow* really take place in our lifetime? Recently the U.S. Defense Department commissioned a report looking at the national security implications of a sudden shift in climate brought on by global warming. The report, "Imagining the Unthinkable," outlines a worst-case scenario in the event of a massive and abrupt shift in global climate, similar to sudden shifts in the past.

The hypothesis: Global warming melts huge quantities of polar ice, reducing the salinity of water in the Atlantic Ocean. Less salt in the water means that a phenomenon called the North Atlantic Conveyor Belt, a broad clockwise circulation of water, could be weakened or stalled altogether. If warm Gulf Stream waters are not swept toward Europe, the result could be a rapid cooling in water temperature, resulting in severe winter conditions for much of the Northern Hemisphere, even a southward expansion of the ice caps!

Some scientists believe that this may be a legitimate, long-term concern for the next century, but a majority of researchers believe that such a sudden, devastating cold wave is unlikely. Statistically, odds favor a continued warming of northern latitudes in our lifetime.

10 Things You Can Do to Help the Environment

Unfortunately, when it comes to matters of the atmosphere and the environment, there are no quick and easy fixes. Treaties between nations to find a consensus will be critical, but so will grass-roots efforts, and parents joining with their kids to take a series of small but significant steps. Here are just a few ideas on what you can do to make a long-term difference:

Stay informed. It's critical to keep an open mind and to get your news and information from more than one source. Don't rely on TV sound bites for information on climate change and possible impact on your local weather. Read a few newspapers, browse the Web, and become engaged in what's happening in your community and the rest of the nation. Start a dialogue with friends and neighbors.

Adopt a hybrid mentality. There is a reason there is such a long wait for the new, breakthrough gasoline-electric hybrid vehicle, the Toyota Prius. It has struck a nerve among consumers who feel a little guilty about our gas-guzzling-SUV nation. The next time you go shopping for a new vehicle, consider something that gets more miles per gallon.

The Sierra Club estimates that if every American car owner switched to a hybrid vehicle, one that got 40 miles per gallon, up from today's average of 20.8, this would save 3 million barrels of oil a day and cut greenhouse gases by nearly half. The mpg of today's average vehicle is actually lower than it was in the 1980s. Although buyers pay a little more initially for gas-electric hybrids, they save on average $5,000 at the gas pump over the 15-year life of a vehicle. Consumers who buy hybrids are eligible for a $2,000 tax deduction. Toyota, Honda, Ford, GM, and Lexus all have hybrid options, which even include fuel-efficient SUVs.

Realistic alternatives. You don't have to plug a hybrid into a wall socket. It uses a combination of electricity and gasoline to maximize efficiency, reclaiming braking energy to charge up an electric motor. Many of these vehicles get 35 to 50 mpg and some even more. Options include the Toyota Prius, the Honda Civic Hybrid, the Honda Insight, and, coming soon, hybrid SUVs.

Right, Ford Motor Company test driver Steven Yuhas looks over the engine of a 2005 Ford Escape Hybrid. It combines a fuel-efficient four-cylinder engine with an electric drive system, thus delivering between 35 and 40 mpg in the city.

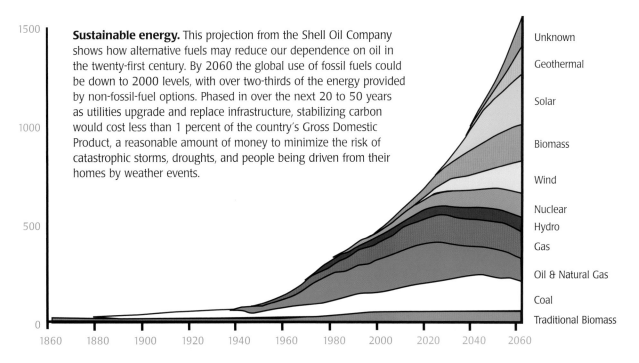

Sustainable energy. This projection from the Shell Oil Company shows how alternative fuels may reduce our dependence on oil in the twenty-first century. By 2060 the global use of fossil fuels could be down to 2000 levels, with over two-thirds of the energy provided by non-fossil-fuel options. Phased in over the next 20 to 50 years as utilities upgrade and replace infrastructure, stabilizing carbon would cost less than 1 percent of the country's Gross Domestic Product, a reasonable amount of money to minimize the risk of catastrophic storms, droughts, and people being driven from their homes by weather events.

Reduce, reuse, and recycle. It all starts at home, in the decisions we make every day. Making recycling a habit is a great first start. The average person creates nearly 2,000 to 3,000 pounds of garbage every year, more than 6 pounds a day! Energy is required to get products and services to your grocery store, and, ultimately, your home. Packaging makes up 30 percent of municipal solid waste. You can reduce the amount of packaging you throw in the trash. Avoid single-serving products in favor of larger servings or buying in bulk. Mixing leftover fruit-and-vegetable food waste with your yard waste helps create high-nutrient compost. When something breaks, take the time to have it repaired instead of rushing out to buy new. Leave grass clippings on your lawn. Remove your name from junk-mail lists to cut down on the amount of paper entering your home.

Get inspired by governments and companies that are switching over to carbon-free energy sources. According to *U.S. News and World Report,* Home Depot buys some of its wood from sustainable forests. The chemical company DuPont is working to cut carbon dioxide emissions by half in the next 20 years. British Petroleum is developing a wide range of cleaner-burning fuels. Nationally we can use tax incentives and market forces to reward companies that think outside the box to generate energy savings. Support politicians who are serious about renewable energy alternatives ranging from cleaner-burning natural gas to biodiesel, geothermal, solar, and wind power. Wind energy already

Trash talk. The average adult in America generates approximately 2000 pounds, one ton, of trash every year. According to the USDA, 27 percent of the nation's total food supply, some 97 billion pounds, is wasted every year. Packaging makes up another 30 percent of solid waste.

provides 1 percent of America's electricity, but it could provide more than 20 percent. Fourteen states have made it a goal to have clean, renewable energy sources within 10 years.

   Think green. A gesture as simple as planting a tree can have a big long-term impact on climate. Trees absorb carbon dioxide and cut down on global warming. Encourage developers to plant three new trees for every tree that they cut down. The American Forestry Association estimates that if only one of every three Americans planted one tree in his or her lifetime, about 100 million trees in all, carbon dioxide could be reduced by 18 million tons a year, saving American consumers $4 billion annually in energy costs.

   Reduce energy use at home and the office. Cooling and heating our homes and water has a huge impact on energy consumption. Keeping your thermostat a few degrees warmer in the summer and cooler in the winter will save significant energy and put cash back in your pocket. Do an audit of your home. Your local utility will be happy to come out and test your home for energy efficiencies. Buy energy-efficient bulbs and appliances; look for the ENERGY STAR label. Fluorescent lights consume roughly half the energy of incandescent bulbs. Better building standards, heat insulation, and use of direct solar energy to heat buildings can result in significant energy savings over time.

Consume wisely. Before you buy a product, look at its ingredients. Are they renewable? Buy products made from recycled materials. Buy milk, water, and other beverages in refillable containers. Look for products labeled "post-consumer," "pre-consumer," or "recycled content."

According to the U.S. Department of Agriculture, 27 percent of the nation's total food supply—97 billion pounds—goes to waste every year! Food is wasted in many ways, such as preparing too much or letting fresh food go bad. Planning your meals and your shopping will help you buy and prepare only what you need.

Educate those around you. Talk really is cheap. Friends, family, and neighbors will respond by seeing your words in action. Tell them what you're doing, and why. Challenge them to take a series of small steps in their lives that will have a favorable impact on the environment.

Planting trees.
Forests are the world's second largest reservoir of excess carbon, second only to oceans. One acre of forestland can absorb an estimated 150 to 200 tons of carbon dioxide in its first 40 years.

Smart growth. Most of us spend entirely too much time in our vehicles every day driving to and from work. New communities are sprouting up close to the downtowns. By moving back into the cities people are saving precious time and money and enhancing their overall quality of life. If there are other options for commuting in your town, take advantage of them. Using subways, trains, and light-rail will help in our quest to reduce greenhouse gases.

Europeans are amazed by how dependent Americans are on their vehicles. The train system serving Europe is world-class. We need to upgrade our own rail systems to that level of service and quality. Our communities deserve more transportation options, and rail is a great place to start.

A new mind-set. Quality of life goes beyond materialism and consumerism. On some level most of us have been collectively brainwashed to believe that happiness can be achieved only through bigger and better and buying and accumulating our way to prosperity. And it's that consumerism that is putting strains on our environment. At some point the lightbulb goes on over your head and you realize that piling up more . . . stuff . . . is not the most satisfying answer. We can get off the treadmill now and realize the true source of genuine happiness: spirituality, friends, family, community, and making connections. Not to sound like Dr. Phil, but think before you buy that next environment-destroying item. Will it really "complete you," or will it provide only a temporary fix and leave you hungering for the next big acquisition?

CHAPTER SEVEN

High-Tech Weather
The Future of Forecasting

The trouble with weather forecasting is that it's right too often to ignore it and wrong too often for us to rely on it.—Patrick Young

THE PHILOSOPHER Aristotle once mused that the second greatest problem known to man, second only to the study of human nature itself, was the problem of the weather. The ancient Greeks marveled over *hydro meteors,* or clouds, *igneous meteors,* lightning, and even *luminous meteors,* rainbows and halos. *Meteors* were defined as "anything in the air," and so came the study of meteorology.

Some of America's first weather forecasters were farmers trading postcards by mail, sharing stories of what the rain, hail, and wind were doing to their livelihoods. They had the right idea. The first order of business: describe what is happening right now. To be able to predict the weather one has to know what's happening now, not just over America, but worldwide.

That brings up a problem: No matter how many supercomputers we employ, there are gaps in the data. We don't have good information from third-world countries and over the oceans, for example. We rely on weather satellites to fill in the missing information, but that's a little like trying to do a jigsaw puzzle with half the pieces missing. One quickly appreciates the sheer complexity, and at times the futility, of trying to anticipate Mother Nature's next move.

Recently, the National Weather Service went through a 10-year, $4.5 billion modernization program that produced a mind-numbing blur of acronyms. But as you'll see, it's also bringing state-of-the-art advances to the American public, saving lives today. The service's stated goal: no unpleasant or potentially deadly weather surprises.

They are turning that vision into reality. Since 1993 the agency has increased the lead time for severe storm warnings from 15 to 18 minutes and improved the accuracy of those forecasts from 65 to over 80 percent. In spite of a marked uptick in severe weather, far fewer Americans are dying from storm-related events every year.

That's a testament to the streamlined National Weather Service. It's also the result of local and national media spending hundreds of millions of dollars on state-of-the-art radar and graphics systems that bring the weather story home to millions of Americans. The American public has become better informed and more weather-savvy, and we need to be. Our weather is among the most severe on the planet. For us it's a simple matter of survival. Technology won't necessarily save us, but new meteorological hardware, software, and services are revolutionizing the weather business. Today, on your own home computer, you can call up a wealth of real-time information that was unimaginable just 15 years ago. The seven-day forecast is still shaky, more a horoscope than a prediction sometimes, but Americans do benefit from some of the most accurate forecasts in the world. As you're about to see, the science of meteorology has come a long way.

Predicting the Weather: An Ancient Science

For as long as people have been outside, at the mercy of the elements, they've tried to anticipate changes in the weather drifting over their heads. From ancient hunters and gatherers to modern commuters, our very survival has depended on the rhythmic arrival of sun, warmth, and rain. The Chinese tried to predict weather nearly 3,000 years ago, with limited success. Ancient Babylonians tried to unravel the mysteries of the skies around 650 B.C. using clouds and the appearance of unusual phenomena like rainbows and halos.

Thomas Jefferson bought his first thermometer while writing the Declaration of Independence and his first barometer a few days after it was signed. Jefferson made daily weather observations until six days before his death, in 1826. He was one of the first to envision a nationwide network of weather observations.

That weather network became a reality in 1847, and by 1860 there were an estimated 600 daily weather observers working with the Smithsonian Institution in Washington, D.C. The launch of the telegraph in the mid-1800s revolutionized the reporting of weather information. On February 9, 1870, the U.S. National Weather Service was instituted as a part of the Department of the Army. Weather

In A.D. 61, the philosopher Seneca complained about the pall of air pollution hanging over Rome.

observations were made at 24 locations by the Army Signal Corps, and the term "forecast" was first used.

The weather service began largely as a reaction to costly storms and to ships' sinking into the Great Lakes in the late 1860s. The resulting public outcry was the nudge that Congress needed to appropriate the money for a weather bureau in the United States, and within a few years timely warnings resulted in cost savings that more than paid for the new forecasting service.

Weather Forecasts and Wartime

Dependable weather forecasts proved to be invaluable during wartime, and one critical forecast may have helped to turn the tide of history. In May 1944 the Allied invasion of France was delayed by wet, windy weather stalled over the English Channel. General Dwight D. Eisenhower consulted with his best meteorologist, who assured him that there would be a narrow break in the weather, with just enough clearing to launch the assault on Normandy. Meanwhile, Hitler's team of meteorologists was convinced that the stormy weather would continue uninterrupted, so they allowed the German army to let its guard down. The forecast Eisenhower received was right on the money, and on the morning of June 6, 1944, under a partly sunny sky, the D-day drama unfolded along the coast of France.

That wasn't the only bad forecast Hitler received. His meteorologists had assured him that weather would not be an issue as German troops pushed toward Moscow. As it turned out, the winter of 1941–42 was one of the coldest and snowiest of the twentieth century. The German invaders were caught off guard by subzero temperatures and two-story snow drifts. Temperatures sank to minus 45 degrees, taking a heavy toll on German troops and morale, leading to their ultimate defeat.

An American soldier with the First Army Division sleeps atop a pillbox bunker during a monsoon downpour following heavy Viet Cong sniper and mortar fire.

During the Vietnam War even the United States military proved to be no match for monsoon rains that boiled up over mountainous terrain, lasting months, turning bombing campaigns into exercises in futility. In his book *To Hanoi and Back: The U.S. Air Force and North Vietnam, 1966–1973,* Wayne Thompson states that "the most effective North Vietnamese air defense has always been the weather." To control that unruly weather, the military instituted Project Popeye, an attempt to increase rainfall and trigger downpours capable of washing out parts

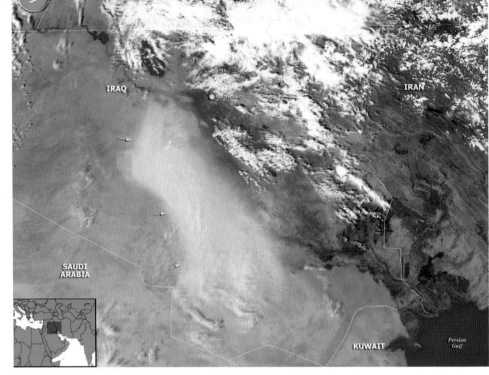

Tracking sand. NOAA weather satellites can track not only clouds and fog capable of impacting military missions, but also 100-mile-long wisps of blowing sand that can damage jet engines and jam high-tech weapon components. On April 15, 2003, a dust storm extended almost all the way from the Saudi Arabian border to the western suburbs of Baghdad.

of the Ho Chi Minh Trail. For the better part of five years, airplanes seeded monsoon clouds with chemicals. Military intelligence claimed that in some parts of Vietnam rainfall may have been increased by a third. Today, weather manipulation is no longer a military option, since the United Nations General Assembly banned environmental warfare in 1971.

THE NATIONAL WEATHER SERVICE

The National Weather Service (NWS), an arm of the National Oceanic and Atmospheric Administration (NOAA), is based in Silver Spring, Maryland. Consisting of more than 120 weather forecast offices scattered across the country, the NWS is in business 24/7 because, when it comes to the atmosphere, there are no weekends or holidays. Each office is staffed by an average of two dozen meteorologists, hydrologists, and technicians, but as many as 11,000 additional weather observers volunteer daily weather data from their backyard weather stations.

NEXRAD

One of the most powerful tools at the fingertips of National Weather Service meteorologists is NEXRAD, which stands for Next Generation of Radar. Today's NEXRAD radars are extremely powerful, with 750,000 watts of radiating power and a range of 450 kilometers, close to 300 miles. Working with the Department of Defense and the Federal Aviation Administration, the National Weather Service now operates a network of 160 Doppler radars, covering most of the United States. This state-of-the-art radar system generates dozens of different products, giving meteorologists new tools to pinpoint and diagnose severe weather.

Much like a physician examines a patient looking for specific symptoms, NEXRAD permits the meteorologist to conduct multiple tests on a potentially severe thunderstorm "cell," determining not only the intensity of rain or hail, but what the wind fields inside the thunderstorm may be like and how the storm varies with altitude. NEXRAD can scan the anatomy of a severe thunderstorm, highlighting twisting and turning circulations that may be precursors to hail, straight-line winds, and tornadoes. That's critical, because on a busy summer day there may be 30 to 50 thunderstorms on radar, only 1 or 2 of which may be severe. Highlighting those storms is a priority for meteorologists from coast to coast. Coupled with reports from storm spotters on the ground, NEXRAD provides a severe weather safety net across most of America, providing citizens with a weather detection and warning system that is second to none in the world.

But the NEXRAD national network, while impressive in scope and power, is still not perfect. There are some gaps in coverage, especially in the Western states, where mountains block the lower scans of the radars and weather in the valleys is unseen. As a result, the lower portions of some storms, under 2 or 3 kilometers, may not be visible at all. NEXRAD also misses some of the shallow storms moving in from the Pacific Ocean. Because of the earth's curvature, by the time the NEXRAD radar beam, or any radar, reaches 125 miles from the radar site, it's scanning clouds 15,000 feet above ground level.

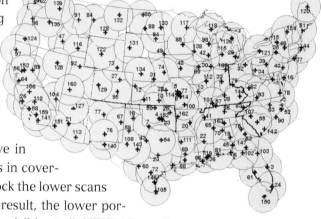

Coast-to-coast coverage. NEXRAD coverage can be spotty in the mountainous Western states, but the radar safety net extends to more than 95 percent of Americans.

Predicting Severe Storms

The National Severe Storms Laboratory (NSSL) in Norman, Oklahoma, is on the cutting edge of severe-storm and tornado research.

The scientists at NSSL have refined the theory of how severe thunderstorms, hailstorms, straight-line winds, and tornadoes form, thus improving forecasting and lead time, and lowering death and injury tolls. NSSL researchers have launched airborne Doppler radars and refined our ability to launch weather balloons in a high-wind environment, obtaining critical weather data in the vicinity of severe thunderstorms.

A tornado intercept program in the 1980s and early 90s (made famous by the

The National Severe Storms Laboratory made the first observations of a tornadic storm ever charted on April 20, 1974, mapping a radar "thumbprint" of the storm at several altitudes.

Turtles. Meteorologist Tim Samaras has remarkable skill and some luck in placing weather instruments called turtles into the path of oncoming tornadoes. An electrical engineer, Samaras built these 45-pound devices crammed full of sensors, the design insuring that the turtle remains stationary as the tornado passes overhead. On June 24, 2003, near Manchester, South Dakota, one of his turtles measured the biggest atmospheric pressure drop ever recorded—100-millibars—as a monstrous F-4 tornado passed directly overhead.

Mobile Mesonet. Led by Erik Rasmussen at NSSL and Jerry Straka at the University of Oklahoma, the mission is to completely surround a tornadic thunderstorm with vehicles that measure temperature, pressure, and winds with onboard weather sensors.

movie *Twister*) evolved into the VORTEX, or Verification of the Origin of Tornadoes Experiment. The goal of the program was to bring tornado researchers and forecasters together to improve warnings and save lives. The VORTEX team has had considerable success in intercepting several weak tornadoes and at least four violent tornadoes, developing a rich data set that is still being analyzed. This information will help scientists determine how tornadoes form, what causes them to strengthen, and why twisters ultimately dissipate. In recent years the VORTEX team has operated a Doppler on wheels, which measured the strongest winds ever recorded on the planet, 318 mph, during the Oklahoma City tornado of May 3, 1999.

Satellites: Weather Eyes in the Sky

Modern meteorologists rely heavily on satellite data to track and predict the weather. The Geostationary Operational Environmental Satellite, or GOES, is a necklace of minivan-size satellites providing continuous coverage for North America and the Atlantic and East Pacific oceans. The satellites, a joint development effort of NOAA and NASA, are parked in orbit 22,240 miles above the equator. At that altitude they rotate at precisely the same speed as the earth below, so they appear to hover over the same location. This allows forecasters to "loop" multiple cloud photographs together without any shift. These spacecraft can provide both day and night imagery of the earth's surface and cloud cover. The onboard imager is amazingly fast and sensitive, scanning an area 1,864 by 1,864 miles in just three minutes, then transmitting this data to the ground in real time. As many as eight images can be generated every hour. During a hurricane approach or major tornado outbreak, the "rapid scan mode" can transmit new pictures every 7 1/2 minutes.

Twelve weather satellites have been launched since 1974 and three are in use now. GOES-8 provides coverage over the Eastern U.S. and the Atlantic, GOES-10 scans the Western U.S., and a back-up satellite, GOES-11, is in standby mode, a spare just in case a new satellite is needed.

Weather satellites provide invaluable information, helping meteorologists observe and predict thunderstorms, tornadoes, fog, flash floods, and even lake-effect snow squalls. An estimated 97 percent of the global data that is entered into computer models comes from GOES satellites. In addition, Polar-orbiting Operational Environmental Satellites, or POES, circle the Earth in low orbit, supporting global weather and marine forecasts, insuring that no observation for any corner of the planet is more than six hours old.

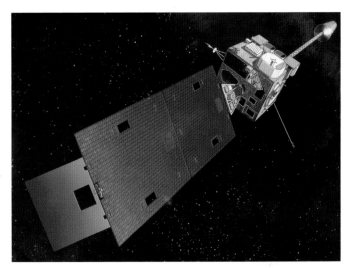

The GOES satellites provide continuous coverage over the Americas, the Atlantic, and much of the Pacific.

X-Ray for Storms

A new generation of weather satellites is helping meteorologists peer into storms with the rough equivalent of X-Ray vision. The Tropical Rainfall Measuring Mission, or TRMM, is operated jointly by America and Japan. Positioned 218 miles high in the sky, it is the only satellite that has a radar system capable of scanning rainfall rates far below. This next-generation satellite helped to confirm the existence of "hot towers" in hurricanes, unusually powerful updrafts within the raging eyewall. Research suggests that a hurricane with one of these hot towers is twice as likely to intensify quickly as a storm that lacks a tower—critical information for meteorologists.

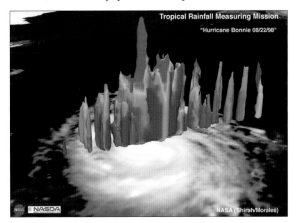

Hot tower. The new Tropical Rainfall Measuring Mission Satellite can scan storms below with radar, identifying hurricanes that have "hot towers" near the eye, statistically more likely to intensify and possibly threaten coastal populations.

The integration of all this raw data can be a monumental challenge for a meteorologist trying to keep up with a rapidly changing weather situation, especially when the difference between an accurate forecast and a "bust" may come down to one precious nugget of information. The National Weather Service has streamlined the flow and display of data with the Advanced Weather Information Processing System, known as AWIPS. The advanced system, deployed to local weather service offices nationwide, allows the meteorologist on duty to look at multiple windows of information and quickly drill down to the one critical, forecast-altering fact that he or she needs to make a successful forecast.

187

The system integrates weather, hydrological, radar, satellite, and rawinsonde (weather balloon) data simultaneously and combines them to get a better handle on what is unfolding in the skies overhead, and why.

In a September 1999 report to Congress, then commerce secretary William Daley cited "substantial improvements in warnings and forecasts as a direct result of modernization." Among the improvements:

- Increased warning times for tornadoes, from 6 to 11 minutes since 1993.
- Increased warning times for flash floods, from 21 to more than 50 minutes since 1993.
- More accurate hurricane landfall predictions, from within 100 to 88 miles since 1993.

Flood risk. The normally gentle Virgin River flowing through the Narrows at Zion National Park can become a deadly torrent when thunderstorms stall nearby.

Will That Raging River Flood?

River forecasters, called hydrologists, analyze soil moisture, current and future rainfall rates, snowmelt, and other factors when determining whether river water levels will rise or fall, and how fast. They assess predicted rainfall amounts for their local area and then issue forecasts for specific locations on major streams and rivers as far as five days into the future.

The technology has paid off on numerous occasions. Scores of people may owe their lives to new tools that allow meteorologists to zero in on areas most prone to flash flooding. One recent example: On the morning of July 27, 1998, National Weather Service forecasters in Salt Lake City studied the latest NEXRAD data and computer models, found the right ingredients for thunderstorms near Utah's Zion National Park, and issued a flash-flood watch.

By 2:00 p.m. three inches of rain had fallen about 20 miles north of the park, and forecasters changed the flood watch to a warning, even though there wasn't a drop of rain over the park. The forecasters urged park rangers to keep hikers out of Zion's most popular slot canyon, the Narrows, a rough slash into the ground with virtually no outlet once into the canyon.

Some of the tourists and hikers probably thought that the forecast had been inaccurate, since skies directly overhead were dry. But that evening, the forecast proved dead right. The North Fork of the Virgin River crested and pushed a three-foot wall of water through the Narrows, killing two hikers and forcing seven others to spend the night stranded on high ground. But dozens of visitors had avoided the spot—and the dangerous flooding—because of the warning. The skill of these forecasters, and technology, saved an unknown number of lives.

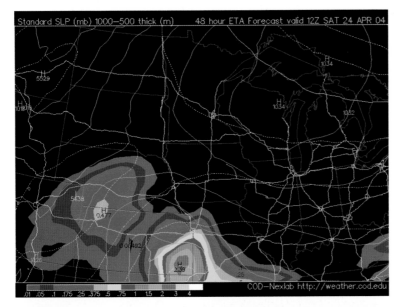

Weather models. Computer accuracy drops off with time, and forecasting 8 days requires skill and experience. The 48-hour ETA forecast map, left, shows a two-inch bull's-eye of heavy rain near Kansas City. The 10-day MRF/GFS model, below, shows a vigorous cold front pushing into the Eastern Seaboard, with the heaviest rains predicted over the Deep South. The question for meteorologists: Based on the current scenario and past history, which model do you believe will be closer to the truth?

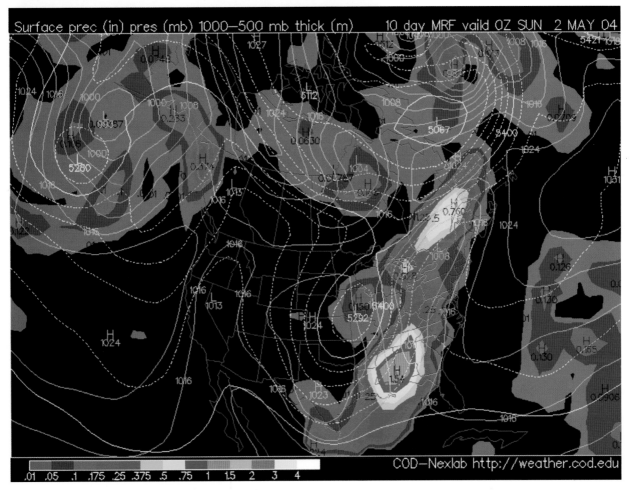

Temperature (K)

282 285 287 290 292 295 297

Sea-surface temperatures.
GOES satellite sensors can
estimate ocean water
temperatures, critical
information for hurricane
forecasters trying to predict
if a storm will weaken or
strengthen.

20dBZ

40 dBZ

0   10   20   30   40   50 dBZ

Space radar. Tropical Rainfall Measuring Mission
is the only weather satellite with onboard radar.
This image from May 6, 2003, shows a squall line
of severe thunderstorms over the Southeast; a
vertical slice or cross section reveals the storms
most likely to produce large hail.

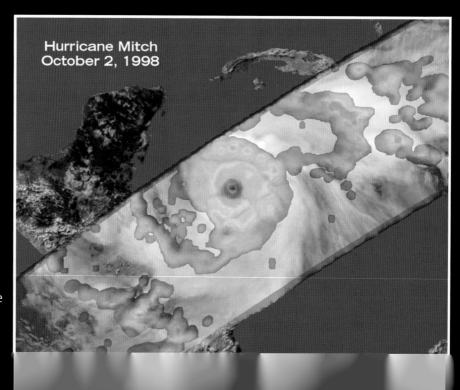

Hurricane Mitch
October 2, 1998

Hurricane Mitch.
The new low-orbit
Tropical Rainfall
Measuring Mission
satellites can measure
rainfall rates and
data from lightning
passing overhead.

Modeling the Weather

Computer weather models, which generate forecasts for up to 16 days into the future, start by using atmospheric observations, including temperature, wind speed, precipitation, and other oceanographic and satellite information. The observations result in the collection of billions of bytes of data. The faster the flow of data, the higher the resolution of the forecasts and the farther into the future forecasters can predict with some degree of accuracy. The models provide vital guidance to meteorologists, allowing them to predict weather events such as hurricanes, floods, and winter storms days in advance.

In the mid-1970s, when I first began to predict the weather, there was only one computer model, the Limited Fine Mesh, or LFM. Today meteorologists are faced with nearly a dozen weather simulations, each one using slightly different physics and mathematical equations to predict how the atmosphere will behave in the days to come. Each computer model has its own unique strengths and weaknesses. Some work better than others under certain circumstances, and this is where the "art of meteorology"—past experience and gut feel—comes in. Faced with a bewildering choice of solutions, which computer do you believe, and why? Sometimes weather forecasters "blend" or average computer predictions to come up with a forecast, but rarely is the outlook black or white. It's almost always some nebulous shade of gray, especially beyond 48 hours, when computer solutions can differ wildly.

Most computer models are run operationally at the National Centers for Environmental Prediction, located at Camp Springs, Maryland. The quality of the forecast is only as good as the data initially flowing into the models. Bad data from weather balloons or incomplete information from airports can blossom into big errors over time. Boundary conditions, the initial data fed into the outer fringes or borders of a weather model, are critical. The quality of that data ultimately determines if the computer simulation handles the track and intensity of a storm well or if the forecast is wrong.

With the ETA model meteorologists can track precipitation, cloud cover, and temperature 60 hours into the future, with 29-kilometer resolution. That means that calculations on multiple levels of the atmosphere are performed every 29 kilometers, across all of North America. This tighter grid permits a more detailed forecast.

The GFS model can crunch atmospheric conditions up to 240 hours into the future, with a steady drop in accuracy over time. Recent studies suggest that there is some reliability to computerized weather prediction (better than a 50-50 flip of a coin) for a specific location as much as 14 days into the future. But don't bet the farm based on the two-week forecast. Today's five-day outlook is as accurate as the three-day forecast was a generation ago, but there are limits to how far into the future we'll ever be able to peer.

191

Fine-Tuning the Short-Range Forecast

Long-range outlooks are still very much up in the air, but meteorologists are increasingly excited about the ability to fine-tune the short-range outlook, or "nowcast." Will it rain over the northern suburbs or the southern suburbs this evening? Will the rain turn to ice in time for the commute home? Will you wake up to 2 or 5 inches of snow tomorrow morning? The RUC model, short for Rapid Update Cycle, integrates current data from monitoring stations around the country, rawinsondes from weather balloons, wind profilers, ocean buoys, satellites, and even commercial aircraft sending back real-time weather observations of wind and temperature, in an attempt to fine-tune and improve the short-range, or 12-hour, forecast.

Hurricane forecasters in Miami take advantage of the GFDL model, from the Geophysical and Fluid Dynamics Laboratory, to fine-tune a prediction of where a hurricane will land. The grid is moveable, meaning that meteorologists can place this 10-kilometer grid directly over the hurricane in the model, increasing the odds of detecting subtle changes in movement and intensity. In 1995, during its first year of operation, the GFDL model showed a 20 percent increase in landfall accuracy 48 to 72 hours in advance, a significant improvement in hurricane forecasting.

On June 6, 2003, the National Weather Service activated a new supercomputer for daily weather simulations, a massive IBM server and storage system. The goal: to increase the lead time for hurricane watches and warnings and improve the tracking and prediction of severe storms over the United States. Researchers estimate it would take one person with a calculator more than 80 million years to perform the number of calculations the supercomputer will eventually be able to crunch in just one second! The new computer processes weather data at speeds of over 3 trillion calculations per second.

Spaghetti Plot Forecasts

Even with all the improvements, perfect predictions of weather remain elusive, and in all probability mathematically impossible. Since 1992 National Weather Service meteorologists have generated ensemble forecasts, slightly changing the starting conditions of various models and running them out over time to get slightly different predictions of storm tracks, precipitation amounts, and future temperatures. By analyzing the ensemble forecast and subsequent data, a "spaghetti plot" of many strands, meteorologists can see how the computer models are trending and come up with a consensus, a rough average of what will probably come to pass.

Physicists often discuss the fundamental challenge of chaos theory for both weather and economics, how very small, seemingly insignificant changes can

00Z 09/20/1999

Wind Speed (m/s)

0 1 2 3 4 5 6 7 8 9 10 11 12 13 14 15 16 17

NASA's QuikSCAT satellite is providing meteorologists with accurate data on surface winds over the global oceans, leading to improved 2- to 5-day forecasts. Data from QuikSCAT can be used to identify potential hurricanes as long as 1 to 3 days before traditional methods, giving forecasters a jump on potential trouble.

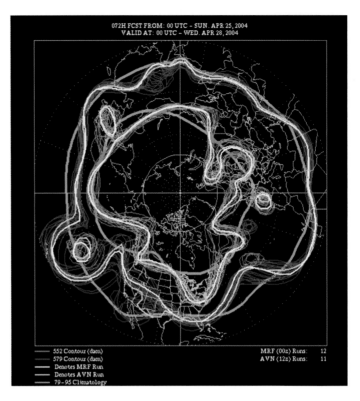

072H FCST FROM: 00 UTC - SUN. APR 25, 2004
VALID AT: 00 UTC - WED. APR 28, 2004

Spaghetti plot. This ensemble plot, from the National Centers for Environmental Prediction, shows a comparison among a dozen computer runs of two weather models, the MRF and the AVN. After only three days, the two models were predicting different jet-stream patterns and subsequent weather for the United States. Many meteorologists would look at this difference and average the two forecasts to lower the risk of a "busted" forecast.

552 Contour (dam)
579 Contour (dam)
Denotes MRF Run
Denotes AVN Run
79–95 Climatology

MRF (00z) Runs: 12
AVN (12z) Runs: 11

have a profound impact on the ultimate outcome. A convergence of otherwise minute factors may lead to a stock market rally, or converge to generate a devastating F-4 tornado.

Faced with the specter of the truly unknowable, scientists have focused on improving the starting point, trying to make the data going into the supercomputers as accurate as possible. But believing we can get a perfect, real-time snapshot of wind, temperature, and moisture at every possible level of the atmosphere, all over the world, is wishful thinking.

Forecast for the Forecasts: Improving Conditions

So how accurate are weather forecasts? People tend to remember the mistakes, rather than the many times that meteorologists come close to the mark. Accuracy depends on a number of factors, such as where you live and how far into the future you're looking.

Short-range forecasts, that is, for the next few hours, are the most accurate. Surprisingly, the accuracy of the 24-hour forecast, the "tomorrow forecast," has not changed substantially in the last 20 years, holding at close to 87 percent.

Accuracy drops off steadily with time, for several reasons. First: As good as the mathematical equations are, they aren't perfect descriptions of how air parcels really behave. Modeling the effect of air passing over mountains, or the exchange of warmth and moisture with ocean water below, is incredibly complex. There are limitations to the physics and calculus that ultimately drive the computer simulations. And gaps in the data, where all we have is scattered satellite input and an occasional ship or floating weather-buoy report, introduce potential errors into the models. The old saying "garbage in, garbage out" holds true. If we begin the models with incomplete or inaccurate data, small errors blow up into "bombs" after 36 to 48 hours, making the computer forecasts unreliable.

Even so, additional sources, especially a steady torrent of satellite information, are improving weather forecasting. For example, the National Weather Service's three-day heavy-rain outlook is now as accurate as the two-day forecast was in 1990. Satellites have given human forecasters a bird's-eye view of weather features for over 40 years, but only in the last decade have atmospheric, mathematical, and computer scientists figured out reliable ways to convert the vast amount of information, several billion bytes a day, into forms that weather models can use.

What Is Happening Now?

Meteorologists rely on what they learned from previous storms when determining what will happen next. But every weather map is different; every weather scenario is unique. Today's pattern may be similar to one four years ago, but it is never identical. Forecasters rely on airport observations, called METARS, to discover what is happening now across the state, the region, and the nation. These reports come in at the beginning of every hour, giving us critical and precise information about temperature, dew point, wind direction and speed, as well as any precipitation falling at the time. Doppler radar can tell us if precipitation is falling, but only METARS can confirm that it's raining and not snowing, or that fog has dropped visibilities to under a quarter mile.

Until recently, most weather observations on or near the ground were made by humans, either NWS personnel or volunteers. Now automation has come to the weather service in the form of ASOS, the Automated Surface Observing System, America's primary surface-weather-observing network. ASOS has doubled the number of full-time observing sites from coast to coast, with reports transmitted every minute of every day from 882 sites, most of them located at America's airports. That number will be increased to nearly 1,500 sites within a few years, providing valuable information about what is happening at ground level. Each reporting station is extremely sophisticated, able to detect everything from lightning nearby to freezing rain, the height of the clouds, visibility, and how much rain has fallen. Although initially greeted with some level of skepticism (how could a machine observe weather better than a human being?), ASOS has proven to be a reliable data source for pilots, meteorologists, and the general public.

An ASOS site located at Walker Field, Colorado, collects temperature, humidity, winds, sunlight, barometric pressure, and precipitation data, but can't accurately measure snowfall.

195

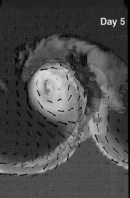

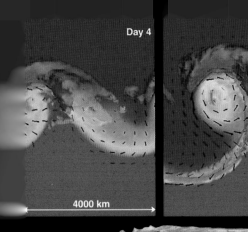

Day 4   Day 5

4000 km

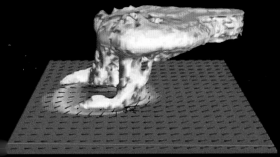

WRF model. The fine-scale detail made possible by the Weather Research and Forecasting (WRF) model will depict small-scale weather features such as showers and thunderstorms with far greater resolution. WRF is being created through cooperation among six government agencies. This simulation shows (top) a developing low-pressure wave and (bottom) a supercell thunderstorm.

Bow echo. NEXRAD shows a bow echo, which resembles a colorful horseshoe, on Doppler radar, a tip-off that the storm contains violent straight-line winds. This storm hit Kentucky on May 5, 1996, triggering straight-line winds up to 70 mph and claiming the life of one boy, who was swept away by raging flood waters. A new generation of satellites, radar, and higher resolution computer models will help meteorologists pinpoint exactly which storms are severe and potentially life-threatening.

Flood potential. The NEXRAD Doppler-radar network deployed across the United States can not only track where rain, hail, and snow is falling, and how the winds are circulating within storms, but also how much precipitation has fallen over time, allowing forecasters to zero in on counties that are most susceptible to flash flooding. From September 14 to September 18, 1999, Hurricane Floyd dumped over 16 inches of rain on central North Carolina.

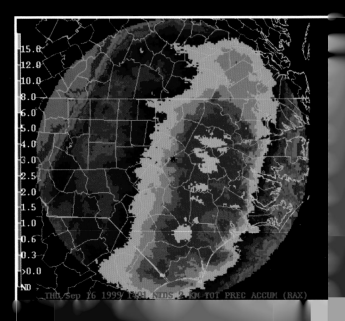

15.0
12.0
10.0
8.0
6.0
5.0
4.0
3.0
2.5
2.0
1.5
1.0
0.6
0.3
>0.0
ND

THU Sep 16 1999 1201 NIDS 2 KM TOT PREC ACCUM (RAX)

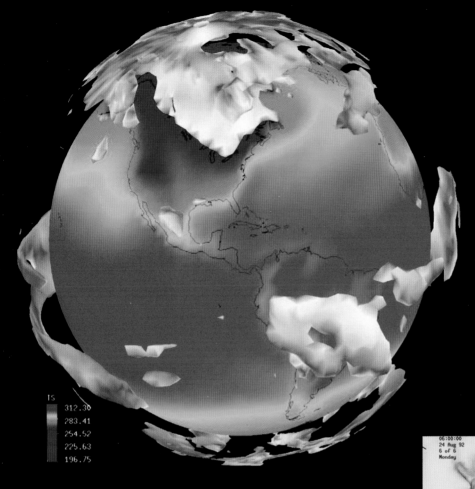

IS
312.30
283.41
254.52
225.63
196.75

Climate modeling.

Faster, more sophisticated weather models will enable climatologists to better track increases in carbon dioxide and effects on global temperature and cloud cover. The Climate System Model project formally began in January 1994 with the long-term goal of building, maintaining, and continually improving a comprehensive model of the climate system. The system is composed of four independent models (ocean, atmosphere, sea ice, and land surface) that communicate with each other for optimum results.

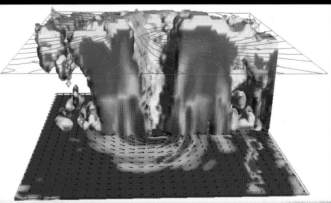

06:00:00
24 Aug 92
6 of 6
Monday

3-D visualization. Researchers are studying storms in all three dimensions in an attempt to improve analysis and forecasting of tornadoes, hailstorms, and hurricanes. This series of images shows Hurricane Andrew, which hit South Florida in late August 1992. The 3-D simulation at right shows the eyewall of Hurricane Andrew, where sustained winds of 150 to 200 mph were recorded shortly before landfall.

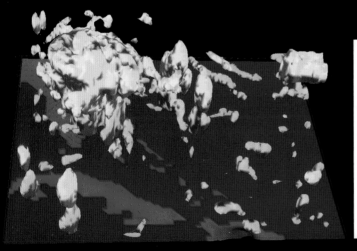

Looking Ahead

As research meteorologists continue to improve the physics in their programs, their models more closely approximate reality, how the atmosphere really works. The launch of new sensing systems will also have an impact on how well the nightly weather predictions play out the next morning. New, state-of-the-art weather instrumentation will put more reliable "current" information into these computer models, increasing the odds of a better forecast hours, days. and even weeks into the future.

The phased array radar system, a possible successor to the NEXRAD Doppler-radar network, is already being tested in Oklahoma. Meteorologists at the National Severe Storms Laboratory are taking advantage of sophisticated Navy radar technology to speed up the transmission of critical data. Today, a normal "volume scan" from NEXRAD, sampling data from multiple levels of the atmosphere, can take up to six minutes. But using SPY-1 radar technology currently deployed on Navy ships for spotting severe weather at sea, phased array radars can cut these volume scans down to only one minute. Phased array radar will allow forecasters to scan the lowest few thousand feet of a thunderstorm with greater precision and detail than ever before, detecting rapid changes in wind fields that often are a precursor to tornado genesis, or tornado formation. The radar is just one more example of technologies created for military applications, for fighting battles and winning wars, trickling down into the public service.

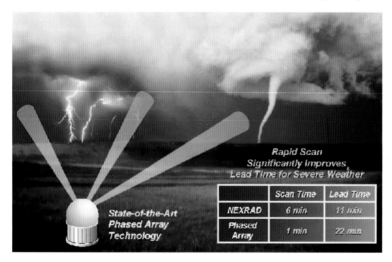

Rapid Scan
Significantly Improves
Lead Time for Severe Weather

	Scan Time	Lead Time
NEXRAD	6 min	11 min
Phased Array	1 min	22 min

State-of-the-Art Phased Array Technology

Fast scan. A phased array radar can take a 3-D snapshot of surrounding precipitation and wind fields in less than one minute, compared to the six minutes now required by NEXRAD.

New and revolutionary methods of remote sensing and high-resolution data gathering are based on the Global Positioning System (GPS), the military's high-altitude satellite network. More than 200 ground-based GPS moisture sensors have blossomed across the United States in the last few years. The system uses a Department of Defense navigation tool, the same technology placed in some cars, which is a free source of coherent radio waves illuminating the earth 24 hours a day. GPS is comprised of a network of 28 satellites orbiting 20,000 kilometers above the earth along with a network of ground tracking stations. By measuring the time required for signals to travel from the satellites to the receivers, the positions of the receivers can be precisely determined.

GPS signals map ocean waves and surface winds, soil moisture, and sea ice below. Soil moisture as well as ice age and thickness are related to the strength of reflected GPS signals and can be retrieved from them, unleashing a torrent of useful information for meteorology, oceanography, and geology.

Future computer models will use these and other ground- and satellite-based data to build increasingly fine-scale depictions, some of them with telescoping grids to zero in on areas as small as a few city blocks! These models will track everything from wildfires, airborne chemicals, and disease vectors to severe thunderstorms, hurricanes, and heavy rains capable of flash flooding.

The challenge is to provide the computational horsepower, the raw computer power and human intelligence, to interpret the flood of data. Turning that torrent into intelligence that can pinpoint a tornadic thunderstorm down to a city block or accurately predict that a massive blizzard moving up the East Coast will hit four days from now, is what drives research meteorology today.

Lightning Forecasts

Lightning, as I said earlier, claims more lives in the United States than hurricanes and tornadoes combined, second only to flash flooding in an average year. Most of these fatalities are preventable, but getting real-time lightning data to people in the path of dangerous electrical storms is a challenge. The National Lightning Detection Network, or NLDN, a private company based in Tucson, Arizona, gathers lightning data for the nation and makes it available to businesses and consumers in a variety of formats.

The NLDN is made up of over 100 ground-based lightning sensors, which can instantly detect the electromagnetic pulse given off by a cloud-to-ground lightning strike, scattered around the country. Using triangulation, gathering data from at least three sensors simultaneously, the network can pinpoint a lightning strike to within 500 yards. Within seconds the location, intensity, and time of the strike is received at the Network Control Center, in Tucson, Arizona, where it is disseminated to customers nationwide. America's only lightning detection network, the NLDN monitors the estimated 20 million to 25 million strikes across the lower 48 states every year, providing essential, mission-critical information to thousands of organizations and businesses, ranging from power utilities to forestry offices, airports, and countless golf courses and the PGA tour.

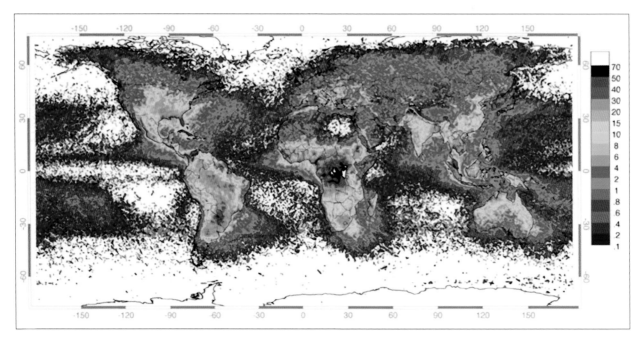

Lightning capital.
Lightning data from 1995 to 2003 recorded by two satellites, NASA's Optical Transient Detector and the Lightning Imaging Sensor. The bright red colors show the areas that receive the most strikes, over central Africa.

Today there are new options for detecting lightning strikes, all of them satellite based. According to NASA, the Lightning Imaging Sensor (LIS) is a space-based instrument used to detect the distribution and variability of the total lightning (cloud-to-cloud, intracloud, and cloud-to-ground lightning) that occurs in the tropical regions of the globe. There is an LIS aboard the TRMM Observatory, which was launched from the Tanegashima Space Center in Japan on November 28, 1997. The TRMM satellite moves in low orbit at roughly 16,000 mph, allowing it to observe one location on the ground for about 90 seconds, enough time to scan for lightning strikes within the clouds.

Severe lightning may tip off the imminent formation of tornadoes. On April 17, 1995, satellite-based lightning observations over southern Oklahoma showed a supercell thunderstorm creating more than one strike per second, with a high percentage of these strikes within the thunderhead itself. Lightning strokes within the storm decreased just prior to tornado formation. Lightning within a storm

LIGHTNING FAST

Within 30 seconds of a lightning strike anywhere in the lower 48 states, the National Lightning Detection Network communicates specific information about the strike to its customers around the nation.

1. Lightning sensors transmit strike information to the satellite.
2. Satellite relays information to the earth station.
3. Data is transmitted to mission control in Tucson, Arizona, via landline.
4. Network Control Center processes data.
5. Processed data is relayed back to satellite.
6. Precise location of lightning is displayed to customers.

may warn meteorologists that a severe thunderstorm is in the "collapse phase," when tornadoes are most likely to develop. In addition, there is significant research suggesting that the most frequent lightning strikes occur in regions where the heaviest rains are falling and the threat of flooding is greatest.

Managing Weather Risk: A New Frontier

Managing weather risk is a new, emerging discipline within the meteorological community, helping businesses to reduce their financial exposure to severe weather and seasonal climate anomalies. The American economy is highly sensitive to changes in the weather, especially those affecting transportation, the production of food, and the distribution of energy. In fact, one-third of the economy is sensitive to weather and the fluctuations around climate normals. Subtle shifts in storms can have a profound impact on commercial aviation, trucking, and "just-in-time" shipping. Utilities, for example, are very interested in more accurate tem-

perature forecasts. If the forecast high for a city is 88 degrees and the actual high temperature is 94, the resulting strain on resources can be severe, forcing utilities to pay a premium for the additional energy to keep homes and businesses cool. The recently deregulated energy industry is one of dozens of businesses that hire weather consulting companies to create more accurate and personalized forecasts for their specific needs.

Weather-risk companies like Weather Ventures (WxVx) can analyze a company's exposure and risk to weather and create a customized plan that helps them make informed business decisions. By analyzing European ensemble forecasts and trying to detect emerging trends in future weather, WxVx meteorologists can forecast with some

skill as far as six months into the future. When dealing with fluctuating prices of commodities, only a 5 percent improvement in accuracy can translate into many millions of dollars in cost savings for businesses ranging from agriculture to insurance and energy.

We'll never be able to change the weather in any appreciable way. But using sophisticated computer models and human experience to improve long-range forecasts to reduce the risk of catastrophic weather losses, and thus help people make smarter business decisions, is one of meteorology's newest frontiers.

Weather sensitive.
An estimated 2 to 4 trillion dollars of the U.S. economy is impacted by changes in weather and climate.

201

It's an Online Weather Revolution!

There is an almost unimaginable amount of weather data on the World Wide Web, and much of it is the result of your tax dollars at work. NOAA and the National Weather Service have put some of the most useful, visual, and up-to-the-second information at the fingertips of anyone with a computer. After trolling the Internet for many years, I've put together a short list of some of my favorites:

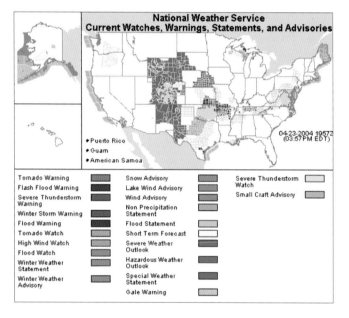

Watches, warnings, and advisories for the U.S. Color-coded watches, warnings, and advisories for the entire nation update continuously and can be looped to see the progression of severe weather across the nation. Click on a specific county to get more information about any severe weather and a detailed seven-day National Weather Service forecast. **www.nws.noaa.gov**

High-resolution radar and satellite maps. The College of Dupage Web site provides full 1-kilometer resolution for visible satellite images and NEXRAD mosaics. Satellite and radar data can be looped over time with amazing clarity. **weather.cod.edu/analysis/analysis.1kmvis.html**

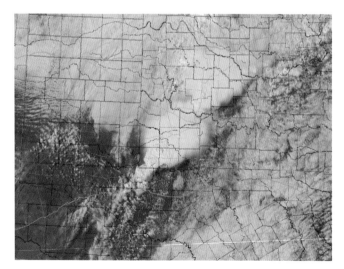

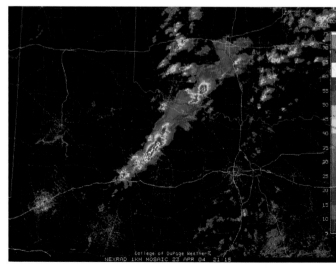

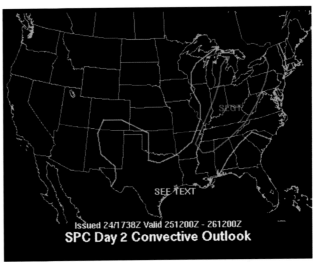

The Weather Channel. The granddaddy of weather sites, weather.com has a wide range of consumer weather information. Allergy and health data, gardening tips, travel maps, event forecasting, airport delays, and global information can be accessed at weather.com. **www.weather.com**

Storm Prediction Center (SPC). Based at ground zero of Tornado Alley in Norman, Oklahoma, the SPC updates severe-weather parameters around the clock. Data includes detailed radar information, severe-weather outlooks with risk levels from slight to moderate to high, and a host of forecasting tools that allow anyone to be an armchair tornado forecaster. **www.spc.noaa.gov**

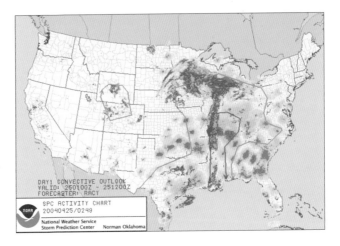

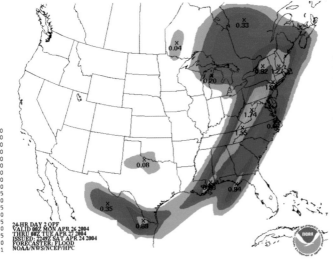

Precipitation outlooks. The images at the Hydrometeorological Prediction Center give detailed rainfall or snowfall predictions three days into the future. **www.hpc.ncep.noaa.gov**

203

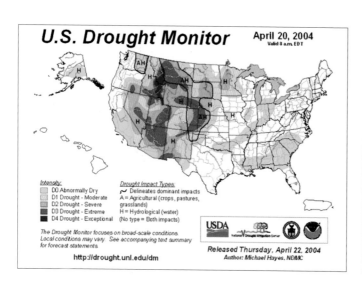

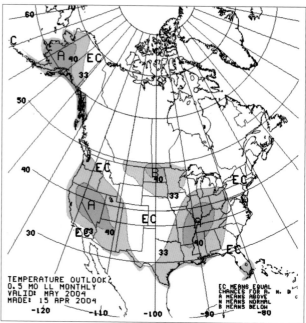

Climate data. The Climate Prediction Center provides drought outlooks along with 30-day, 60-day, 90-day, and even an experimental 12-month outlook!
www.cpc.ncep.noaa.gov

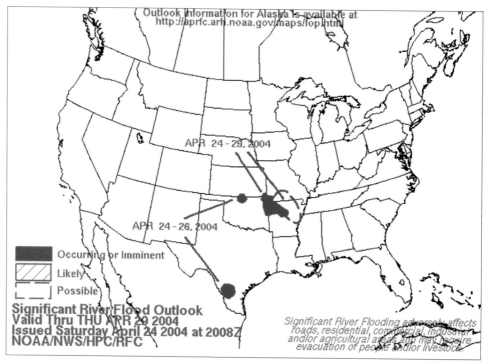

River flooding potential. This five-day outlook issued by the National Weather Service displays the potential for large-scale river flooding (not flash flooding).
www.hpc.ncep.noaa.gov/nationalfloodoutlook

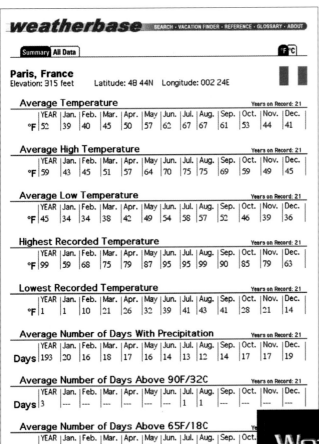

Worldwide weather.
Detailed average weather conditions for more than 16,000 cities around the world are available at no charge. Curious about the average snowfall in October in Vermont? Want to know if you'll have good weather in March in St. Thomas or Rome? Wondering about the average temperature in July in Paris? You'll find it here.
www.weatherbase.com

WeatherMatrix. WeatherMatrix is more than a Web site; it's a community of weather enthusiasts on the Web, a worldwide organization of over 8,000 online amateur and professional weather enthusiasts—meteorologists, storm chasers and spotters, and weather observers. Members trade weather data and help maintain external links on WeatherMatrix.net. The Web site serves as a database of WeatherMatrix members, their interests, and their contact information, which fosters local communication between members. There's nothing like it.
www.weathermatrix.net

Getting Personal With the Weather

We are a mobile nation; everyone seems to be on the move. There are times when many of us are away from our computer or TV and yet still need weather information. New options allow us to see the weather on devices as small and portable as a cell-phone screen or even a watch. No, it's not your grandpa's weather forecast anymore!

Instead of twentieth-century, "one size fits all" forecasting, new technology can pinpoint weather down to a city block, so that everyone is seeing something slightly different, based on his or her current location, day planner, and lifestyle.

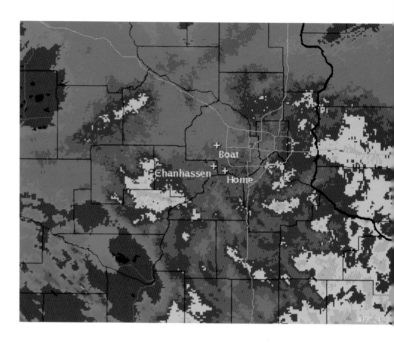

www.my-cast.com/mobile

Doppler radar on your cell phone. My-Cast, personalized weather graphics and e-mail alerts, is a free Web service I launched with a friend, meteorologist Craig Burfeind. In 1997 we set up Mobile My-Cast with the vision of giving people a complete weather report on their cell phones, one tailored for their individual location and lifestyle. The cell service is not free, but for the price of a fancy cup of coffee you can sign up for a monthly subscription on your color cell phone, then zoom into Doppler Radar, a moving weather map, an hour-by-hour forecast for your neighborhood, or a seven-day lookout. You'll need a data contract, but almost every cell phone today has data capabilities.

Now there are new detailed versions of the technology. Pilot My-Cast tracks weather for pilots, everything from satellite data to maps displaying visibility conditions. For sportsmen there is Weather Scout, from Gander Mountain, which factors barometric pressure trends, and sun and moon phases to highlight when fish should be biting!

For Mobile My-cast, go to www.my-cast.com. For Weather Scout, go to www.gandermountain.com.

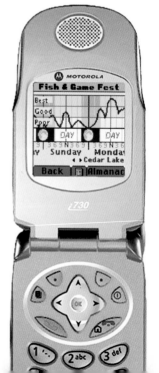

Weather Watch Pro. Weather Watch Pro builds Swiss-made technology into watches to deliver wind speed and direction. In addition, you can call up the temperature and windchill, chart the barometric pressure, and, oh yeah, even tell the current time. This device is guaranteed to bring out your hidden inner weather geek.

Handheld weather. With the Kestrel 4000 you can monitor barometric pressure, altitude, temperature, humidity, wind speed, windchill, dew point, and heat index, charting parameters over time to determine trends.

Smart TV. A television set is married to NOAA Weather Radio to produce RCA Alert Guard Television. Six different-size sets, ranging from 20 to 32 inches, warn viewers of approaching severe weather, even if they're watching a TV show or playing a video game. Equipped with technology that allows the TVs to be tailored for specific countries, the sets detect alerts for 30 kinds of severe weather, including tsunamis, tornadoes, flash floods, hurricanes, and earthquakes. Local and state alerts cover chemical spills, nuclear power plant emergencies, gas line breaks, train derailments, and refinery fires, among other crises. The system also provides for high-level state or federal emergencies such as terrorist alerts, bio-warfare alerts, bombing threats, and immediate life-threatening emergencies.

Wireless weather stations. Several companies offer wireless weather stations that monitor everything from solar radiation to wind speed, humidity, moon phase, and rainfall right down to

the minute. You can have a professional weather station in your yard without tripping over cables. The wireless Vantage Pro tracks the weather floating over your house every 2 1/2 seconds, and can set off an alarm if weather conditions reach a certain level (for example, if the mercury drops close to freezing or winds exceed a certain speed).

Lightning data on your PC. The Boltek LD-250 direction-finding antenna, below, can track lightning up to 300 miles away, setting off an audible alarm when a strike hits too close to home.

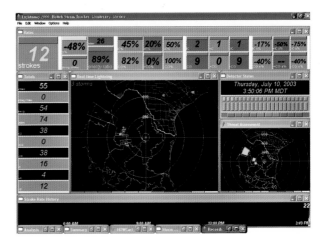

CHAPTER EIGHT

Your Local Weather
Bringing the Forecast Home

Forecast for tonight: dark.—George Carlin

L OCAL WEATHER is the number-one reason most people turn on their televisions to watch news shows, the late news in particular. In fact, there's a truism in television news: If you can "win weather" you stand a good chance of walking away with the viewing audience in your area.

The reason? The weather affects everybody. No other story has as much widespread local impact, day after day. That's why the weather forecast, usually delivered by a professional meteorologist, is the last segment on news shows, and promoted heavily during the show. The goal: to hold that audience through the entire newscast.

But why would stations need their own meteorologist? One would think that with all the highly technical refinements of recent decades, and the vast resources of the federal government's National Weather Service, the forecast would be a piece of cake. It's all there in the computers, isn't it?

It may be in the computers, but getting it out of the machines accurately and in real time on the local level is the trick. Most of the raw data local forecasters use come from the National Weather Service. But the daily weather forecast you see on TV or hear on the radio is the interpretation of that data by the local meteorologist. And if we respectfully disagree with the national service, we are free to issue our own forecast. (This is not true in most other countries, including European countries, where by law local broadcasters must adhere to the official government weather report. This means that if, for example, there are two television stations in a city, they must both give the same report. It makes for less confusion, but not necessarily the most accurate forecasts.)

Cross promotion.
The author delivering daily radio reports on Minnesota's WCCO-AM. The same weather forecast is packaged differently for radio, television, and the Web.

How variable is the art of weather prediction? Well, drop a twig in a nearby stream and then try to predict exactly where that twig will be, downstream, 24 hours from now. How about seven days from now? That's the problem. There are thousands of variables—rocks, boulders, bends, speed of water—that affect where that twig will ultimately wind up.

Meteorologists deal with streams too, jet streams, and storms swept up in that stream, areas of rain that may be only five miles in diameter—but which five miles? Every day is different; every day is a new meteorological creation. As fronts and storms track across America, they mutate; they become wetter or drier. They may speed up or slow down, even stall. Sometimes the computers catch these changes, but often these random events are not predicted in advance.

Your Local Forecast: How It Gets to You

When your local meteorologist walks into the weather center, he or she will first examine the current information: radar data, satellite maps, soundings from

In recent years meteorologists have also begun to assume the role of graphic artists. Much of our time is spent creating those moving maps and clouds that will flash by on your screen in less than 10 seconds. But these maps are critical to creating a memorable weather report, one that viewers at home will come to trust.

weather balloons, and nearby airport observations. We have a choice of several computer models and will choose the one we think will wind up closest to reality. We can, if we wish, issue our own vision of what we think will happen, based on everything from science, to past history, to an educated hunch.

The computers will tell us what is happening "upwind," what's about to drift overhead, the temperature and moisture composition of the atmosphere. For a first guess at today's high we'll track the 850-millibar temperature, the air temperature at roughly 4,000 feet, and then translate that temperature down to the ground, knowing that the air warms nearly five degrees for every thousand feet.

What else can affect the local forecast? The jet stream, for one thing. What is its configuration? Is there a moisture source from the Gulf of Mexico or the Atlantic coming into play? If clouds are predicted, temperatures may be at least 5 degrees cooler during the daytime in the summer and significantly warmer at night in the winter. Where is the storm track predicted to be? If we're north of the track, we should stay in the cooler, more stable air; south of the track, the threat of severe storms will be higher. Will the sun come out for your barbecue? If there is a stubborn layer of stratocumulus clouds, it may take hours, even days, to erode before high pressure makes the sun come out again.

We can see the weather on satellite photos, but just moving that weather east or west is too simplistic. Chances are it will morph and mutate over time. Storms will get wetter, bigger, and then drier, slipping slightly south. Winds will shift and the storm will blow away, or come right at us. Or dissipate completely. The computers do an increasingly good job of telling which way a storm will go, but they're still not perfect.

Other factors we look at when making a forecast:

Persistence

The first forecast option is to just take today's weather and assume that it will linger on tomorrow. That's called persistence. It works best in the summer, especially in southern climates where jet-stream winds are lighter and large, organized storms are less frequent. But usually weather systems are clipping across America at 20 to 40 mph, so persistence is rarely the best alternative.

Urban heat island

Cities tend to be warmer and drier than the surrounding suburbs. If the rain-snow line is projected to be directly overhead (temperatures in the lowest mile of the atmosphere projected to be below freezing) then we might nudge the forecast over to "rain" in the metro areas, since it's going to be 2 to 4 degrees warmer because of more asphalt and concrete. If skies clear and winds subside on a crisp autumn night, we may forecast frost for the outlying suburbs but not the downtowns, where the growing season can be two weeks longer.

Sea breeze

It happens like clockwork nearly every summer day. The sun comes out and heats the land faster than the surrounding water. This heated air rises, pulling cooler, maritime air inland. That can mean a fresh breeze setting up for coastal residents, but the leading edge of this mini cool front can spark showers and thundershowers inland by afternoon. Even smaller lakes can trigger these afternoon showers, due to uneven heating of water and land.

Orographic showers

Hills receive more sunlight than valleys and heat more rapidly, increasing the potential for afternoon showers and thundershowers in hilly terrain. Sometimes these showers, called orographic, persist, but often they are swept downstream, over a city, complicating the local forecast.

Downslope

If winds are predicted to blow from the west, and there are hills to the west, chances are skies will clear. The reason? As air sinks on the lee side of the hill or mountain, it warms and dries, and clouds often dissipate. That's why a west or northwest wind in Washington, Philadelphia, or New York often means clearing, while an east wind is more likely to be accompanied by clouds, rain, or snow.

What the Weather Words Mean

Part of the real challenge of forecasting is communicating what the meteorologist is picturing in his head to his listeners. We choose our words carefully, but as we all know, communication can be a difficult art. And some of the weather words have precise meanings that the public is not always aware of.

Do you know, for example, what a 30 percent probability of precipitation means? It does not mean that there is a 30 percent chance of rain in your backyard. It means that on 3 out of 10 days with a similar weather pattern, one county will pick up .01 inch or more of rain in the next 12 hours. Pretty confusing, right?

I prefer to use different terminology to convey the probability of bumping into a summer shower or storm:

- **Isolated showers:** 5 to 20 percent of the area will experience rain.
- **Scattered showers:** 20 to 50 percent of the area will get wet.
- **Numerous showers:** 50 to 80 percent of the viewing or listening area will need umbrellas.
- **Rain:** 80 to 100 percent of the viewing or listening area will see puddles; just about everyone will get wet; rain will last longer than a typical shower, usually for many hours.

The same applies to winter precipitation:

- **Flurries:** Very light, intermittent snow that rarely accumulates.
- **Light snow:** Steadier, more persistent snow; visibility over 5/8 mile; a light accumulation possible.
- **Moderate snow:** Visibility from 5/16 to 5/8 of a mile; accumulation likely.
- **Heavy snow:** Visibility under 1/4 mile; snow piling up at the rate of at least 1 inch per hour.

You may be surprised to learn that "partly cloudy" does not mean the same thing as "partly sunny." Partly cloudy actually implies more sunshine than partly sunny! Here is a sunshine scale that may help you interpret what the sky outside your window will look like tomorrow.

Terminology	Percentage of the day with sunshine
Sunny	95–100%
Mostly sunny	90–100%
Partly cloudy	60–90%
Variable clouds	50–60%
Intervals of clouds/sun	40–50%
Considerable clouds	30–40%
Partly sunny	20–30%
Mostly cloudy	10–20%
Cloudy/overcast	0–10%

War Stories From the Weatherman

While doing the weather outdoors, I have been pelted with snowballs, sprayed by a skunk, nearly mauled by a drunk black bear, and visited by friendly motorcycle gangs wanting to be on TV. Every day has been a new adventure, all right. One night a filling fell out of a tooth as I was reading the current conditions and I wound up spitting while on the air. Another time an anchorman came on with a fogging machine, and after 30 seconds he'd completely wiped out both the weather map and me—yes, the forecast had called for dense fog. While on-screen, all news broadcasters have a small earphone in one ear, warning them how much longer they have in their segments. A "wrap" means hurry it up. A "hard wrap" is a polite way to say "Get the heck off the air!" I had a producer once firmly tell me to "shut up!" No wonder TV meteorologists sometimes have a deer-in-the-headlights look.

Why Weather Forecasters Over-Warn

It's happened to you, no doubt. You're watching your favorite television show, and the programming is interrupted by the local news station, bringing a weather warning. How annoying! Why don't they just wait until the end of the broadcast? The switchboards at TV stations light up. We've interrupted Oprah!

When a tornado or hurricane touches down, it affects a tiny percentage of the viewing area, maybe less than one-tenth of 1 percent. Most people will experience only heavy rain, lightning, and maybe some downed trees and power lines.

But when a tornado warning is issued for an area, there is a high probability that someone is going to get clobbered, and the rest of us need to realize that in an effort to reach those people in the path of this terrible storm, those who are not affected will be temporarily inconvenienced.

New technology, the Internet, cell phones, and NOAA Weather Radio can pinpoint the warnings, getting essential information to where it's needed, and only where it's needed. But not everyone has access to those devices. Most people depend on mass media, television and radio, for their weather information. And mass media will over-warn the population. Everyone in a tristate area will hear the tornado warning issued for only one county. But look at it this way: If the storm was headed for your hometown, would you expect anything less?

When TV meteorologists go into "continuous coverage mode," staying on the

213

Chasing a Tornado

Finding a tornado is the atmospheric equivalent of locating a turbulent needle in a haystack of towering clouds, requiring skill and a big dose of sheer luck. Arrive 10 minutes too late and you'll be in a wall cloud with hail capable of turning your car hood into tapioca pudding.

Believe it or not, if you know what you're doing, there is a relatively safe way to approach a tornado—from the south or south-east, with the tornadic storm in front of you, in clear view. But it's not something I recommend to amateurs.

At one early point in my career, a photographer and I—hoping to get a good shot of a tornado for a broadcast during the May sweeps ratings period—tagged along with the professional storm chasers from the National Severe Storms Laboratory (NSSL). The NSSL team was trying to deploy a 55-gallon drum crammed full of weather instruments, nicknamed TOTO,

TOTO
(Totable Tornado Observatory)

which stands for Totable Tornado Observatory, into the path of an oncoming tornado. On April 26, the last day of our two-week adventure, we stumbled onto something big.

The NSSL meteorologists had gotten word that a huge thunderstorm anvil was exploding near Ardmore, Oklahoma: extreme divergence aloft, mushrooming out of control. It was just ahead, maybe 10 miles or so. We raced up Interstate 35, probably ignoring several posted speed limits. Minutes later we were bumping over dirt roads, now muddy from rain. It was getting dark, and the sky overhead was churning, looking green and angry.

"Deploy. Deploy!" Josh Wurman from NSSL yelled, and on cue researchers began to unload TOTO from the back of a pickup truck. They flipped a switch and left TOTO on the side of the road. The thunderhead base was morphing into a wall cloud now, spinning slowly and lowering to the ground. We got back into our vehicles and started to drive again, not knowing where we were headed. We were on old country roads, off the maps.

Only in retrospect do I realize how dangerous, and comical, this was. I was driving a hail-dinged Ford Taurus, with one hand on the steering wheel and the other holding the legs of Bob Durland, my photographer. He was sitting in the open window of the passenger side door, aiming his camera behind us, shooting as we lurched and careened down this dark, muddy road somewhere in the heart of Oklahoma.

"Tunnel! Tunnel!" he shrieked. I looked around. We were in a field. I was confused. There were no tunnels anywhere.

"Tunnel! Dammit, there's a tunnel!" he insisted.

I looked in the side mirror and gasped. A tornado was forming behind us now, an inky, oily swirl rising up from the horizon. In his excitement Bob had combined tornado and funnel into one word, tunnel.

"Oh my God," I muttered, saying a silent prayer under my breath. This was not the way I wanted to meet my maker.

Seconds later we were out of the car with cameras rolling, watching as a fat F-2 tornado spun up on the edge of the mesocyclone less than a quarter-mile away. There was no sound, only the occasional growl of thunder and the excited shouting of the storm chasers now snapping pictures and screaming observations.

Close encounter. I took this picture in April 1986 near Ardmore, Oklahoma, of photographer Bob Durland tracking the F-2 tornado that moments earlier had struck TOTO and knocked it into a ditch. TOTO is now "retired," resting in a NOAA museum in Silver Spring, Maryland.

Crouched down, I did a stand-up segment, delivering a stunned sentence or two into a microphone as the tornado lifted up behind me, clearly visible in the frame.

"And here is what we've been waiting to see, a tornado," I said into the microphone. "Possibly F-1 or F-2, which has just formed in the last couple of minutes. And let me tell you, these last couple of minutes have been some of the most terrifying moments of my life!" I wasn't exaggerating. My heart was pumping, my mouth dry, and I had a sense of terror tinged with sheer exhilaration.

"It's getting too dark now," the lead NSSL chaser yelled out. "I don't want to go any farther in this." It was a smart decision. Chasing, however dangerous (and foolish) during the day, becomes exponentially more dangerous at night, when it can be even more difficult to see the tornado and avoid a potentially lethal track.

We returned to find TOTO knocked over on its side in a ditch, scuffed up but still intact. There was more jubilant hollering as the meteorologists examined their tornado sensor. Later, magnetic tape inside TOTO would confirm that for the first and, as it would turn out, only time, the weather instrument had been grazed by a tornado.

air for many minutes and sometimes hours, interrupting regular programming, it means that the threat of severe weather is ongoing somewhere, and the location of those "somewheres" could change quickly. The system isn't perfect, but I would rather stay on the air with updated information than take the phone call from the injured tornado victims wondering why I didn't warn them when the tornado hit.

TV stations are licensed by the Federal Communications Commission to "serve the public interest." As Dennis Swanson, vice president of Viacom Television, puts it, "We have an obligation to get weather information to people quickly, accurately, and in an intelligent fashion. It could mean the difference between putting people at risk or putting them in a safe position." I can't think of anything more important that we do than provide real-time, blow-by-blow accounts of what the weather is doing now, and tell which neighborhoods, which streets, are in the path of dangerous weather.

Chroma Key. People are still baffled when they stop by the station and see me pointing to a green wall. In the control room computer effects can substitute that shade of green with any of my weather sources or Doppler radar. But to see what I'm actually pointing at, I have to look at TV monitors strategically placed on either side of the Chroma Key. It takes a little practice, but it's not too hard to master. As I'm talking to the camera I'm getting time cues from the producer, counting me down to the end of my weathercast. "Sixty . . . thirty . . . wrap. Hard wrap!"

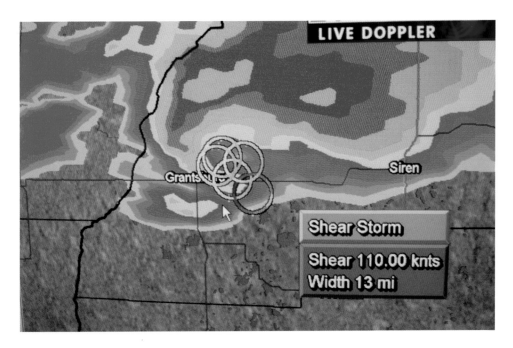

Tracking Weather Down to the Street Level

NEXRAD radar images from the National Weather Service provide a nationwide network of data, but they have limitations. To start with, they are delayed in time. There is no such thing as "live NEXRAD."

NEXRAD scans the skies in all 360 degrees, and at different levels to get a three-dimensional view of the weather. Gathering that wealth of 3-D data takes time, about four to six minutes. That means that ground-level scans of precipitation and wind velocity and direction are captured in six-minute increments, which can be problematic when a fast storm is moving through the area. In six minutes a storm traveling at 40 mph can move four miles.

The only way to know what's happening right now is to invest in a live Doppler radar, and scores of television stations around the nation have done just that. At my station, WCCO-TV, we have a network of five live Doppler radars, which allows us to get closer to any storm, scanning the lowest few thousand feet, increasing our confidence that rotation may be translating into a tornado on the ground.

We also have two radar displays from Baron Services, based in Huntsville, Alabama. Bob Baron founded the company after a particularly violent and deadly tornado ripped through his hometown in 1989, killing 22 people and injuring hundreds more. He set out to create technology that could identify and track tornadic storms.

Our live radar displays allow us to zoom down to street

Tornado tip-off. This 3-D Storm Alert view allows TV meteorologists to zero in on the spinning thunderheads most likely to produce large hail and tornadoes. City names are automatically programmed into the radar's software, so tracks showing threatened neighborhoods and towns can be called up, live, on the air, giving viewers critical lead time to seek shelter in their basements.

STREET-LEVEL WEATHER

The forecast is no longer "one size fits all." New technology permits meteorologists to zoom down to specific neighborhoods, showing how weather will change from one part of town to the next. Doppler radar and automated weather instruments can give viewers an appreciation of how different the weather can be from one end of the city to the next. This zoom sequence shows predicted rainfall over Minneapolis during a heavy rain event. An estimated 1.48 inches of rain is expected at the Metrodome, home of the Minnesota Twins and Vikings.

level, showing data that are live, happening right now. We look for "shear markers" that highlight areas of rapid rotation. Yellow circles on the screen show a "mid-level lock," meaning that rotation in the mid levels of the thunderstorm have been detected. A red circle means a "low-level lock," with dangerous rotation at the lowest levels of a severe thunderstorm, a tip-off that a tornado may be about to form. We can use diagnostic software to estimate wind speeds within a thunderhead, the size of hailstones, and even how much rain has fallen in the last 24 hours to zero in on parts of counties that may be most prone to flash flooding.

Once a tornado is detected, we can project the track into the future, showing those towns, landmarks, and intersections that are in its path and estimating what time the tornado will hit each location.

The Future of Local Forecasting

Weather forecasting continues to evolve. It's only within the last 15 years or so, as station managers began to understand how important the weather was to their viewers, that professional meteorologists have been hired for television forecasts. In the early '60s, the weather was reported by weather "bunnies," attractive women in skimpy outfits. Or it was reported by clowns and comedians who

In the years ahead, local meteorologists will continue to focus on bringing the forecast down to your neighborhood.

worked a little weather into their routines. In the '70s, professorial types in smoking jackets took their turn, but their forecasts left a lot to be desired. It wasn't until the 1980s that local news directors began hiring professional, degreed meteorologists, though a pleasant personality was and still is a requirement.

In the years ahead, local meteorologists will continue to focus on bringing the forecast down to your neighborhood. The seven-day outlook will always be iffy—we just can't tell what nature will bring us that far out. But real breakthroughs may come in the first 12 hours of a forecast. What time will the showers hit my house? Will the storms that hit the northern suburbs spare the outdoor wedding downtown? What time will the rain turn to ice, before or after I get home? Technology will increasingly dazzle viewers with street-level forecasts timed to the hour or even the minute, capabilities that would have been unthinkable a decade ago. Future innovations and breakthroughs will weave together some combination of the Internet and local television, giving everyone his or her own personalized, one-of-a-kind forecast.

I can predict one thing with rare 100 percent accuracy: The weather presentations will not be dull.

CHAPTER NINE

Facts, Fibs, and Weather Trivia

Some people are weatherwise, but most are otherwise.—Benjamin Franklin

THE WEATHER affects more than our harvests and heating bills. There is little question that swings in temperature, moisture, and wind can tug at our health and our moods, leaving us feeling stressed or cheered, anxious or optimistic. An estimated one in five Americans has allergies, and for them daily shifts in weather are nothing to sneeze at. Man-made pollution can make matters worse; ask anyone with asthma living in or near a major city.

Think about it. We live at the bottom of a vast pond of air, moisture, and wind. We shouldn't be at all surprised to discover that an approaching storm or frontal passage may affect how well we feel, or how long it takes us to get to sleep. Kids in school seem to be more active, even hyperactive, when a big storm is moving in. Ask any teacher. People with arthritis are in pain when a front is moving through; they can feel the changes right in their bones.

So don't discount some of those old, dusty proverbs you grew up with. Some of those clichés have scientific validity. The meaning behind a halo around the moon, birds flying low before a storm, or a red sky greeting you at dawn—you may be surprised to find out how many of those old weather tales you grew up with are true. In the high-tech world of weather there is plenty of room for the old world and the low tech.

Understanding the link between weather and human physiology is critically important. If we can interpret tomorrow's forecast, predicting not only what clothes to wear and whether to lug along an umbrella, but also how changes in the weather will make us feel, we gain a slight but important edge on Mother Nature. Man's understanding of how the atmosphere works, and how we react to these changes, both mentally and physically, is a new and evolving story, one that needs to be told.

Painful Forecast: Cloudy and Wet With a Falling Barometer

An approaching storm or frontal boundary is the worst kind of weather for many people, triggering assorted aches and pains. People with arthritis and rheumatism dread damp, chilly weather when relative humidity levels are high, the barometer is falling, and winds are gusty.

> **BIOMETEOROLOGY**
>
> Biometeorology is the study of how weather affects health and wellness. Pioneered in Germany, the field is very popular throughout Europe and interest is building in the United States, for good reason. Some of us are more affected than others, but there is little question now that science can prove a link between changes in the sky overhead and our moods, attitudes, and even our ability to ward off illness.

There may be a physiological reason why so many people are hurting when a storm approaches. A rapidly falling barometer causes fluids in the membranes of joints to expand, increasing friction and reducing range of motion, making every step an effort. The same holds true for people who have recently broken a bone; they feel sharp discomfort at the site of the bone break when the weather is about to turn foul. People with bad teeth, corns, and bunions are often sensitized to drops in pressure before a storm.

Reaction times go down when a storm system is moving in, posing more of a threat to people driving vehicles and operating machinery in factories, possibly even affecting the performance of professional athletes. Talk about the ultimate excuse: Just blame it on the weather! Mental acuity and sharpness may be dulled by a rapidly falling barometer and gathering clouds and this can show up in lower test scores and reduced job productivity.

Hospitals report that when the barometer drops sharply, more pregnant women go into labor, with the best chance of giving birth happening as a storm or front passes directly overhead. A woman's womb may, in fact, act as a barometer, expanding and contracting with changing air pressure overhead. The sharper the drop in pressure, the more the womb can expand, possibly setting off the labor process. So have your obstetrician consult with the local seven-day forecast before estimating a due date!

Feeling SAD

For many people a gray, midwinter day is more than an inconvenience. A string of cloudy, dreary days can be depressing and debilitating. There is a physical reason why millions of Americans feel down during the dark days of winter. It's called SAD, for Seasonal Affective Disorder. *Affective* is a psychiatric term relating to mood, and as many as 1 in 10 of us can sink into a dark blue funk when skies turn cloudy during the winter months, when sunlight is sparse to begin with. An estimated 3 out of 4 people who suffer from SAD are women, and there is growing evidence that this malady is hereditary, passed on from one generation to the next. Many mammals hibernate during the winter, but, unfortunately, that's not a viable option for most people.

Why do some of us have this kind of reaction? All of us have a biological internal clock that regulates when we sleep and when we're awake and alert. Generations ago people slept when it was dark and worked during the daylight hours, but today most of us are expected to be wide awake during the darkest days of winter, even though our biological clocks are telling us to work less and sleep more. A lack of sunlight in the winter months can stimulate production of a hormone in the body called melatonin. The release of melatonin promotes sleep; that's why many people take it as a supplement when they get on an airplane and want to reset their body clocks to a new time zone. But if our bodies are still producing high levels of the hormone in dim winter daytime weather, we can feel groggy throughout the day. And when we can't get to sleep because it is daytime, we begin to feel anxious and depressed.

Most people feel best when skies are clear or clearing, with a rising barometer on the back of a storm system, and temperatures that are comfortable, within a few degrees of 70.

There are effective treatments for SAD. Many doctors prescribe bright light therapy, which means spending as little as an hour a day in front of a full-spectrum light that mimics the sun. Newer full-spectrum bulbs are fluorescents, screw into a normal light fixture, and cost about $30 to $40, but they can be worth every penny. In addition to light therapy, standard antidepressant medications can provide some relief.

Commonsense solutions that may leave you feeling a little better include trying to get as much natural sunlight as possible during the winter months, removing window obstructions like blinds and curtains. Sit near windows when possible (some people are immune to the effects of artificial light), and consider taking a daily walk. Research suggests that taking a one-hour walk in the midwinter sunlight can lift your spirits considerably, as will a sunny, southern vacation.

If you suspect that SAD is bringing you down, consult with your physician before embarking on any kind of a treatment program, but know that you do not have to suffer the ill effects of SAD in silence.

An Evil Wind

Chinook. Santa Ana. Ask people who live in the West what happens when a hot, dry wind comes whipping through the valleys and canyons: Bad things happen. Brushfires erupt, tempers flare, and arguments degenerate into full-blown brawls. No, you're not imagining the ability of steamy weather to make a bad situation worse.

The Simon Fraser University criminologist Ehor Boyanowsky has spent more than three decades studying the link between weather and people who display a

223

"hot temper." He believes that hot weather lowers the threshold for violence, and that a higher brain temperature plays a significant role in crimes of passion. His studies show that when the mercury rises, inhibition drops, causing some people to become more aggressive and potentially violent.

This is not just an American problem. Europeans are always on the lookout for a hot, dry *foehn* that blows across the Alps. In the south of France and Italy the *tramontana,* a hot, dry wind, has been linked to mental illness, aggression, even suicide. People in Greece, Israel, and Libya complain of the *sirocco* moving in from the Sahara Desert. Hot winds may affect serotonin levels in the brain, ultimately affecting behavior and leaving us more than a little hot under the collar.

The *Farmer's Almanac*

This venerable publication has been around for centuries and publishes forecasts that extend as far as a year. In the old days, farmers needed to have some idea of how well their next crop would do, and they did, literally, sometimes bet the farm on the *Almanac's* forecasts.

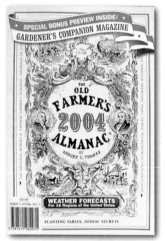

The Almanac relies on subtle changes in the sun's energy, specifically the sunspot cycle, to tailor its forecasts.

But the question arises: How much science is involved in making these long-range weather predictions? The *Almanac* uses roughly the same formula devised by its founder, Robert B. Thomas, back in 1792. It relies on subtle changes in the sun's energy, specifically the sunspot cycle, to tailor its forecasts. The people at the *Farmer's Almanac* believe that by comparing solar patterns and historical weather records they can spot trends and predict future events. Their meteorologist tries to forecast how temperatures and precipitation will vary from long-term 30-year "normals," and they claim an 80 percent success rate looking as far as 18 months into the future. This purported track record does raise eyebrows among more traditional meteorologists wrestling with their beleaguered seven-day outlooks.

To be sure, sunspots, slightly cooler regions of gas that freckle the sun's surface like clockwork, have been linked to drought cycles on the earth, but expanding this to predict specific weather events is something of a stretch. There are times when the *Almanac* is amazingly on-target, but other times when forecasts are way off. Don't bet your farm (or vacation) on what you might read in the *Farmer's Almanac.*

That said, here's a true confession. I keep a copy of the *Almanac* locked away in one of my desk drawers. I treat it as a curiosity, a third opinion. Long-range forecasting is the holy grail of meteorology. We realize that people are hungry for guidance weeks and even months into the future. But I do not envision a time in this century when you'll be able to get a reliably accurate forecast of temperature or rainfall for a specific day weeks or months into the future. That is simply beyond the scope of science, and will be for the foreseeable future.

Those Old Weather Proverbs: True or False?

We've all heard those old proverbs that have been traded about for as long as people have stepped gingerly outside, peering up at an uncertain sky. Proverbs are based on observations and stories that have been handed down over many centuries. They have not been tested for validity using the scientific method. Some are altogether bogus, others a source of fascination, and many even have some validity. Separating fact from fib can be challenging, but read on to see which of the stories you've been told are tall tales and which are wise nuggets of information that may just keep you out of trouble!

**"Red sky at night, sailor's delight;
red sky at morning, sailors take warning."**
True. At dusk a red sky is often the result of sunlight passing through particles of dust, salt, smoke, and pollution. The blue end of the white sunlight spectrum is scattered (or bent) more than the red colors by all these particles, giving the sun a redder appearance. High pressure is associated with sinking air, which also confines these particles closer to the ground, making the reds look even redder. However, a red sky in the morning, coming when winds are blowing from the east or northeast, often means that mid- or high-level clouds are present, and since the atmosphere always moistens up from top to bottom, that often means rain.

"The heaviest rain falls following a full or new moon."
False. The moon exerts a gravitational tug, which obviously affects tides around the world, especially near the poles, but there is no known link between a full or new moon and the tendency for major storms to spin up. The atmosphere is considered to be a fluid, and that has caused some to speculate that the moon may be able to nudge the weather in a certain direction, but this has never been proven scientifically. A full moon may have some subtle effects on human behavior, but the next time your yard is bathed in the light of a full moon, don't worry about your outdoor plans for the weekend.

**"When the wooly bear caterpillar's brown band is wide,
a bad winter abides."**
False. Every year people call and e-mail ominous reports of black wooly bear caterpillars and wonder out loud how rough the winter will be. I tell them to relax. Studies done as far back as the late 1940s show that the coloring marks on the

225

wooly bear have nothing to do with weather, and everything to do with where the caterpillars grew up. Wide black bands are the result of living in a wet environment, and wider brown bands arise from living in a dry climate.

"If cats lick themselves, fair weather."
True. When high pressure is drifting overhead and skies are sunny, relative humidity levels are usually low, the air quite dry. Under these conditions static electricity can build up on a cat's fur, making it feel unclean. Licking and moistening the fur can cause static electricity to slowly bleed off the cat, reducing the risk of an uncomfortable shock. This is especially true during the dry winter months, when charges can build up, resulting in unpleasant little shocks. That may be why some cats don't like being petted.

"When spider webs in the air do fly, the spell will soon be very dry."
False. Spider expert Dr. Henry McCook disputes this saying. His research suggests that spiders are creatures of habit; they do the same things at the same time of day, every day, no matter what the weather.

"Halo around the sun or moon, rain or snow soon."
True. This is one of the more reliable tip-offs that a storm may be brewing. Remember that the atmosphere always moistens up from top to bottom before a storm. The first clouds to arrive are cirrus, ice crystals at 25,000 feet. These crystals act like tiny prisms, bending white moonlight to form a ring around the moon, a halo. The brighter the halo, the thicker the cirrus overcast, and the greater the likelihood of rain or snow within 24 hours. It's not foolproof, but a halo, combined with a falling barometer and an easterly wind, suggests that you had better have a plan B (indoors) for tomorrow's activities.

"Clear moon, frost soon."
True (some of the time). The coldest temperatures come on crystal-clear nights, when warmth is radiated rapidly into outer space and the ground can cool most rapidly. A deck of clouds, especially low clouds, usually acts as a blanket, trapping warmth near the ground, often preventing a frost or freeze. So yes, on a clear, dry night in the autumn with little or no wind, the probability of a frost goes up.

"Swallows high, staying dry; swallows low, wet will blow."
True. A fine, sunny day is usually characterized by high pressure and sunshine heating the ground, which generates thermals, regions of warm, rising air capa-

ble of carrying insects aloft, forcing birds to fly higher than usual to find a snack. A rapidly falling barometer is thought to exert pressure on a bird's ears, forcing it to fly closer to the ground.

"When the groundhog sees his shadow, expect six more weeks of winter."

False. Poor Punxsutawney Phil. Every year that unfortunate, overexposed groundhog is trotted out for national television. It makes for great shtick, but, stating the obvious, no animal is capable of predicting the weather six weeks out. Add man to that list, come to think of it.

"Feels like earthquake weather out there right now."

False. Some quake survivors relate stories of how the weather preceding the big shake was unusually warm and humid, with an eerie stillness in the air. In spite of what you may hear from friends in California, there is no sound scientific evidence that weather conditions can trigger an earthquake. Tremors occur in all different kinds of weather—rain, sunny, warm, cold—in all seasons of the year, and at all times of the day.

"Deer feed heavily before a storm."

True. Many mammals appear to be hypersensitive to even small changes in atmospheric pressure. Falling barometric pressure ahead of a storm may be a cue to fill up on food before the rain or snow hits and conditions for finding the next meal may not be as good.

"Fish bite best before a cold front."

True. Avid anglers will tell you that a falling barometer ahead of a cold front will often result in a fish feeding frenzy, with the slippery creatures gorging themselves on whatever they can find. Fish almost always go deep and dormant on the lake bottom after a cold front passes and the barometer begins to rise. It may be a little windy and wet out there on that boat, but your best odds of catching a fish occur a few hours before the cold front arrives and winds shift to the northwest.

227

"When the cicada falls silent, look to the sky for thunder."
True. When the humidity level rises, cicadas usually cannot vibrate their wings to produce their telltale sound, so the insects are often quiet immediately before a rainstorm.

"A wind from the south has rain in its mouth."
True. As a storm approaches, winds usually increase from the east or northeast, and then swing around to blow from the south as the center of low pressure moves in. Rain and strong thunderstorms are most likely to arrive when winds at ground level are blowing from the south, ahead of a cold front.

"Cows lie down before a storm."
True. A rapidly falling barometer ahead of a storm's arrival may affect the digestive systems of cows, creating discomfort, and getting off their feet seems to help.

"A cow with its tail to the west makes weather the best; a cow with its tail to the east makes weather the least."
True. This old New England saying has a lot of truth to it. Instinctively, animals graze with their tails pointing into the wind, to keep tabs on potential adversaries. So if you see a cow with its tail pointing east, know that an easterly wind would have a higher probability of bringing rain than a westerly breeze.

"When leaves show their backs, it will rain."
True. Prevailing (westerly) winds cause a tree's leaves to grow in a specific pattern. When a storm is approaching, the winds usually blow from the opposite direction, and the leaves will be ruffled backward to show their lighter underside.

"Flies bite more just before a rain."
True. Higher humidity levels and warmer temperatures immediately before a storm can trigger more perspiration; that, coupled with lower pressure's releasing more natural body odor, could make us appetizing targets before a storm moves in. Yes, flies and other pests seem to be more interested in us before a storm than after one.

"Chimney smoke descends, our nice weather ends."
True. Smoke from a campfire or chimney going straight up implies little or no wind, which in turn suggests that a fair-weather high-pressure system is parked overhead. If the smoke curls back toward the ground, winds are stronger, or an inversion may be trapping the smoke, and the odds of clouds and rain developing are higher.

"The higher the clouds, the better the weather."
Questionable. High clouds may imply fair weather in the short term, but if those cirrus clouds are increasing rapidly, accompanied by an easterly wind and a rapidly falling barometer, expect a good chance of rain or snow within 24 hours.

"This is the calm before the storm."
True. The saying "Calm continueth not long without a storm" dates back to an anonymous source in 1576! During the Vietnam war, bomber pilots were instructed to wait until the approach of a typhoon (same thing as a hurricane) to insure crystal-clear conditions and unobstructed views below. It may seem counterintuitive, but if the air is rising violently in one place, producing rain, thunder, hail, and worse, then the air must be sinking nearby. As air sinks, it warms and dries, resulting in clear skies. Hurricanes are often preceded by a day or two of flawless blue sky. Thunderstorms are often preceded by an eerie period of calm, where the air is still and birds seek shelter. Don't count on a calm before every storm, but there is a meteorological reason why, in many cases, this old proverb appears to be true.

> ### WEATHERFACT
> Which weighs more, a puffy little "popcorn" cumulus cloud or an elephant? Not even close. The cloud, by a wide margin. According to *Weatherwise* magazine, a typical cumulus cloud, occupying roughly a cubic kilometer, contains water weighing approximately 440,000 pounds, enough to fill up a swimming pool. A mature thunderstorm may contain a thousand times more than this!

"When clouds appear like rocks and towers, the earth's refreshed by frequent showers."
True. "Rocks and towers" refer to the imposing, bloated appearance of cumulus congestus and cumulonimbus, heavy storm clouds that can tower as much as 10 miles into the atmosphere. When you see turrets of gray rising above you, there's a pretty good chance your picnic may be moved into the garage as the skies open up.

Weather Quiz

Just how weather-wise are you? Take a few minutes and try this quiz. It starts out fairly easy and gets more difficult near the end. You may be pleasantly surprised to see some of the answers, and how well you ultimately do. (Hint: Some of the multiple choice questions can have more than one correct answer.) See page 234 for the answers.

1. Meteorologists study meteorites, true or false?

2. Which of the following is a fair-weather cloud? A) Cirrus. B) Stratus. C) Cumulus. D) Nimbus.

3. If you are at least 20 miles inland from the coast when a hurricane hits, you're safe, true or false?

4. Which of the following feel the true wind-chill effect? A) People. B) Pets. C) Cars and trucks. D) All of the above.

5. A baseball player stands a better chance of hitting a home run when the weather is: A) Cool and dry. B) Warm and humid. C) Calm. D) Weather makes no difference!

6. What is the safest place to ride out a tornado? A) Basement, under the stairs. B) Basement, southwest corner. C) Closet. D) Attic.

7. If you're in your car or truck and you can't outrun a tornado or seek shelter in a building, the safest place is: A) In your vehicle. B) Under your vehicle. C) Under the nearest concrete bridge overpass. D) In the nearest ditch.

8. Which of the following have relatively calm eyes? A) Tornadoes. B) Hurricanes. C) Low-pressure systems. D) Typhoons.

9. You become stranded on a cold, snowy road. What should you do? A) Stay with your vehicle and wait for help to arrive. B) Walk to the nearest home. C) Push the vehicle to the nearest gas station. C) None of the above.

10. Which kind of wintry precipitation is the most difficult to drive on? A) Sleet. B) Snow. C) Freezing rain. D) No difference in traction.

11. Steadiest rains tend to be associated with a(n): A) Cold front. B) Warm front. C) Occluded front. D) Stalled high-pressure system.

12. If someone nearby is hit by lightning, wait at least 30 minutes before administering CPR, true or false?

13. If you count 20 seconds between seeing a flash of lightning and hearing the thunder, how many miles away was the strike? A) 1 mile. B) 4 miles. C) 10 miles. D) 20 miles. E) Impossible to estimate.

14. Doppler radar can detect: A) Rotating super-cell thunderstorms. B) Hail and snow. C) Dust and insects. D) Temperatures.

15. Weather forecasts in the United States tend to be most accurate in the: A) West. B) Central states. C) East. D) Location makes no difference—they're bad everywhere.

16. Where would you be most likely to hydroplane? A) Driveway. B) Freeway or interstate. C) Backyard. D) None of the above.

17. Which of the following can reduce the amount of carbon being released into the atmosphere? A) Planting more trees. B) Switching to hybrid vehicles. C) Purchasing energy-efficient lightbulbs and appliances. D) All of the above.

18. Which word used in a weather forecast implies heavier, steadier precipitation lasting many hours, a situation where nearly everyone will get wet? A) Shower. B) Thunderstorm. C) Rain. D) Drizzle.

19. Which of the following will wake you up in the middle of the night if a warning is issued for your county? A) FM radio. B) Home Doppler radar. C) NOAA Weather Radio. D) Loud mother-in-law.

20. Splashes of colored light on either side of a rising or setting sun are called: A) Halos. B) Rainbows. C) Sun dogs. D) Hallucinations.

21. Computer models can predict temperature and precipitation with some accuracy as far ahead as: A) 6 hours. B) 7 days. C) 14 days. D) 1 year.

22. Which of the following are symptoms of a warming sky overhead? A) Greater frequency of droughts and heat waves. B) More severe storms and tornadoes. C) Rising ocean water levels. D) Greater potential for the West Nile virus and malaria.

23. A hurricane is approaching your location and you can't escape inland. The safest place to ride out the storm is: A) The nearest basement. B) Any vehicle. C) A boat. D) An interior room on an upper floor of a well-built home, office building, or hotel.

24. A thunderstorm has just passed through and the rain has tapered off. When is it safe to go outside again? A) Immediately. B) 30 minutes. C) 1 hour. D) Trick question!

25. Which of the following clouds are sometimes mistaken for UFOs? A) Cumulus. B) Pileus. C) Cirrus. D) Lenticularis.

26. Compared to the suburbs, cities tend to be: A) Warmer. B) Drier. C) Less prone to small tornadoes. D) More susceptible to flash flooding.

27. A sunburn is much more likely on a hot day, true or false?

28. El Niño events tend to result in: A) More storms for California. B) Wetter weather for the Deep South. C) Fewer hurricanes. D) All of the above.

29. The energy expended by shoveling heavy snow is roughly equivalent to: A) Changing a diaper. B) Playing a vigorous round of golf. C) Brisk walking. D) Jogging at 9 mph.

30. Heat lightning is the result of: A) Distant thunderstorms. B) Unusual heat and humidity. C) Curvature of the earth. D) El Niño.

31. Which phenomenon poses the greatest threat to flying near area airports: A) Lightning. B) Heavy rain. C) Snow. D) Downbursts and microbursts.

WEATHERFACTS

Three out of four of all the tornadoes reported worldwide touch down on U.S. soil.

Nine out of 10 lightning bolts hit land rather than oceans.

It takes about one million microscopic cloud droplets to make one raindrop.

If you suffer from an irrational fear of tornadoes and hurricanes, the name of your phobia is lilapsophobia.

Feeling the weight of the world on your shoulders? Well, no wonder! While the atmosphere flows and is considered a fluid—it is composed of hydrogen, oxygen, nitrogen, and other trace gases—it has weight. The trend of this weight (falling or rising barometer) is more important than the actual value of the air pressure. A falling barometer is often a tip-off that stormy weather is coming. If you could somehow weigh the entire atmosphere, it would tip the scales at about 5 trillion tons!

32. On dark, gray days in the winter you feel especially tired, anxious, or depressed. You may be suffering from: A) Allergies. B) Scurvy. C) The flu. D) Seasonal affective disorder, or SAD.

33. Which of the following weather conditions, on average, claims the most American lives every year? A) Lightning. B) Tornadoes. C) Floods and hurricanes. D) Extreme heat.

34. The accuracy of the "tomorrow" forecast has improved dramatically in recent years, true or false?

35. Which of the following moves fastest? A) A large hailstone. B) An F-1 tornado. C) A category-4 hurricane. D) Snowflakes in a blizzard.

Weather Quiz Answers

Ready to see how well you've done? Here are the answers and some brief explanations. Keep score and see how many questions you got right.

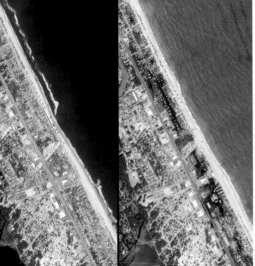

1. **False.** A meteor is "anything in the air," so meteorologists study hydrometeors (clouds), electro meteors (thunder), and luminous meteors (rainbows and halos).

2. **C) Cumulus.** When you see cumulus clouds combined with a north or northwest wind and a rising barometer, expect fair weather for at least the next 24 hours.

3. **False.** Recent research suggests that more people are killed by flash flooding hundreds or even thousands of miles inland, in some cases days after the hurricane reaches land, than by the storm itself. Coastal residents are threatened by the "storm surge," unusually high tides pushed ashore by the combination of strong winds and low pressure—but just because you live inland, there is no reason to be complacent about a hurricane's approach.

These high-resolution IKONOS satellite images were taken on September 4, 2002, left, and September 21, 2003, right, just two days after Hurricane Isabel passed overhead. Some homes have been entirely swept away, with sand deposited hundreds of feet inland from the ocean.

4. **A) and B) People and pets.** Unless your vehicle perspires, it does not experience the same windchill effect as people and pets do. Remember that the evaporation of perspiration off your skin has a cooling effect. That's why you feel chilled stepping out of the bath. The stronger the wind in the winter, the greater the evaporation and the colder you feel. It is true that a cold wind will cool your vehicle's engine block down to the current air temperature faster, making it a little more difficult to start your car or truck.

5. **B) Warm and humid.** Air density is lower when relative humidity levels and dew point temperatures are higher. Statistically, the odds of hitting a home run are greater on a sticky, humid day than on a cool and comfortable day. Now professional ballplayers have a good meteorological excuse!

6. **A) Basement, under the stairs.** During the 1950s, '60s, and '70s, officials recommended the southwest corner of a basement as the safest place to seek shelter during a tornado. Subsequent research showed that debris often fell into the southwest corner, making it unsafe. Statistically, the safest place to be during a tornado is in the basement under the stairs, and under a heavy table or workbench, if available. You can ride out even the most severe tornado, an F-4 or F-5, there.

7. **D) In the nearest ditch.** Famous video from a television news crew hiding under a bridge during the Andover, Kansas, tornado on April 26, 1991, sent the wrong message. The cameraman left his camera on as the tornado passed nearby, only grazing their location. But the F-5 tornado that hit Oklahoma City on May 3, 1999, was a monster, and, sadly, three people lost their lives hiding under bridge overpasses. You are safer getting out of your vehicle and seeking shelter in the nearest ditch.

8. **A), B), and D). Tornadoes, hurricanes, and typhoons.** Remember that *typhoon* and *hurricane* are different names for the same phenomenon, a large ocean-forming storm that gets its strength from warm water. Amazingly, tornadoes also appear to have eyes, but few people live to see them and tell their story. On March 29, 1998, a huge—F-4—tornado hit Comfrey, Minnesota. A group of at least 10 people were outside a local church when the first blast of wind moved in. They described a period of eerie calm, looking up inside the swirling tornado and then having about 20 to 30 seconds to run into the church's basement before the second, even more devastating, side of the tornado smashed the church. They were very, very lucky.

Supercells. Shortly before this GOES satellite image was taken, a total of four tornadoes touched down on Deshler, Nebraska, destroying 100 homes and 25 businesses.

9. **A) Stay with your vehicle and wait for help to arrive.** The initial instinct is to be a hero and go to get help, but this increases your risk of frostbite, hypothermia, and getting stranded. Research shows that you stand a better chance of a successful outcome if you stay with your vehicle and wait for help to reach you. Tie something to the antenna, run the engine infrequently, clear snow away from the exhaust pipe, and crack the window slightly to avoid carbon monoxide poisoning. Remember that when walking in a major snowstorm or blizzard, it is very easy to become disoriented, lost, and in serious trouble.

10. **C) Freezing rain.** Four-wheel drive provides improved traction on snow and sleet, but freezing rain is another matter altogether. Rain that freezes onto power lines, trees and highway surfaces is especially insidious. Front-wheel drive and four-wheel drive will not provide much, if any, additional traction. The only thing you can do is slow down to a crawl, or, better yet, wait for temperatures to drop or road crews to put down a salt/sand mix capable of melting the glaze ice.

11. **B) Warm front.** Warm air rising up and over cold air near the ground usually results in steadier rain, snow, or drizzle, lasting many hours. Precipitation in the vicinity of cold fronts tends to be "convective," or showery. When a cold front catches up with a warm front, the system is said to "occlude." Occluded fronts near the center of low-pressure systems usually bring showery weather as well.

12. **False!** There is no danger of electrocution after the strike, and there is at least a 50 percent chance that if you begin CPR immediately, the lightning victim can be revived.

13. **B) 4 miles.** Thunder travels at the speed of sound, covering one mile roughly every five seconds. So take the number of seconds between seeing the lightning and hearing thunder, and divide by five to find out how many miles away the strike was.

14. **A) Rotating supercell thunderstorms. B) Hail and snow. C) Dust and insects.** Doppler radar detects not only the location of dust, insects, and precipitation, but also the movement toward or away from the radar site. All thunderstorms that produce tornadoes spin—they rotate—and these supercell thunderstorms often show up on Doppler radar, in some cases 10 to 30 minutes before a tornado forms on the ground, allowing National Weather Service forecasters to issue timely warnings.

15. **C) East.** Recent studies seem to confirm that weather forecasts are more accurate the farther east you live in the United States. The reason: If you live in the East, there are thousands of airports upwind, to your west, that feed or "initialize" the computers with raw weather information—temperature, moisture, wind speed, and direction. The greater the quantity and quality of this data put into the weather computers, the better the odds of an accurate forecast, especially during the first 48 hours.

16. **B) Freeway or interstate.** During a heavy rainfall, your vehicle's tires can temporarily leave the highway surface at speeds over 25 to 30 mph, because of a thin film of water between the rubber of your tires and the

Tornadic supercell with tornado on southwest edge of storm. Tornado outbreak of October 4, 1998.

road below. This can result in a loss of steering and braking, increasing the potential of getting into an accident. The only remedy: Slow way down when heavy rain is falling.

17. **D) All of the above.** The increase in carbon in the atmosphere in the last 250 years is unprecedented in history, and may already be triggering some unpleasant side effects in daily weather and longer-term climate. Taking a series of small steps to reduce carbon release will help to reduce some of the ill effects of global warming and climate change in the years ahead.

18. **C) Rain.** A forecast of "rain" implies a longer-duration precipitation event where nearly everyone will get wet. In contrast, a prediction of "showers" implies a quick burst of heavier rain, perhaps an hour or two of rain in any given day. Much of the challenge of broadcast meteorology is accurately portraying, through the terminology we use, what we think the skies will look like over your house tomorrow. Choosing the right words to paint that mental picture is important to reduce the potential for confusion.

19. **C) NOAA Weather Radio.** NOAA Weather Radios are sold at most electronic stores, and they set off an alarm when warnings are issued, any time of the day or night. Some come equipped with SAME technology, which allows you to input just your county, so you won't be needlessly alerted when warnings are issued for neighboring counties. NOAA Weather Radio should be part of your family's severe-weather safety net, which includes sirens, radio and television, cell phones, and the Internet. When storms hit late at night, when you're asleep, NOAA Weather Radio can wake you up and give you time to reach the basement if threatening weather is moving in.

NOAA Weather Radio. Part of your family's safety net, this radio triggers an alarm when a warning is issued for your county.

20. **C) Sun dogs.** Refraction, or bending, of white sunlight through tiny, prism-like ice crystals focuses the light into these little colorful splashes of light on either side of the sun, often visible shortly after sunrise or before sunset.

21. **C) 14 days.** There is some success, better than 50-50, as far as 14 days into the future. But accuracy drops off rapidly after the three-day forecast, and anything longer than a five-day forecast is riddled with doubt. Meteorologists can sometimes detect trends in weather patterns, many times linked to what is happening in the Pacific Ocean (El Niño and La Niña). New, experimental long-range forecasts from the Climate Prediction Center are for more than one year!

The first hurricane
ever observed in the Southern Hemisphere—it may be another byproduct of climate change and global warming—hit Brazil in March 2004. It surprised a lot of people, including scientists who thought this couldn't happen because the water offshore has always been too cool—hurricanes require at least 80 to 82 degrees.

22. **All of the above!** Severe weather is on the rise, not just in the United States, but around the world. A warmer atmosphere, even by just a couple of degrees, increases the potential for not only drought, but also extreme weather events, including flash floods, hail, and tornadoes. Warming temperatures are impacting migration patterns for animals, and also increasing the potential for the rapid spread of infectious diseases like malaria and the West Nile virus.

23. **D) An interior room on an upper floor of a well-built home, office building, or hotel.** In a tornado you want to seek shelter below the ground, in a basement, if possible, due to the risk of being hit by flying debris. But if you live on or near the coast, one of the major threats of a hurricane landfall is the "storm surge," a rapid rise in water level, which can inundate escape routes on the ground floor of homes and businesses. If you can't evacuate inland, try to ride out the storm in an interior room, on the third or fourth floor, if possible. Avoid outer walls and windows, and stay tuned to local television and radio stations for continuous updates. Remember not to venture outside when the eye passes overhead, but wait until the storm is over to assess damage and check on neighbors.

24. **B) 30 minutes.** Remember the 30-30 rule. It may save your life. A majority of lightning victims are struck at the tail end of a storm, after the heavy rain has tapered off. But just because the rain is over does not mean that the lightning threat has passed. Wait at least 30 minutes after hearing the last thunderclap before heading back outdoors. And when a storm approaches and the sky blackens, do not wait until you can see lightning before seeking shelter. When you hear the first rumble of thunder, you should immediately go into your vehicle or a nearby building. Lightning can travel as far as 10 miles away from the parent thunderhead.

25. **D) Lenticularis.** Lenticularis, wave clouds, are usually the result of air rising violently up and over a mountain range. When the air is warming with altitude, this upward motion will produce a smooth, rounded, sculpted cloud that appears to hover over the same location, prompting some to call 911 with UFO reports!

26. **All of the above!** The "urban heat island" arises as concrete and asphalt release stored radiation back into the atmosphere, keeping temperatures as

much as 5 to 10 degrees warmer, especially at night. Because there is less moisture available to evaporate, cities tend to be drier as well, and this may reduce the odds of a small tornado. But larger (F-2 or more) tornadoes draw in air from a 10- to 20-mile radius, and a metropolitan area with a few skyscrapers won't deter a major tornado from coming through an urban area. Paving over our downtowns means that rainwater can't soak into the ground, resulting in rapid runoff and an enhanced potential for flash flooding.

Urban twister. On September 24, 2001, a rare inner-city tornado hit College Park, Maryland, ripping through the University of Maryland between 5:15 and 5:30 p.m. Two students were killed when their car was hurled into a tree.

27. **False.** The potential for sunburn has nothing to do with air temperature, and everything to do with time of year and sun angle. The higher the sun is overhead, the more direct the sunlight and the greater the potential for sunburn, which can significantly increase the risk of melanoma, skin cancer. In general, you should try to avoid the midday sun, and if you do work or play outside, wear lightweight, light-colored clothing and a hat whenever possible.

28. **D) All of the above.** El Niño, a periodic warming of the ocean water off Central America, results in higher-velocity jet-stream winds blowing from California across the southern states. This produces violent storms for San Francisco, Los Angeles, and San Diego, more rain for the Deep South, and fewer hurricanes over the Caribbean, since strong winds aloft can interfere with a hurricane's warm updrafts near the eye.

29. **D) Jogging at 9 mph.** Keep that in mind the next time the flakes fall. "Heart attack snows" are more likely when temperatures range from 27 to 32 degrees, when there is a higher water content in the snow, making it heavier and harder to get off your driveway or sidewalk.

30. **A) Distant thunderstorms.** There is no such thing as heat lightning. When you see the flickering of lightning on a warm, sultry night, it is probably from a storm 50 to 150 miles away, over the horizon. Lightning can often reflect off high clouds and haze and be seen hundreds of miles away, while thunder is rarely heard from a storm that is more than 12 to 15 miles away.

31. **D) Downbursts and microbursts.** A violent thunderstorm downdraft that reaches the ground and spreads out horizontally is called a downburst. This sudden rush of rain and hail-cooled air can trigger violent straight-line winds capable of giving an airplane a sudden surge of lift, followed by a loss of lift, sending it into an uncontrollable stall. That's why airplane take-offs and landings tend to be delayed when a thunderstorm is over or near an airport.

Microburst. Smaller than downbursts, microbursts are fewer than 2 1/2 miles in diameter. These downward-rushing surges of rain and hail-cooled air present an ongoing threat to aviation.

32. **D) Seasonal affective disorder, or SAD.** SAD is most likely to sneak up and make you feel blue during the dark days of winter, when a low sun angle can combine with consecutive cloudy days. Light treatment can be especially effective, helping to pull most people out of a deep, dark funk.

33. **D) Extreme heat.** Flooding claims the most storm-related deaths, but complications brought on by exposure to prolonged heat and humidity claim more lives overall than any other weather phenomenon. Researchers believe that nighttime temperatures are even more critical than daytime temperatures. If people can't find relief at night by opening windows (or turning on the air conditioner) and cooling down, then stress can accumulate, possibly resulting in heat stroke or heart attack.

34. **False.** Today's five-day outlook is as accurate as the three-day outlook was 30 years ago. But in spite of new sensing technology and improved physics in weather models, the nationwide accuracy for the 24-hour, or "tomorrow," forecast is still holding at about 87 percent.

35. **A) A large hailstone.** F-1 tornadoes have been clocked with winds over 100 mph, but most track well below that. A hurricane can churn westward across the Caribbean at up to 20 mph. But large, baseball-size hailstones can hit the ground at more than 125 miles an hour, fast enough to shatter windows, dent car hoods, and even trigger concussions in people struck on the head.

Aggregate hailstone. A large hailstone with smaller stones visible. The ruler shows the radius of this remarkable hailstone—the diameter is approximately six inches, the size of a grapefruit.

So, let's see just how weather-wise you are:

30–35 correct: Meteorology master

Congratulations on a job well done! You are a weather genius. Have you ever considered a job in the weather business?

20–29 correct: Weather wizard

You have nothing to be ashamed of; in fact, you got more questions right than some meteorologists just starting out. You are more than capable of making intelligent weather chitchat at the coffeemaker every morning. Tune in to the Weather Channel for a little after-hours tutoring.

10–19 correct: Weather intern

OK. You need a little more work. You need to seriously brush up on your weather trivia.

6–9 correct: Weather Luddite

Forgive me for asking, but do you ever get outside? Turn off the TV or computer once in a while, sneak out the front door, lift your gaze skyward, and drink in the kaleidoscope of clouds drifting overhead. I know you can do better.

0–5 correct: Hello, cave-dweller!

You spend entirely too much time in your cubicle, but there's still hope for you.

Epilogue

PERHAPS I AM JUST WEATHER-OBSESSED, but I am becoming increasingly concerned about what I'm seeing, both on television and outside my window. The nightly weather report describes record floods, historic tornado outbreaks, devastating heat and drought, advancing brushfires and awe-inspiring hurricanes pin wheeling offshore. These aren't Hollywood special effects, but our new reality.

It could be that the weather has always been this extreme, and now we're just more plugged in and aware. But part of me has to wonder if we're on the leading edge of a new chapter in the weather story, one with ever-increasing extremes. There's a fine line between hype and due diligence, but we seem to be spending more and more time in the grip of great changes in our climate, as significant shifts in winds, moisture and temperature take place, right before our very eyes.

That said, my concern is tempered by the fact that Americans are a). adaptable, and b). ingenious. As a nation we have always encouraged creative solutions. Our can-do mentality is buried deep within our genes. We've figured out so much—we'll figure this out too. Entrepreneurs will find new energy sources that will allow us to use less oil and stabilize carbon in the atmosphere. We and our children will work to conserve what we have and do more with less. A new, green mindset is already catching on. I'm confident we are only seeing the first stages of a transformation in how we work, commute and play.

I'm planning to do my part by continuing to study our amazing weather. As I do, I have to admit that, though my beloved Penn State professors would beg to differ, there really is no such thing as a weather expert. Truth be told, the term is almost laughable, an authentic oxymoron, ranking right up there with jumbo shrimp and Senate Intelligence Committee. So while I don't pretend to have the answer key, I'm going to keep on asking questions.

And speaking of answers, I close with a prediction that has rare 100% accuracy. In a world of uncertainty there is one thing you can count on with a great level of certainty. Our skies will remain forever volatile, enchanting, wondrous, impossible to predict, wild, and at times, forbidding. And yet we can't help but look up as we leave the house, scanning the horizon, waiting and wondering what will come next. The extended outlook continues to call for restless skies. Count on it.

—Paul Douglas

Index

X

ACKNOWLEDGMENTS

True story. As a self-confessed weather fanatic, I make it a habit to visit bookstores in any new town I visit, searching for that special book on weather that has great pictures, charts, and useful information. Over the years I've found good textbooks and kids' books on meteorology, but precious little in between. I want to thank Alan Kahn and Barbara Morgan at Barnes & Noble Publishing for sharing my vision and allowing me to write the book I've always imagined in my mind's eye. Marjorie Palmer edited my words with precision and care, helping me manage a veritable flood of facts, acronyms, and trivia—no small task. Designer Richard Berenson skillfully weaved together photographs, charts, and text into a coherent narrative that captures what I set out to create.

My literary agent, Jonathon Lazear, has become a dear friend, and I want to take this moment to thank him for his continued friendship and encouragement over the years. His tenure in Minnesota turned Jonathon into a reluctant armchair meteorologist, and he believed in this book as much as I did. Craig Edward is the meteorologist in charge of the local Twin Cities National Weather Service office. His support and help in the ongoing research for this book proved invaluable. Thanks also to Becky Helgeson and Peter Ciborowski at the Minnesota Pollution Control Agency for helping me to stay current with air-quality issues and climate change. It's a rapidly changing scientific landscape with a constantly evolving stream of data and new research to digest. Being surrounded by professionals willing to share cutting-edge findings has proven invaluable.

I'm lucky to be working at one of America's best local television stations. WCCO-TV is known nationally for its commitment to solid news gathering and award-winning journalism. Thanks to news director Jeffrey Kiernan and general manager Ed Piette for supporting me as I set out to write *Restless Skies*. These two news executives have fostered an atmosphere of innovation and excellence and it's an honor to work for them. Step one of any job is to be equipped with the right tools; this requires vision at the very top levels of management, a willingness to invest in state-of-the-art technology and people. Executive vice president Dennis Swanson and president and CEO Fred Reynolds head up Viacom's Television Stations Group. They oversee weather-programming decisions made at

the CBS-owned stations around the nation, investing many millions of dollars in live Doppler radar systems and sophisticated computer graphics to keep their stations firmly on the cutting edge of weather. Thanks to their leadership, local television viewers around the nation are receiving information second to none in the world. I, for one, do not take that privilege for granted. Thank you also to J. Drake Hamilton, Science Policy Director for Minnesotans for an Energy Efficient Economy (ME3) for his input on Chapter 6 and climate change.

Penn State has turned out more than great linebackers and gifted engineers. An estimated one in four meteorologists in America today is a graduate of the Pennsylvania State University, and I was blessed to be able to get instruction from some of the best professors and research scientists on the planet. Thanks to Dean Eric Barron at the College of Earth and Mineral Sciences for lending his support and the resources of this great university. Mike Seidel also attended Penn State for meteorology, and in addition to being a great forecaster he is my favorite on-air meteorologist at The Weather Channel in Atlanta. He is a perfectionist and meticulous, and I am indebted to him for taking the time to go over the manuscript carefully and methodically.

A belated thank-you to my wife of 20 years, Laurie, for her endless patience and love over the years. Being married to a meteorologist is no walk in the park, but there's a roughly 90 percent probability that Laurie, a gifted architect, has adapted to my strange line of work. I'm still passionate about the weather and for that I can ultimately thank my parents, Grace and Volker Kruhoeffer, who live in Lancaster County, Pennsylvania. Growing up they both encouraged my crazy desire to study and document the weather drifting overhead. Dad had a clipping service going, saving newspaper and magazine articles about particularly bad storms and technological breakthroughs, recommending books, and fueling my interest in everything weather. He still sends me articles and trivia, but now it's by e-mail. He is a master storyteller and I hope I inherited his love of a good yarn. Getting one's arm around the weather is a big job and I am indebted to a long list of friends and colleagues for giving me the confidence to give it a try.

—Paul Douglas

EDITORIAL CREDITS

EPA = Environmental Protection Agency
NASA= National Air and Space Administration
NOAA = National Oceanic & Atmosphere Administration
NWS = National Weather Service

Page 10 Billion-dollar U.S. weather disasters, 1980-2003 NOAA, National Climatic Data Center, Feb. 3, 2004 William Cosgrove, World Water Council, Feb. 27, 2003.mindfully.org. weatherwatchers.org; 12 Infoplease.com, virtualny. cuny.edu; **13** *Isaac's Storm: A Man, A Time, And the Deadliest Hurricane in History* Erik Larson, Isaac Monroe Cline; **14** *Dust Bowl Diary* Ann Marie Low; **16** Tornado Super outbreak: www.april31974.com; **17** Geocities.com/hurricane/ hurricanecamille.htm "Thirty Years After Hurricane Camille, Lessons Learned, Lessons Lost" Center for Science and Technology Policy research, U. of Colorado/Cires; **18** 1993 Flood summaries, central region headquarters, NWS; **20** "Charting El Nino" www.cnn.com/2002/weather K\ NOAA:www.elnino. noaa.gov.; **21** "East Coast Winter superstorms" David Dildine "Superstorm 1993" www.2010.atmos.uiuc.edu/; **22** "Preliminary Report, Hurricane Andrew. 16–28 August, 1992"-Ed Rappaport, National Hurricane Center, Dec. 10, 1993 www.nhc. noaa.gov/1992andrew.html; **24** "Dying Alone" an interview with Eric Klineberg; **25** "Southern New England Tropical Storms and Hurricanes, a 98-year Summary 1909–1997, David Vallee and Michael R. Dion, NWS; **27** Tornado Track, 1925. Tri-state tornado, 75th anniversary www.crh.noaa.gov; **29** "The Blizzard of '96 in the Northeast" Northeast Regional Climate Center, Cornell University; **31** Hurricane Hugo, September 22, 1989: http://www.geocities.com/hurricanene/hurricane-hugo.htm; **33** Johnstown Flood, National Park Service, www.nps.gov "A Roar like Thunder". **36** windchill facts: www.weatherimages.org, The new windchill formula: Francis Massen, MeteoLCD; **37** Weather-proofing your pet: Humane Society of the U.S.; 38-39 Climate data courtesy of NCDC, the National Climatic Data Center, Asheville, NC; **40** Frostbite info: Steve Dowshen, M.D., Kim Rutherford, M.D., at kidshealth.org, Hypothermia info: medline plus, U.S. National Library of Medicine and the National Institute of Health; **41** "Snow Trivia: Crystallizing the Truth", John Carey. *National Wildlife,* Dec/Jan 1985. **43–44** Science facts, weather and exploration of the forces that drive the world's weather, Peter Lafferty. Snow Trivia courtesy of "The Snow Booklet" Colorado Climate Center; 43 National Weather Service Event Definitions, Ice Safety: MN Dept of Natural Resources; **44** Avalanche info: www.avalanche.org., America's snowiest cities: NOAA, National Weather Service; **46** Notable Nor'easters "Notable winter snowstorms: historical list". NDIDC.org; 47 "One year later: another look at an infamous ice storm and its aftermath" Michele, Turk. disasterrelief.org; **50** fema.govpage; **51** Petroleum Equipment Institute; **52** NCDC, National Climatic Data; **53** NWS, NOAA; **54** sciencepolicy.colorado.edu, *Applied Behavioral Science Review,*

1999, Roger A. Pielke, Jr.; **56** river flooding safety tips, NWS, NOAA; **60** NOAA, NWS; **61** Pet Safety, Holden, MA, Police Dept.; **62** www.earth-policy.org; **63** FEMA; **66–67** NCDC (National Climatic Data Center) **69** Geophysical Institute of Alaska, Fairbanks, Time Life Books; **70** SUNY College of Environmental Science and Forestry; **72** Environmental Protection Agency; **78** *The Tornado: Its Structure, Dynamics, Prediction and Hazards.* C. Church, D. Burgess, C. Doswell, R. Davies Jones. American Geophysical Union, 1990, *What Is a Tornado?* Charles A. Doswell, III. Cooperative Institute for Mesoscale Meteorological Studies; **79** National Severe Storms Lab (NSSL) Norman, Oklahoma; **81** On-line Tornado FAQ, Roger Edwards, SPC (Storm Prediction Center); **82** NSSL; **85** NOAA; **86** Tornado Capital of the U.S.: VorTek, LLC; **87** "Inside a Tornado": 1930 Monthly Weather Review, "Tornado Oddities," *WeatherWise* Magazine, July/August 2002; **88** The Tornado Project; **92** Storm Prediction Center; **93** Gene Rhoden. *Highway Overpasses: Are They Safe for Shelter?;* **94** FEMA; **97** The Tornado Project; **99** Storm Prediction Center; **100** Spectrum Educational Enterprises; **102** Seattle Tornado: seattlepi.com; **106** NOAA; **112** National Hurricane Center; **114** American Meteorological Society; **115** Hurricane Hunter fact sheet; **115** NHC tracking charts; **118** Hurricane Hunter fact sheet; **120** Collin McAdie, NHC.; **120** www.mcwar.org **124** Vicki Lankarge, insure.com, Air Worldwide Corp.; **125** Joe Morgenstern, *New Yorker,* May 29, 1995. "The Fifty Nine Story Crisis"; **126** AMS policy statement, October 2, 1998; **127** floridadisaster.org, disasterrelief.com; **137** National Safety Council, FAQs; **138–139** NSSL.NOAA.gov; **140** *Lightning. The Whys and Wherefores of Nature's Fireworks.* Ron Hipschman, exploratorium.edu, *Guinness Book of World Records;* **143** Lightning Strike Survivor's Resource; **144** fma-research.com; **145** scientificamerican.com. Virtual Times Astronomy; **146** Andrew Alden geology.about.com; **149** Hail fact sheet, UCAR. *Historical Hail: It's Raining Frogs and Fishes,* Jerry Dennis; **150** *The Indestructible Pilot, Q&A in the World of Aviation.* AMS; **152** Mentalfloss.com. Fact of the Day, June 5, 2003. Hail deaths; **153** NOAA, American Red Cross; **158** Paleoclimatology. Henry N. Pollack, Shaopeng Huang, Po-Yo Shen (NOAA); **160** *Northern Hemispheric Temperatures of the Last 6 Centuries.* Michael E. Mann, Raymond S. Bradley. Malcolm K. Hughes NOAA Paleoclimatology. NCDC; **161** "The Future of Earth" *U.S. News and World Report.* Spring, 2004; **162** Global Warming FAQs. NOAA; **164** MN Office of Environmental Assistance; **165** IPCC Climate Change Report, 2001 International Action About Global Warming. Professor. of Atmospheric Science, John Houghton. Oxford University; **166** World Meteorological Organization; **167** Atmospheric Measurement Program (ARM); **170** EPA; **175** Natural Resources Defense Council (NRDC); **177** "Unlikely Eco-Warriors," Mark Hertsgaard, *Salon.* Jan. 13, 1996; **182** NASA; **187** "Learning from Lightning". Annie Strickler "Heart of the Hurricane". Patrick L. Barry; **224** *Farmer's Almanac;* **227** United States Geological Serivce (USGS) earthquake hazards program.

PICTURE CREDITS

Corbis Stormchaser CD; **77** courtesy NOAA Photo Library/Historic NWS Collection; **78** Melanie Metz, twistersisters.com; **79** Wild Weather CD; **80** top Storm Chaser CD; bottom left courtesy Tornado Chaser; right © Bettmann/CORBIS; **81** courtesy NOAA/NSSL; **82** left © Paul Douglas; top Corbis Stormchaser CD; bottom courtesy www.weatherpix.com; **83** top, bottom left Paul Douglas; bottom right Corbis Stormchaser; **84** courtesy The Storm Prediction Center and NOAA; **85** top courtesy NSSL; bottom Corbis Stormchaser CD; **86, 87, 88** Corbis Stormchaser CD; **89** courtesy NSSL; **91** top courtesy NSSL; bottom © David Hies/CORBIS SYGMA; **92** Corbis Stormchaser CD; **93** © J. Pat Carter/Associated Press; **94** courtesy FEMA; **95** © CORBIS SYGMA; **96** top Paul Douglas; bottom courtesy NOAA; **97** © Jim Reed/CORBIS; **98** © Reuters/CORBIS; **100** top www.aerialok.com; bottom © Jim Reed/CORBIS; **101** top left and right photos by Alfred K. Schroeder, courtesy Massachusetts Historical Society; bottom NOAA/Historic NWS Collection; **103** Weatherstock CD; **104** courtesy NASA; **106** SeaWIFS Project. ORBIMAGE; **107** courtesy Mike Trenchard, Earth Sciences and Image Analysis Laboratory, Johnson Space Center; **108** © Raymond Gehman/CORBIS; **110** left Corbis Stormchaser CD; right courtesy NOAA/Historic NWS Collection; **112** Berenson Design & Books, Ltd.; **113** courtesy NASA/National Center for Atmospheric Research (NCAR); **114** FEMA; **115** © Michael Ainsworth/Dallas Morning News/CORBIS; **116** courtesy NOAA/NASA; **117** courtesy NOAA; **118** Air Force Reserve Command; **120** top left © Jim McDonald/CORBIS; map Berenson Design & Books, Ltd.; **121** top courtesy NOAA/NWS; bottom courtesy NOAA/Historic NWS Collection; **122** © Annie Griffiths Belt/CORBIS; **123** courtesy NOAA/Historic NWS Collection; 124 © CORBIS SYGMA; 125 © James Leynse/CORBIS; **126** © Bettmann/CORBIS; **127** © Jim McDonald/CORBIS; **128–129** Corbis Stormchaser CD; **131** National Weather Service; **132** top Wild Weather CD; courtesy Ron Swanson, Oakdale, MN; **133** top Corbis Stormchaser CD; bottom Jolie Sasseville; **134** courtesy NASA; **135** © Bill Ross/CORBIS; **136** © Doug Kiesling; **138–139** Berenson Design & Books, Ltd.; **141** © Ray Bird; Frank Lane Picture Agency/CORBIS; **142** courtesy www.co.pasquotank.nc.us; **143** © Bettmann/CORBIS; **145** top © Firefly Productions/CORBIS; bottom photo taken by an unidentified Japanese student in Nagano, Japan, in 1987; **146** left courtesy University of Alaska, Fairbanks; right courtesy NASA; **147** courtesy Carlos Miralles (AeroVironment) and Tom Nelon (FMA); **148** © Aaron Horowitz/CORBIS; **149** courtesy NCAR (National Center for Atmospheric Research); **150** courtesy NOAA; **151** courtesy Lori Jo Turner, Mow Lake, Akeley, MN; **152** top courtesy NOAA/NSSL; bottom courtesy NWS; **153** Corbis Stormchaser CD; **154** © Raymond Gehman/CORBIS; **155** © Mark L. Stephenson/CORBIS; **156** © Premium Stock/CORBIS; **159** top courtesy NCDC (National Climatic Data Center)/NOAA; bottom World Meteorological Organization; **160** top courtesy NOAA Paleoclimatology Program; **161** courtesy NOAA; **162** left courtesy Scripps Institution of Oceanography/NOAA; right © Gavriel Jecan/CORBIS; **163** courtesy NASA; **164** courtesy University of Maryland College Park, Department of Meteorology; **166** courtesy The Intergovernmental Panel on Climate Change (IPCC); **167** top courtesy Earth Science and Image Analysis Laboratory, Johnson Space Center; bottom courtesy Geophysical Fluid Dynamics Laboratory; **168** courtesy Geophysical Fluid Dynamics Laboratory; **169** courtesy Environmental Protection Agency (EPA); **171** courtesy Kengo Sudo, University of Tokyo; **172** courtesy NASA, Goddard Space Flight Center; **173** courtesy NOAA/ National Weather Service, National Centers for Environmental Prediction, Climate Prediction Center; **174** top courtesy NASA Tropical